BLACK POLITICIANS AND
RECONSTRUCTION IN GEORGIA

BLACK POLITICIANS AND RECONSTRUCTION IN GEORGIA

A Splendid Failure

EDMUND L. DRAGO

Louisiana State University Press / Baton Rouge and London

To my wife, Cheryle

Designer: Albert Crochet
Typeface: Linotron Trump Medieval
Typesetter: G & S Typesetters, Inc.
Printer: Thomson-Shore, Inc.
Binder: John Dekker & Sons, Inc.

LIBRARY OF CONGRESS CATALOGING IN PUBLICATION DATA

Drago, Edmund L.
    Black politicians and Reconstruction in Georgia.

    Bibliography: p.
    Includes index.
    1. Afro-Americans—Georgia—Politics and suffrage.
2. Reconstruction—Georgia. 3. Georgia—Politics
and government—1865–1950. 4. Georgia—Race
relations. I. Title.
E185.93.G4D7   975.8'04   82-232
ISBN 0-8071-1021-3   AACR2

Contents

Illustrations

Preface

In preparing the official biography of members of the state legislature of 1871–1872, Alexander St. Clair-Abrams excluded Georgia's black reconstructionists, claiming it would have been absurd "to have written the lives of men who were but yesterday our slaves, and whose past careers, probably embraced such menial occupations as boot-blacking, shaving, table-waiting and the like." Since that time, no book-length monograph on these men has been published. Moreover, much of what has been written is inadequate. E. Merton Coulter's *Negro Legislators in Georgia During the Reconstruction*, a collection of articles that had previously appeared in the *Georgia Historical Quarterly*, dealt with only three of Georgia's black leaders. It also suffered from the usual shortcoming of the traditional histories of Reconstruction: it was written from a viewpoint sympathetic to the ex-slaveowners.[1]

Georgia's black politicians have fared little better in state histories of Reconstruction. C. Mildred Thompson's *Reconstruction in Georgia: Economic, Social, Political, 1865–1872*, the best of the traditional state studies, devoted minimal space to the black political leaders. Similarly, Elizabeth Studley Nathans (*Losing the Peace: Georgia Republicans, 1865–1871*) and Alan Conway (*The Reconstruction of Georgia*) wrote from revisionist perspectives, ignoring Georgia's black politicians. This lack of attention to the black politi-

1. Alexander St. Clair Abrams, quoted in E. Merton Coulter, *Negro Legislators in Georgia During the Reconstruction Period* (Athens, 1968), 179.

cians would have surprised their contemporary political foes, who credited them with single-handedly bringing about the Second Reconstruction of Georgia.[2]

There still remains something mystifying about Radical Reconstruction in Georgia. Why was it that the Republican party did so little for blacks, even though it received the great majority of its votes from them? Why was Reconstruction in Georgia so short-lived? How was the racism of white Republicans able to sabotage the whole effort in Georgia? Why were black leaders completely unable to secure even a brief period of political freedom for their people?

Building on earlier works by W. E. B. Du Bois, Vernon Wharton, and Joel Williamson, the scholars of the seventies have greatly expanded our knowledge of the black reconstructionists. Charles Vincent, in his *Black Legislators in Louisiana During Reconstruction*, employed a collective biography to refute the traditional view that the black reconstructionists were ignorant, vindictive, and corrupt. Products of Louisiana's relatively large and affluent free black community, these men came from various occupations, including teaching, business, the Union army, the ministry, and the Freedmen's Bureau. They did not promote corrupt or narrowly racial legislation, and "most of their programs were intended to benefit citizens of both races." More recently, Thomas Holt confirmed Vincent's findings but cast them in a new light. Holt conceded in *Black over White: Negro Political Leadership in South Carolina During Reconstruction* that the black politicians were not ignorant, vindictive, or selfishly race-oriented, but he nevertheless blamed much of the failure of Radical Reconstruction on them. Relying on impressive research in the federal census and a sophisticated analysis of voting behavior, Holt concluded "that the key leaders were basically bourgeois in their origins and orientation and oftener than not failed to act in the interest of the black peasants."[3]

2. C. Mildred Thompson, *Reconstruction in Georgia: Economic, Social, Political, 1865–1872* (New York, 1915); Elizabeth Studley Nathans, *Losing the Peace: Georgia Republicans, 1865–1871* (Baton Rouge, 1968); Alan Conway, *The Reconstruction of Georgia* (Minneapolis, 1966); John M. Matthews, "Negro Republicans in the Reconstruction of Georgia," *Georgia Historical Quarterly*, LX (Summer, 1976), 145–64.

3. Charles Vincent, *Black Legislators in Louisiana During Reconstruction* (Baton Rouge, 1976), xv, 219; Thomas Holt, *Black over White: Negro Political Leadership in South Carolina During Reconstruction* (Urbana, 1977), 3.

Like their counterparts from Louisiana and South Carolina, Georgia's black politicians came from a black elite that stressed political and civil rights over economic issues. However, they were less affluent and educated, and most of them were ministers. These differences played a crucial role in shaping the course of Radical Reconstruction in Georgia. To place these men more fully in their times, I have discussed at length the economic situation of the freedmen from their initial response to freedom to the evolution of the labor system. Through an examination of one black-belt county, I have tried to show how successful blacks were in fulfilling their aspirations after emancipation. I have also devoted a chapter to the methods the white conservatives used to intimidate their black and white political opponents to regain political power.

Analyzing Congressional Reconstruction in Georgia, August Meier concluded that it was "really not a genuine revolution, not even an abortive one . . . southern whites actually dominated the state's government, and by 1872, the Redeemers or Democrats had returned to power. Thus the period of so-called Radical or Black Reconstruction can scarcely be said to have existed in Georgia." By understanding the context of the times, however, I hope to show that W. E. B. Du Bois was closer to the truth when he called Radical Reconstruction a "splendid failure."[4]

In the course of my research many librarians have been helpful—Lilla M. Hawes of the Georgia Historical Society particularly so. I am also grateful to Leon Litwack, Lawrence Levine, Kenneth Stampp, and Andrew McFarland of the University of California, Berkeley. They, as well as Eric Foner, Jack Sproat, Harold Woodman, and Theodore Rosengarten, read and criticized earlier versions of the present manuscript. I am indebted to them for their invaluable assistance. I also owe a great deal to the late Horace Mann Bond, who offered fruitful suggestions in the initial stages of my research. Part of this book was originally published as an article, "How Sherman's March Through Georgia Affected the Slaves," in the *Georgia Historical Quarterly.* I thank the editor for permitting me to reprint it here. I

4. August Meier, "Negroes in the First and Second Reconstructions of the South," *Civil War History,* XIII (1967), 114, 116; W. E. B. Du Bois, *Black Reconstruction in America: An Essay Toward a History of the Part Which Black Folk Played in the Attempt to Reconstruct Democracy in America, 1860–1880* (New York, 1975), 708.

would like to acknowledge the cooperation I have received from Louisiana State University Press, especially from Beverly Jarrett, assistant director and executive editor. I am likewise grateful to my editor, Judy Bailey, for her painstaking and thorough preparation of the manuscript for publication.

BLACK POLITICIANS AND
RECONSTRUCTION IN GEORGIA

CHAPTER I

Glory Be to God, We Are Free

Blow ye the trumpet, blow,
The gladly solemn sound,
Let all the nations know
The year of jubilee has come.
—George Whitefield Pepper

By 1864 the desperate Confederate government had been forced to cancel military exemptions for overseers, although they were needed to maintain plantation discipline. The son of prominent planter Colonel David C. Barrow, when he asked that his father's overseer be exempted, was informed that because of so many similar requests all had to be turned down. The harried planters were also unable to completely protect their slaves from conscription, but many planters failed to provide the one out of every five slaves the Confederate government requested of them. Not only were the slaves needed on the plantation, they were also valuable property vulnerable to abuse in the wrong hands. One planter lost a slave worth four thousand dollars, who died working on some Savannah fortifications. Conscription was even more resented by the slaves themselves, and some resisted. Mrs. Irby Morgan, who lived near Augusta, recalled how the soldiers would invade black religious meetings to round up laborers. Her own slave eluded impressment by donning a makeshift sling and feigning a limp. Nevertheless, as one Confederate general wrote, "If the people and government of the State of Georgia mean Savannah to be defended, they must themselves furnish the necessary labor." In spite of planter and slave resistance, thousands of slaves were impressed to work on fortifications throughout the state, draining the plantations of manpower.[1]

1. Pope Barrow to Henry C. Wayne, October 10, 1864, J. Hardman, Jr., to Barrow, October 17, 1864, both in Col. David C. Barrow Papers, University of Georgia Library,

1

With so many planters and overseers gone, it was not unusual for a plantation and its remaining slaves to be left almost entirely in the hands of its mistress. Plantation discipline could not be as stringently enforced, as it had been before the war, and the old, troublesome problem of slave control grew increasingly difficult. Some slaves became openly hostile. In 1863 eighteen blacks were arrested in Hancock County for attempting to incite insurrection. A year later three blacks in another county were hanged for a similar offense. Perhaps some of these reported insurrections were imaginary, the products of southern hysteria, but newspapers, letters, and diaries all record an undeniable increase in slave rebelliousness.[2]

The growing restlessness among the slaves was nourished by their belief that the approaching northern army would liberate them. As early as 1862 when Federal ships threatened the Sea Islands, dozens of slaves escaped. Susie King Taylor, a slave who lived in Savannah during the war, wrote in her memoirs: "I wanted to see these wonderful 'Yankees' so much, as I heard my parents say the Yankee was going to set all the slaves free. Oh, how those people prayed for freedom!" Confederate stories of Yankees burning and drowning blacks, forcing them to fight, harnessing them to carts, or shipping them to Cuba seldom succeeded in engendering fear among the slaves. "Massa hates de Yankees," they reasoned, "and he's no fren'ter we; so we am de Yankee bi's fren's." Susie Taylor's grandmother had encouraged such reasoning in her granddaughter. "Don't mind what the white people say," she had warned. "[They] did not want slaves to go over to the Yankees, and told them these things to frighten them." This old woman was later arrested at a black religious meeting, which the slave patrol broke up because of the suspicion that the slaves, singing about the almighty Lord, really meant the Yankees.[3]

Athens; Allen D. Candler (comp.), *The Confederate Records of the State of Georgia* (Atlanta, 1909–1911), II, 239, 276, 375, 313; Charles R. Armstrong to John A. Cobb, April 4, 1864, in Howell Cobb Papers, University of Georgia Library, Athens; Mrs. Irby [Julia] Morgan, *How It Was: Four Years Among the Rebels* (Nashville, 1892), 103–104, 119–20.

2. Eliza Frances Andrews, *The War-Time Journal of a Georgia Girl, 1864–1865* (New York, 1908), 19; Thomas Conn Bryan, *Confederate Georgia* (Athens, 1953), 122–27, 134.

3. Thomas Wentworth Higginson, *Army Life in a Black Regiment* (East Lansing,

Some southerners were fully aware that the slaves yearned for their freedom. As early as 1861 a Savannah rice planter, Louis Manigault, had commented, "This war has taught us the perfect impossibility of placing the least confidence in any Negro. In too numerous instances those we esteemed the most have been the first to desert us. House Servants, from their constant contact with the family become more conversant with passing events are often the first to have their minds polluted with evil thoughts." Ironically, the Confederate war effort itself was a source of such pollution. As Clarence Mohr has suggested, war-related institutional changes, especially rapid urbanization, brought large numbers of plantation blacks into the cities where they had greater opportunities for freedom and autonomy. "To a very considerable extent," Mohr concluded, "Georgia's black people had ceased to act, think, or function as slaves long before slavery itself legally passed out of existence."[4]

While the reverberations of the manpower drainage were still being felt, Georgia was shaken anew in the spring of 1864. A Union army of nearly a hundred thousand men, under the command of General William T. Sherman, invaded the state with the objective of occupying it and thereby dividing the Confederacy. As Sherman's army marched relentlessly southward from Atlanta to Savannah, planters along the route fled into the southwest part of the state. Many of them, encouraged by Confederate directives, took their slaves along to keep them out of the path of the invading army.[5]

1960), 53, 212–14; Susie King Taylor, *Reminiscences of My Life in Camp with the 33d United States Colored Troops, Late 1st S.C. Volunteers* (Boston, 1904), 7–8. See also John Townsend Trowbridge, *The South: A Tour of Its Battle-Fields and Ruined Cities, a Journey Through the Desolated States, and Talks with the People; Being a Description of the Present State of the Country—Its Agriculture—Railroads—Business and Finances—Giving an Account of Confederate Misrule, and of the Sufferings, Necessities and Mistakes, Political Views, Social Condition, and Prospects of the Aristocracy, Middle Class, Poor Whites, and Negroes* (Hartford, Conn., 1867), 481; M. A. DeWolfe (ed.), *Marching with Sherman: Passages from the Letters and Campaign Diaries of Henry Hitchcock, Major and Assistant Adjutant General of the Volunteers, November, 1864–May, 1865* (New Haven, 1927), 70–72; George Ward Nichols, *The Story of the Great March: From the Diary of a Staff Officer* (New York, 1865), 59–60.

4. Albert V. House, Jr. (ed.), "Deterioration of a Georgia Rice Plantation During Four Years of Civil War," *Journal of Southern History*, IX (February, 1943), 102; Clarence Lee Mohr, "Georgia Blacks During Secession and Civil War, 1859–1865" (Ph.D. dissertation, University of Georgia, 1975), 209–210.

5. William Tecumseh Sherman, *Memoirs of William T. Sherman by Himself*

The invasion shattered the last remnants of slave control, and the breakdown of the plantation system became irreversible. The slaves, eager for freedom, deserted en masse. Some nineteen thousand blacks left the plantations to follow Sherman's army. Negro men, women, and children joined the columns at every mile of the march. It was a shock to many slaveholders, one of whom wrote: "We went to sleep one night with a plantation full of negroes, and woke to find not one on the place—every servant gone to Sherman in Atlanta. . . . We had thought there was a strong bond of affection on their side as well as ours!" Another planter recalled: "They didn't even come to ask for advice. . . . when Sherman came along . . . every last skunk of 'em run away."[6]

Some slaves stayed behind with their masters. On a plantation in Clarke County the slaves grieved at the news of their freedom, and the ancient cook, who remained with the family until her death, assured them that freedom "don't make no difference to me." The Reverend Edward R. Carter, a black biographer of successful Atlanta Negroes, claimed that some blacks remained on the plantation because of past kindnesses, and many southerners shared his belief. They tended to interpret a slave's failure to flee as evidence of loyalty and the lasting bond of affection between slave and master. However, self-interest undoubtedly played its part. Many of the slaves who stayed on the plantation were tied down by age or by their families. Others were sceptical about the benefits of freedom. One old black man told Sherman that the northerners would soon be gone and "anudder white man'll come." Another slave concluded more harshly, "look at the poor, white trash them niggers is running after. If they was in the gutters they wouldn't pick them up, unless

---

(Bloomington, 1957), II, 23–24; Sidney Andrews, *The South Since the War, as Shown by Fourteen Weeks of Travel and Observation in Georgia and the Carolinas* (Boston, 1866), 321; Allen D. Candler (comp.), *Confederate Records of Georgia*, II, 779.

6. *The War of the Rebellion: A Compilation of the Official Records of the Union and Confederate Armies* (Washington, D.C., 1880–1901, additions and corrections inserted in each volume, 1902), Ser. I, Vol. XLIV, pp. 75, 159, 410, hereinafter cited as *Official Records*; Myrta (Lockett) Avary, *Dixie After the War: An Exposition of Social Conditions Existing in the South During the Twelve Years Succeeding the Fall of Richmond* (New York, 1906), 190; Stephen Powers, *Afoot and Alone: A Walk from Sea to Sea by the Southern Route, Adventures and Observations in Southern California, New Mexico, Arizona, Texas, Etc.* (Hartford, Conn., 1872), 61–62.

they wanted them to fight for them."[7] These two men seem to have considered the Yankees as just another set of white men passing through, not deeply concerned with or perhaps even hostile to the slaves' well-being. They belonged, however, to a small minority.

Most blacks welcomed Sherman and his army with hardly any reservations. "Every black face was the face of a friend," reported one Union soldier, and "every black hand was open with the proffer of its little all." The fervor with which most of the slaves received the army and freedom gave Sherman's march the intensely emotional religious quality of a revival. One union soldier recalled, "The whole land seemed to be inhabited by negroes, and the appearance of the army inspired them with a profound religious sentiment and awakened in them the most extraordinary religious emotion." James M. Simms, a black Baptist preacher who served as an assemblyman during Reconstruction, eloquently and vividly expressed the feelings of his fellow blacks: "When the morning light of the 22d of December, 1864, broke in upon us, the streets of our city were thronged in every part with the victorious army of liberty; every tramp, look, command, and military movement told us that they had come for our deliverance, and were able to secure it to us, and the cry went around the city from house to house among our race of people, 'Glory be to God, we are free!'" A soldier from Wisconsin observed, "To them it was like the bondsmen going out of Egypt," and Major George W. Nichols, one of Sherman's staff officers, added, "the majority accept the advent of the Yankees as the fulfillment of the millennial prophecies." Countless blacks believed Sherman's army to be the instrument of Almighty God, who was at last delivering his people from bondage. It seemed clear to the freed slaves that the Yankees were the hand of Providence, and throughout Georgia, they unrestrainedly demonstrated their gratitude and joy. A Wisconsin soldier remembered this poignant scene near Milledgeville: "The colored people hailed with demonstrative delight the advent of the

7. Augustus Longstreet Hull (ed.), *Annals of Athens, Georgia, 1801–1901* ([Athens], 1906), 291–92; Edward R. Carter, *The Black Side: A Partial History of the Business, Religious, and Educational Side of the Negro in Atlanta, Ga.* (Atlanta, 1894), 198; Nichols, *The Story of the Great March*, 59; Morgan, *How It Was*, 145; Edwin Quattelbaum, "The Absence of Sambo in Georgia Reconstruction" (unpublished research paper, University of California, Berkeley, 1967–68), 3–4.

union army. 'Bress the Lawd! Tanks to Almighty God, de Yanks is come,' they cried, and wanted to hug the soldiers, often touching the dress of some of the officers, who marched nearest the sidewalks, as the afflicted of old touched the garments of the Great Master." In Savannah the first cries of "Glory be to God, we are free!" came to be expressed more fully in a hymn of praise and thanksgiving: "Shout the glad tidings o'er Egypt's dark sea, / Jehovah has triumphed, his people are free."[8]

The abandon with which the slaves fled the security of the plantations to follow the Yankee columns struck some observers as irresponsible. "These wretched creatures . . . don't know what freedom is," remarked an Illinois officer. It is true that many of the slaves were simply running as far as possible away from the scene of their enslavement. After all, in the slave community freedom had long been defined in terms of running away. A slave from northern Georgia probably expressed the sentiments of numerous refugees when he said, "I wanted to be free; dis nigger wanted to own hisself." But many slaves had good reason to leave. Some, for example, went off to search for family members who had been separated from them.[9]

The security of the plantation, in any case, was often more apparent than real. During the last part of the war, meat was replaced in the diet of the slaves by syrup and other substitutes to such an extent that the *Southern Cultivator*, an influential planters' journal, warned against entirely eliminating meat from the slave's diet. Sherman's army discovered numerous examples of ill-fed and ill-clothed slaves, many of them idle and lacking the means of subsistence.

8. John Richards Boyle, *Soldiers True: The Story of the One Hundred and Eleventh Regiment Pennsylvania Veteran Volunteers and of Its Campaigns in the War for the Union, 1861–1865* (New York, 1903), 263, 262; James Meriles Simms, *The First Colored Baptist Church in North America. Constituted at Savannah, Georgia, January 20, A.D. 1788* (Philadelphia, 1888), 137; Edwin Eustace Bryant, *History of the Third Regiment of Wisconsin Volunteer Infantry, 1861–1865* (Madison, 1891), 282, 283; Nichols, *The Story of the Great March*, 72; Corydon Edward Foote, *With Sherman to the Sea: A Drummer's Story of the Civil War, as Related by Corydon Edward Foote to Olive Deane Hormel* (New York, 1960), 215–17.

9. Avary, *Dixie After the War*, 190; Oscar Osburn Winther (ed.), *With Sherman to the Sea: The Civil War Letters, Diaries, and Reminiscences of Theodore F. Upson* (Baton Rouge, 1943), 136; Paul M. Angle (ed.), *Three Years in the Army of the Cumberland: The Letters and Diary of Major James A. Connolly* (Bloomington, 1959), 311; David Power Conyngham, *Sherman's March Through the South* (New York, 1865), 84; Nichols, *The Story of the Great March*, 71.

"The negroes on all these plantations," one officer reported, "tell us their masters have given them no meat to eat during the past two years, and as a consequence the negroes have been in the habit of prowling about the country . . . stealing chickens, hogs."[10]

To many hungry and jobless but able blacks Sherman's army brought hope for employment and decent subsistence, as well as the opportunity to participate in a crusade to destroy slavery. "An immense number of 'contrabands' now follow us. . . . who intend going into the Army," wrote an Illinois soldier to his family. "They [the army] offer $12 pr month," an unhappy southerner complained. "Many are going off with them." And off they went in the hundreds to become servants, scouts, teamsters, foragers, and pioneers. They repaired roads, built bridges, and wrecked railroads. Many fed Sherman's soldiers not only by cooking their food but by finding it as well. They also provided the northerners with a steady stream of military intelligence. To the end of the march they went, "earning their way as part of the army."[11]

Although many southerners still clung to their belief in a strong bond of affection between slave and master, the specter of tens of thousands of blacks flocking to Union lines haunted them. Incidents of urban looting in which blacks participated with whites confirmed their worst fears. Milledgeville residents watched helplessly as trophy-seeking Yankees and blacks "revelled" about the statehouse. In Washington, Georgia, blacks participated with a Confederate regiment in the plundering of the local commissary. In describing the looting of his store, an Atlanta merchant reported, "Yankees, men, women, children and niggers were crowded into the store each one scrambling to get something to carry away." With great emotion Confederate General John B. Hood wrote to Sherman, "You came

10. Athens *Southern Cultivator*, XXII (January 22, 1864), 20; Nichols, *The Story of the Great March*, 58–59; Angle (ed.), *Three Years in the Army of the Cumberland*, 313.

11. [Mary E. Kellogg] (comp.), *Army Life of an Illinois Soldier, Including a Day by Day Record of Sherman's March to the Sea: Letters and Diary of the Late Charles W. Wills. . . .* (Washington, D.C., 1906), 330; Mary Sharpe Jones and Mary Jones Mallard, *Yankees A'Coming: One Month's Experience During the Invasion of Liberty County, Georgia, 1864–1865*, ed. Haskell Monroe (Tuscaloosa, Ala., 1959), 74; Edmund L. Drago, "How Sherman's March Through Georgia Affected the Slaves," *Georgia Historical Quarterly*, LVII (Fall, 1973), 366.

into our country with your Army, avowedly for the purpose of sub-
jugating free white men, women, and children, and not only intend
to rule over them, but you make negroes your allies, and desire to
place over us an inferior race, which we have raised from barbarism
to its present position. . . . Better die a thousand deaths than submit
to live under you or your Government and your negro allies!"[12]

Despite these incidents, southerners had little to fear from their
former slaves. There are only a few recorded instances of black violence, and those involved overseers. Apparently, it was the overseers,
not the masters, that embodied the worst aspects of slavery and
plantation discipline to most blacks. One southern family survived
the aftermath of the Yankee invasion because a former slave hired
himself out to support them in the summer of 1865. Northerners
were surprised at slave docility and the near absence of violence. "It
is surprising to all of us," Major Nichols wrote, "to see how admirably
the negroes of the city [Savannah] behave, in view of their knowledge
that our coming sets them at liberty from the control of their masters. They take no advantage of their freedom in any way in their
conduct to those who ill treated them in former days." A year after
the war was over, the *Colored American*, an Augusta newspaper co-
edited by a Negro, reminded white Georgians, "When Sherman's
army marched through the South, did we take advantage of this (as
we might) to commit acts of lawlessness and violence? No, never!"[13]

Blacks tended to express their hostility toward their former masters and other southerners in ways less extreme and more indirect.
Some resorted to taunting. "Today," a Savannah woman wrote in her
diary dated January, 1865, "a little negro amused herself by jumping
up and down under my window, and singing at the top of her voice:

12. Conyngham, *Sherman's March Through the South*, 254; Eliza Frances Andrews, *The War-Time Journal of a Georgia Girl*, 193–94; S. P. Richard Diary (MS in
S. P. Richard Papers, Atlanta Historical Society), September 2, 1864; John Bell Hood,
*Advance and Retreat: Personal Experiences in the United States and Confederate
States Armies* (Bloomington, 1959), 235.
13. Joseph Le Conte, *'Ware Sherman: A Journal of Three Months' Personal Experience in the Last Days of the Confederacy* (Berkeley, 1937), 32, 56; Eliza Frances Andrews, *The War-Time Journal of a Georgia Girl*, 286; DeWolfe (ed.), *Marching with
Sherman*, 71; Nichols, *The Story of the Great March*, 103; Augusta *Colored American*, January 6, 1866.

'All de rebel gone to h—— Now Par Sherman come.'" More often slaves turned to open betrayal as an outlet. Mary Sharpe Jones recounted in her memoirs how her baby's nurse unhesitatingly took every opportunity to inform the Yankees that the child's father was C. C. Jones, Jr., a colonel in the Confederate army. One of his own slaves guarded Savannah planter Zachariah Winkler while the Yankees burned his house. Many slaves willingly disclosed to the Yankees where their masters hid the family valuables. Betrayal of this kind was such a common occurrence that a Union army chaplain remarked, "They [the slaves] very readily tell us where anything is concealed, and seem well pleased when we find various articles." The slaves took particular pleasure in watching Federal soldiers destroy the relics of plantation discipline. "It was odd," Major Nichols observed, "to see the delight of the negroes at the destruction of places known only to them as task-houses, where they had groaned under the lash." Another of Sherman's officers, Major Henry Hitchcock, noted in his account of the march that the blacks were quick to point out to them the function of the plantation dog: "Catch nigga, Sah, and catch de soldiers dat run away." When a large red dog was shot by the Yankees, "the darkies . . . were in great glee over it. No wonder," sympathized Major Hitchcock.[14]

Many Union officers and soldiers shared Major Hitchcock's sympathy. Sherman himself helped distribute provisions to destitute slaves. No doubt the genuine concern the Yankees showed toward the slaves fostered good will and hope among them. The Yankees, in turn, must have been touched by such acts of selflessness as an old black's giving his shoes to a reluctant trooper. "Massa soldier boy," he admonished, "you can't fight widout no shoes . . . doan't you know dat *I'se glad to go barefooted* to help you fight de battle of freedom?" There were undoubtedly many such examples of amity

14. Frances Thomas Howard, *In and Out of the Lines: An Accurate Account of Incidents During the Occupation of Georgia by Federal Troops in 1864–1865* (New York, 1905), 204; Jones and Mallard, *Yankees A'Coming,* 71; Mary Granger (ed.), Savannah Writers' Project, *Savannah River Plantations* (Savannah, 1947), 87; Nichols, *The Story of the Great March,* 112, 62; George S. Bradley, *The Star Corps; or, Notes of an Army Chaplain During Sherman's Famous "March to the Sea"* (Milwaukee, 1865), 188; DeWolfe (ed.), *Marching with Sherman,* 152, 78.

between blacks and Yankees. Indeed, the Tenth Regiment Michigan Volunteer Infantry marched toward Savannah lustily singing the hymns of jubilee they had learned from blacks.[15]

Despite the many instances of good will, however, the Yankees' feelings toward the blacks were complicated, inconsistent, and not always favorable. Sherman's men brought with them the diverse political and racial prejudices of their local communities. Moreover, as they came into greater contact with the blacks, they became increasingly ambivalent, perplexed, and uncertain. For many, especially easterners like General O. O. Howard, their concern for the Negro was most likely bolstered by their abolitionist principles. Some were paternalistic in their treatment of the blacks. Sherman, for example, did not think it below his rank to personally dole out provisions to former slaves, but he also reminded them emphatically that "Massa" Lincoln had given them their liberty. An Illinois officer could vehemently denounce Union mistreatment of blacks, but he could also unhesitatingly affirm, "Many of those [rice plantation blacks] I saw to-day were scarcely a single remove from brutes."[16]

The blacks were certain that God had sent the Union army to free them, but not all of the Yankees were convinced that their mission included freeing the slaves. The emotional turmoil many of Sherman's men wrestled with is reflected in a Michigan soldier's dismay over the exuberance with which the blacks were greeting the army: "Tain't right . . . to have them thinking we're here just to free the slaves. We're fighting secession. This slavery business has just been hung onto us." An Indiana soldier told his southern captives, "There was a great dissatisfaction in the Army on account of the present object of the war, which now was to free the negroes." Apathetic towards abolitionism and weary after years of fighting, some, especially the westerners, blamed the blacks for the war and expressed undisguised racism. A Yankee told some southerners in Liberty County that "all he wished was the powder to blow their [the blacks']

15. Nichols, *The Story of the Great March*, 59; Boyle, *Soldiers True*, 263; Foote, *With Sherman to the Sea*, 215–16.
16. Sherman, *Memoirs*, II 245; Nichols, *The Story of the Great March*, 61; Angle (ed.), *Three Years in the Army of the Cumberland*, 354–55, 367, 359.

brains out." Another soldier, a westerner, declared to a southerner that he would fight another seven years to wipe out all the blacks.[17]

To a large extent the directives of its commander shaped the army's attitudes toward the war and the blacks. General William T. Sherman was not an abolitionist. He was interested not in emancipation, but in maintaining the Union. "We don't want your negroes," he told the mayor of Atlanta, "but we do want and will have a just obedience to the laws of the United States." Sherman believed that emancipation was valuable only insofar as it aided Union victory and that the needs and wishes of the newly freed slaves must be subordinated to military objectives. He refused to allow blacks to enlist as soldiers because he feared alienating white Unionist sentiment in northern Georgia, and he gave instructions that blacks were to be tolerated only so far as they aided the war effort. Never were they to be allowed to encumber the moving columns. Sherman also made it clear to his commanders that their first duty was to feed and supply their troops, not the blacks.[18]

General Jeff C. Davis was one of Sherman's subordinates who interpreted the guidelines literally and thereby caused the deaths of hundreds of blacks. As Davis' columns marched towards Savannah, they were often hindered by refugees at river crossings. In each instance, the pontoon bridges were raised before the refugees could cross, and they were left to the mercy of the approaching Confederate cavalry. "The waters of the Ogechee and Ebenezer Creek can account for hundreds who were blocking up . . . [the Union] columns, and then [were] abandoned," a northern journalist reported. "Wheeler's cavalry charged on them, driving them, pellmell, into the waters, and mothers and children, old and young, perished alike!" John J. Hight, a chaplain from Indiana, recalled the terror he witnessed at another crossing: "The bridge was taken up, and these people were left on the other side, without any means of crossing. . . . there went up from that multitude . . . a cry of agony. . . . [then the shout] 'The

17. Foote, *With Sherman to the Sea*, 217; Jones and Mallard, *Yankees A'Coming*, 67, 77; Sidney Andrews, *The South Since the War*, 382; William King Diary (MS in William King Papers, Southern Historical Collection, University of North Carolina, Chapel Hill), July 24, 1864.
18. Sherman, *Memoirs*, II, 126, 174–76, 245, 249.

rebels are coming.' This was all that was needed to turn the grieving refugees into a panic-stricken mob. . . . Some of them at once plunged into the water, and swam across. Others ran wildly up and down the bank, shrieking with terror. . . . Some were drowned—how many is not known."[19]

Chaplain Hight called General Davis a proslavery military tyrant. A doctor in another unit went one step further, declaring that Davis should be hanged as "high as Haman." But Sherman steadfastly defended him: "General Jeff C. Davis was strictly a soldier, and doubtless hated to have his wagons and columns encumbered by these poor negroes, for whom we all felt sympathy." Whatever sympathy Sherman may have felt, his attitude throughout the campaign struck black chaplain Henry M. Turner as anti-Negro. Turner coined the term *Shermanized officers* to refer to "officers partaking of the ignoble prejudice of that General."[20]

This ignoble prejudice, present in all ranks of the northerners, found expression in numerous ways. Northern bounty hunters evaded Sherman's order against the enlistment of Georgia slaves, and a number were transported to South Carolina against their will and impressed into the army. In Atlanta, Federal troops demolished a black church. Some black women found it unsafe to be outside with the Yankees around; their husbands "were obliged to stay at their houses for the protection of their wives." Nor were blacks safe from foraging Yankees, who took from blacks and whites alike.[21]

Blacks were especially vulnerable to Yankee foraging and confiscation in Liberty County, where there was a greater ownership of

19. Conyngham, *Sherman's March Through the South*, 276–77; Gilbert R. Stormont (comp.), *History of the Fifty-eighth Regiment of Indiana Volunteer Infantry, Its Organization, Campaigns, and Battles from 1861–1865. From the Manuscript Prepared by the Late Chaplain John J. Hight, During His Service with the Regiment in the Field* (Princeton, Ind., 1895), 426–27. See also Bryant, *History of the Third Regiment*, 282.

20. Robert G. Athearn (ed.), "An Indiana Doctor Marches with Sherman: The Diary of James Comfort Patten," *Indiana Magazine of History*, XLIX (December, 1953), 419; Sherman, *Memoirs*, II, 244–45; Benjamin Tucker Tanner, *An Apology for African Methodism* (Baltimore, 1867), 416. See also Angle (ed.), *Three Years in the Army of the Cumberland*, 354–55, 367, for Major Connolly's disgust with General Davis.

21. Sherman, *Memoirs*, II, 249; Carter, *The Black Side*, 15; Trowbridge, *The South*, 454; Robert Manson Myers (ed.), *The Children of Pride: A True Story of Georgia and the Civil War* (New Haven, 1972), 1230; Frances Thomas Howard, *In and Out of the Lines*, 22–25.

property by blacks. Settled by Puritan Congregationalists who were opposed to slavery, this county adopted a milder form of bondage than existed elsewhere in the state. According to Chaplain Turner, "They did not allow man and wife to be parted . . . they would church-try one another [for mistreatment of slaves], and without evidence of reformation, the party was expelled, and denounced throughout the country." Under this system of Christian paternalism, many black carpenters, blacksmiths, drivers, and managers had been able to accumulate modest holdings in livestock and crops. After the war, a lawyer sent to investigate Unionists' claims against Sherman's army in Liberty and adjoining Chatham County discovered that twenty-seven of the forty-four claimants were blacks. The damages these twenty-seven suffered totaled over thirty thousand dollars. There were seventeen ex-slaves among their number, whose claims amounted to more than ten thousand dollars. The simple testimony of the wife of one of these ex-slaves details the laborious process by which her husband, and perhaps other Georgia blacks, had accumulated wealth: "In the first place my husband bought a mare colt which was the beginning of his raising. He planted corn & sold it to buy the mare. . . . He got the other things mentioned in his petition by buying, raising & trading—My husband was manager on his Master's plantation." Federal troops had seized his possessions along with his master's.[22] Such indiscriminate confiscation of black property, and the other anti-Negro acts committed by Sherman's army, had a corrosive effect on the enthusiasm with which many had welcomed them.

In Washington, critics began attacking Sherman for his handling of the refugees both during and after the campaign. His friend General H. W. Halleck warned him of the dissatisfaction spreading among administration officials: "They say that you have manifested an almost *criminal* dislike to the negro, . . . you drove them from your ranks, prevented their following you by cutting the bridges in your rear, and thus caused the massacre of large numbers by Wheeler's cavalry." Blacks were also disillusioned with Sherman; their millen-

22. Philadelphia *Christian Recorder*, June 18, 1874; Linda Roberts, Office of the Georgia Commission of Claims, Washington, D.C., January 30, 1875, claim #21,467 in W. W. Paine Papers, Georgia Historical Society, Savannah.

nium had become a nightmare. The lament of a black nurse reveals their frustration and anger: "Dey've took ebry ting I had. . . . Ebry body say de Yankees goin' to free us. Like a fool I belieb 'em, an' now dis what dey do. I might a-knowed it. What kin you spec fum a hog but a grunt."[23]

Regardless of Sherman's intentions, his invasion of Georgia had created a severe refugee problem that could not be ignored. Some blacks began drifting back to the plantations, but by January, 1865, thousands of refugees had reached the coast "after long marches and severe privations, *weary, famished, sick,* and *almost naked.*" Concern in the administration over the refugees and the mounting criticism of Sherman's methods of dealing with them prompted a visit to Savannah in January, 1865, by Secretary of War Edwin M. Stanton. He and Sherman met with twenty black religious leaders to discuss the problem. At one point, Sherman, much to his chagrin, was asked to leave the room while Stanton queried the black representatives about the general. Garrison Frazier, a Baptist minister whom the blacks had elected spokesman, confirmed the pro-Unionist sentiment most blacks still felt and their respect for Sherman. But he also tactfully reminded Stanton of the misery many refugees had suffered and were still enduring. He complained, in addition, that able young blacks were being impressed into the army. Asked how his people could become self-sufficient, he replied, "We want to be placed on land until we can buy it and make it our own." All of the black leaders but one agreed that their people would have a better chance of becoming self-sufficient if they were allowed to live by themselves, "for there is a prejudice against us in the South that will take years to get over," Frazier said.[24]

This meeting soon bore fruit. His military mission accomplished, Sherman issued Field Order No. 15, which forbade impressment of blacks and gave freedmen land on which to live. The islands south of Charleston and the abandoned rice fields along the adjoining coast

23. Sherman, *Memoirs*, II, 247–48; Frances Thomas Howard, *In and Out of the Lines*, 23–24.

24. Powers, *Afoot and Alone*, 62–63; Jones and Mallard, *Yankees A'Coming*, 83; Augusta *Daily Constitutionalist*, January 29, 1865; Sherman, *Memoirs*, II, 245–47; "Colloquy with Colored Ministers: A Civil War Document," *Journal of Negro History*, XVI (January, 1931), 88–94.

to thirty miles inland were to be set aside for freedmen. No whites, except the military, would be allowed on these lands. Whenever three freedmen, heads of families, were to inform the Federal inspector of the location they desired in the prescribed area, he was to issue them a license and aid them in establishing a "peaceable agricultural settlement." No family was to be allowed more than "forty acres of tillable ground," and all were guaranteed protection "until such time as they can protect themselves, or until Congress shall regulate their title."[25]

Field Order No. 15 had little immediate impact on the economic and social well-being of Georgia's nearly half a million blacks, most of whom lived in areas outside the path of Sherman's army. However, the promise of forty acres of land probably did much to stem for a while the growing disillusionment among these blacks. Eventually the promise of forty acres was incorporated into their folklore although it actually remained only a dream.

25. Sherman, *Memoirs*, II, 250–51. For blacks before Sherman's March, see Clarence Mohr, "Before Sherman: Georgia Blacks and the Union War Effort," *Journal of Southern History*, XLV (August, 1979), 331–52. For another view of the impact of Sherman's March on the slaves, see Paul D. Escott, "The Context of Freedom: Georgia's Slaves During the Civil War," *Georgia Historical Quarterly*, LVIII (Spring, 1974), 79–104.

CHAPTER II

Overcoming a Prejudice of Generations

In describing the African Methodist Episcopal church's efforts to win black converts in the South immediately after the Civil War, contemporary church historian John Wesley Gaines noted, "There was a prejudice born of generations of the recognized dominion of the whites which we had to meet and overcome in leading the bodies of Negroes to seek a church where they could be free and untrammeled in their religious worship."[1] The obstacle Gaines was referring to was the hegemony whites had established over blacks during slavery. For two centuries blacks had been made to feel inferior to whites and incapable of self-government. It would strain the imagination to believe the Georgia freedmen had not internalized some feelings of inferiority. Yet, within two years after the war, the ex-slaves created autonomous institutions that both attracted the masses of black people into the Republican party and countered the prevailing cultural belief that blacks were innately inferior to whites. The means they used to overcome this prejudice of generations were the black church and the educational or convention movement. In freedom the blacks moved toward a complete religious autonomy without which there would have been no black political movement.

Georgia's slave-owners, in Christianizing their slaves, did not intend thereby to create an autonomous black institution. Most plant-

1. John Wesley Gaines, *African Methodism in the South; or, Twenty-five Years of Freedom* (Atlanta, 1890), 13.

ers viewed religion as a means of making their slaves more efficient, dutiful, and docile workers. Some allowed their slaves to attend a white church each Sunday, where a separate gallery was usually set aside for them. Others hired white or black preachers to give weekly instruction to their bondsmen. They carefully chose preachers who would encourage obedience to authority. As one slave recalled, "seldom did the text vary from the usual one of obedience to the master and mistress, and the necessity for good behavior." Another slave remembered, "A white minister invariably preached the then worn-out doctrine of a slave's duty to his master, the reward of faithfulness and the usual admonition against stealing." Black ministers were required to preach from a prescribed text often under the watchful eye of a white man, and those who deviated from the text were whipped. "Dey let de colored preachers preach," conceded an ex-slave, "but dey give 'em almanacs to preach out of. Dey didn't 'low us to sing such songs as 'We Shall Be Free' . . . Dey always had somebody to follow de slaves to church when de colored preacher was preachin' to hear what wuz said and done. Dey wuz 'fraid us would try to say something 'gainst 'em."[2]

Religious instruction designed to indoctrinate the slave often failed. "How could anybody be converted on dat kind of preachin'?" an ex-slave asked. "And 'sides it never helped none to listen to dat sort of preachin' 'cause de stealin' kept goin' right on evvy night." As Lawrence Levine has suggested, "the doctrine they [the whites] were attempting to inculcate could easily subvert the institution of slavery—and both they and the slaves realized it." Minnie Davis attended the First Presbyterian Church with her masters each Sunday where she sat in the slave gallery. "I recall," she told an interviewer, "that Dr. Hoyt used to pray that the Lord would drive the Yankees back. He said that 'Niggers were born to be slaves.' My mother said that all the time he was praying out loud like that, she was praying

2. Federal Writers' Project, Georgia Narratives, Nos. 1–4 of "Slaves Narratives: A Folk History of Slavery in the United States from Interviews with Former Slaves" (Typewritten records, assembled by the Library of Congress Project, Work Projects Administration for the District of Columbia, 1936–1938, in Library of Congress), No. 1, pp. 25, 197, 303, 195, No. 2, p. 16, No. 4, p. 129, hereinafter cited as "Slave Narratives, Georgia."

to herself, 'Oh, Lord, please send the Yankees on and let them set us free!'"[3]

Several historians have already described the importance of religion to the slaves. It allowed them some autonomy of personality, a way of ordering the world that explained the existence of evil and injustice, a defense against the psychological evils of slavery, solace, and the possibility of future liberation. But more importantly, even during slavery blacks were developing their church as a semiautonomous institution. In major cities like Savannah and Augusta, free blacks and slaves established their own churches. On the eve of the Civil War, Savannah's black First Baptist Church had a congregation of nineteen hundred people with church property worth eighteen thousand dollars. In these black churches, black preachers exercised a degree of independence. In 1851 a Savannah black preacher named Bentley was singularly unimpressed when the president of the United States came to the city and addressed only the wealthy. The minister told his congregation: "Now, did Christ come this way? Did he come only to the rich? Did he shake hands only with them? No! Blessed be the Lord! He came to the poor! He came to us, and for our sakes, my brothers and sisters!"[4]

Once freed, the most dramatic way for the ex-slaves to assert their religious independence was to organize their own churches. "Soon atter dey was sot free," declared former slave Nicey Kinney, "Niggers started up churches of dey own." This, of course, brought conflict with the whites, particularly over the issue of who controlled the church property. The blacks argued that they had paid for the property as slaves and that the whites had held it in their names only to circumvent the laws against slaves' owning property. In 1866 a freedman's convention declared, "We claim all such property as our own, and that we not only have the right to hold and control it, but the

3. *Ibid.*, No. 2, p. 131, No. 1, p. 258; Lawrence W. Levine, *Black Culture and Black Consciousness: Afro-American Thought from Slavery to Freedom* (New York, 1978), 46.

4. John W. Blassingame, *The Slave Community: Plantation Life in the Antebellum South* (New York, 1972); Eugene Genovese, *Roll, Jordan, Roll: The World the Slaves Made* (New York, 1976); Albert J. Raboteau, *Slave Religion: The "Invisible Institution" in the Antebellum South* (New York, 1980); Ralph Betts Flanders, *Plantation Slavery in Georgia* (Chapel Hill, 1933), 174–75; "Colloquy with Colored Ministers," 88; Levine, *Black Culture and Consciousness*, 49.

right to unite in brotherhood with any christian body that may, in its teachings and sympathies, accord with our feelings."[5]

The history of Methodism in postwar Georgia demonstrates the extent to which the ex-slaves preferred black-controlled institutions. Four Methodist groups actively proselytized Georgia freedmen. Two were white, the Methodist Episcopal Church, South, and the Methodist Episcopal Church, North. The Southern Methodists had little success in retaining the ex-slaves in their black affiliate, the Colored Methodist Episcopal church, because it was too closely identified with the former slave-owners. Black opponents labeled it the "Rebel," "Democratic," or "old Slavery Church." More blacks joined the M E Church, North, but soon found themselves powerless and discriminated against. In 1872 its black ministers, citing the German Conference as a precedent, petitioned for a separate conference. They contended it would give blacks a greater say in the government of the church and "relieve the Church of even a suspicion of a spirit of caste and make us feel as men, and the peers of our white brethren." In 1875, fearing an exodus of its black members, the church subdivided the existing conference, but it was not until 1895 that the blacks had their own conference.[6]

The contest between the African Methodist Episcopal Zion church and the African Methodist Episcopal church, the two black Northern Methodist churches, ended when the AMEZ church lost the influential Trinity Church in Augusta to the AME church. From then on, the AME church had little difficulty overcoming its white competitors. "Other denominations had the money, we had the blood," a contemporary AME historian noted, "and the contest could not long remain uncertain. The fires of oppression have melted down the Anglo-Africans into one." Another church official reported that the

5. "Slave Narratives, Georgia," No. 3, pp. 29–30; *Proceedings of the Freedmen's Convention of Georgia, Assembled at Augusta, January 10th, 1866. Containing the Speeches of Gen'l Tillson, Capt. J. E. Bryant, and Others* (Augusta, 1866), 30.

6. Charles Henry Phillips, *The History of the Colored Methodist Episcopal Church in America: Comprising Its Organization, Subsequent Development, and Present Status* (Jackson, Tenn., 1898), 71–72; Atlanta *Methodist Advocate*, May 1, 1872; Edmund Jordan Hammond, *The Methodist Episcopal Church in Georgia, Being a Brief History of the Two Georgia Conferences of the Methodist Episcopal Church, Together with a Summary of the Causes of Major Methodist Divisions in the United States and of the Problems Confronting Methodist Union* ([Atlanta], 1935), 139.

AME church appealed to southern blacks because it was "the negro's own Church" with a uniquely black religious content and "no undue repression of the emotions which possess us."[7]

As the churches gained greater independence from the whites, they became the center of black Georgia's social life. The church educated the children, imparted morality, strengthened black family life, married the young, and buried the dead. "The typical church," wrote W. E. B. Du Bois, "stands at some cross-roads and holds services once or twice a month. These meetings are great reunions and are the occasions of feasting, country gossip and preaching." Moreover, yearly revivals offered the black churches the opportunity to check the spread of evil, a chance to recruit new members, and a reason to celebrate. According to David Barrow of Oglethorpe County, these yearly meetings were the bulwarks of the black church. "Once a year," he observed in 1880, "during August there is a big meeting at Spring Hill church. From far and near friends come in, and all the houses of all the members are thrown open. They kill pigs, kids, lambs, chickens, everything by the wholesale, and for three or four days they do little else, but preach, sing, and eat." E. P. Thompson might well have been describing the importance of the black church to Georgia freedmen when he said, "Within this religious community there was . . . its own drama, its own degrees of status and importance, its own gossip, and a good deal of mutual aid . . . men and women felt themselves to have some place in an otherwise hostile world when within the Church." As might be expected, the church became the focal point of black political life during Reconstruction. It was the only black institution capable of providing the organization and leadership necessary to mobilize black voters. The churches gave financial support to political compaigns, registered voters, and hosted political rallies. The church also produced most of Georgia's black political leaders during Reconstruction.[8]

7. Gaines, *African Methodism in the South*, 298; Tanner, *An Apology for African Methodism*, 368–69.
8. W. E. B. Du Bois, *The Negro American Family* (1908; rpr. New York, 1969), 130; W. E. B. Du Bois, *The Souls of Black Folk: Essays and Sketches* (Greenwich, Conn., 1964), 142–43, 102; "A Georgia Plantation," *Scribner's Monthly*, XXI (April, 1880), 835; Edward P. Thompson, *The Making of the English Working Class* (London, 1965), 379; Drago, "How Sherman's March Through Georgia Affected the Slaves," 372–73. See also the Appendix.

At the center of the black church stood the preachers. During slavery, as Eugene Genovese discovered, they were the "teachers and moral guides" who kept "the people together with faith in themselves." After emancipation, they became the unchallenged political and social leaders of black Georgia. The president of Emory University noted that black "churches are the centers of their social and religious life. No man has more influence with his following than has the negro pastor." According to Du Bois: "In the Black World, the Preacher and Teacher embodied at once the ideals of this people, —the strife for another and juster world, the vague dream of righteousness. . . . The preacher is the most unique personality developed by the Negro on American soil. A leader, a politician, an orator, a 'boss,' an intriguer, and idealist." Moreover, these men had experience in dealing with the white world. It was logical for newly freed and largely illiterate blacks faced with crucial political decisions to turn to their local preachers for advice. "The colored people are generally very ignorant," wrote black Baptist pastor and politician Thomas Allen. "In my county the colored people came to me for instructions, and I gave them the best instructions I could. I took the New York Tribune and other papers, and in that way I found out a great deal, and I told them whatever I thought was right. I said to them that I thought they had been freed by the Yankees and Union men, and I thought they ought to vote with them; to go with the party always." Baptist minister-politician James M. Simms recalled: "The ministers were almost the only ones capable of looking out after our people, and we were interested in them politically. And my profession as minister-missionary was the only one in which I could go to our people and freely advise them."[9]

For these preachers, political action was a natural extension of their ministry, and even those with little or no political ambition found themselves drawn into politics. In 1867 African Methodist

---

9. Genovese, *Roll, Jordan, Roll,* 273; Atticus G. Haygood, *Our Brother in Black: His Freedom and His Future* (New York, 1881), 222; Du Bois, *The Souls of Black Folk,* 68, 141; "Ku Klux Klan Report, Georgia Testimony: Report of the Joint Select Committee to Inquire into the Affairs of the Late Insurrectionary States," *Senate Reports of Committees,* 42nd Cong., 2nd Sess., Vol. II, Pt. VI, p. 615, hereinafter cited as "Ku Klux Klan Report"; *House Miscellaneous Documents,* 40th Cong., 3rd Sess., No. 52, p. 9.

Episcopal minister Theophilus G. Steward arrived in Lumpkin, a small town located in a black-belt county in southwestern Georgia. He had come to replace the pastor of a local AME church, Thomas Crayton, who had left the pulpit to make a successful bid for a seat in the Constitutional Convention of 1867–1868. Although a new-comer with no abiding political interests, Steward found it impossible to avoid the election campaign activities. As one of the few literate blacks in the county, he felt obliged to accede to the request of the military that he serve as a voter registrar. In 1868 Steward accepted a new pastoral assignment at the AME church in Macon. Its most prominent member was Jefferson Long, Georgia's only black congressman during Reconstruction. The church had recently separated from the Methodist Church, South, and was engaged in a legal dispute with it over the ownership of church property. When Steward defended the property rights of his congregation, he became a target of the Ku Klux Klan.[10]

Most black preachers expounded a providential version of history according to which the blacks were a chosen race and, like the Jews of the Old Testament, were favored by the hand of Providence, which would deliver them from bondage. In the meantime, these preachers counseled, the slaves must be patient. When the war broke out, Lincoln and the Republican party were perceived as the instruments that God would use to free his people. "The day was dark," remembered AME minister Andrew Brown, "but, thank God, we waited on and on. God's horse was tied to the iron stake. The day the first fire was made at Sumter, I saw the Gospel Horse begin to paw. He continued to paw until he finally broke loose and came tearing through Georgia. The colored man mounted him and intends to ride him." Similarly, Garrison Frazier told Stanton at Savannah that Georgia blacks looked upon Sherman "prior to his arrival, as a man, in the providence of God, specially set apart to accomplish this work." In a speech to Augusta blacks in 1867, minister Simeon Beard, a delegate to the constitutional convention, sounded the same providential theme: "When God wanted to deliver the Hebrew children out of Egypt, he sent a means to those children, and God intended, through

10. Theophilus G. Steward, *Fifty Years in the Gospel Ministry* (N.p., n.d.), 90–92, 94–95, 105, 116–25, 128–29.

this war, that, like the Red Sea, while the nation rended itself asunder, you should pass through free. This war was God's work. . . . Wars are the instruments of God's hands unseen to carry out his great purpose."[11]

The religious, or providential, history preached by the ministers provided the postwar black political movement with the unifying ideology and cohesiveness needed to surmount numerous obstacles. It helped the ex-slaves to overcome feelings of inferiority and nourished the growth of republicanism among them. Under this biblical view, political setbacks could be seen as temporary, as God's way of testing their faith. According to preacher-assemblyman Henry M. Turner, "the fires of persecution" were the necessary prerequisites of salvation. Similarly, political advances were also part of God's plan. In 1870 Turner hailed the passage of the Fifteenth Amendment as the "chariot of fire that is to roll us beyond the reach of our persecuting Ahabs and perfidious Jezebels." "Je[ho]vah hath triumphed," Turner declared; "his people are free." It was this deep faith in a benevolent Providence that enabled the black politicians to remain patiently optimistic despite their expulsion from the Georgia legislature in September, 1868. "It is astonishing to see," a white Republican colleague of the black assemblymen observed, "notwithstanding they are certain of being expelled, the calmness . . . and the faith which they have, that although they may be expelled now, they will come back again, and come to stay." James M. Simms compared the expulsion of the blacks to the trials of Jonah and insisted that, like Jonah, the blacks would ultimately triumph if they kept the faith.[12]

The African Methodist Episcopal ministers were the most politically active. Unlike the black Baptists, whose churches were local, the AME ministers were members of a northern-based national organization and were, therefore, less susceptible to pressures from local whites. In addition, their grounding in a long tradition of protest gave them impetus to political activism. The church had been founded in 1816 as a reaction against racial discrimination within the Methodist

11. Gaines, *African Methodism in the South*, 18; "Colloquy with Colored Ministers," 93; Augusta *Daily Constitutionalist*, April 14, 1867.

12. Atlanta *Daily New Era*, May 4, 1870; J. H. Caldwell to Wm. Caflin, September 1, 1868, in William E. Chandler Papers, Library of Congress; Atlanta *Constitution*, August 30, 1868.

church. Its ministers were imbued with the missionary zeal of their church, concerned about religious liberty, and opposed to slavery. The Declaration of Independence, with its promise of equality for all men, was as much a part of African Methodist Episcopal theology as the Old Testament, and the church's ministers saw little distinction between politics and religion. Even before Appomattox, James Lynch had helped to organize the black ministers' meeting with Stanton and Sherman. Some AME ministers who had entered the Union army as chaplains remained in the South after the war to win converts. In their missionary work, they fostered race pride to help the ex-slaves overcome the sense of inferiority ingrained in them under slavery. They also urged blacks, in the face of white hostility, to organize their own African Methodist Episcopal churches.[13]

In late 1864 the organizing campaign of the AME church in Georgia received a boost with the arrival of Henry M. Turner. Born of free parents in South Carolina in 1834, Turner joined the Methodist Church, South, at the age of fifteen. In 1853 he became a licensed preacher, and two years later he migrated to Macon, Georgia, where whites found him "too smart a nigger." Turner joined the AME church in 1858, and in 1862 he was as an elder of Israel Church, a large black congregation in Washington, D.C. There, he attracted the attention of Secretary of War Stanton. He became the country's first black chaplain in 1863 when Lincoln appointed him chaplain to the First United States Colored Troops. After his unit was disbanded, Andrew Johnson reassigned him to the Freedmen's Bureau in Atlanta, but he soon resigned his commission to devote full time to the organizing efforts of the AME church.[14]

According to Turner and his fellow AME ministers, the Civil War had been the consequence of white America's failure to live up to its mission as delineated in the Declaration of Independence. God had sent the war on behalf of his chosen people. At a Fourth of July rally

13. "Colloquy with Colored Ministers," 90: Tanner, *An Apology for African Methodism*, 416, 16–36.

14. Clarence E. Walker, *A Rock in a Weary Land: The African Methodist Episcopal Church During the Civil War and Reconstruction* (Baton Rouge, 1981), 122; William J. Simmons, *Men of Mark: Eminent, Progressive, and Rising* (Cleveland, 1887), 805–812; Tanner, *An Apology for African Methodism*, 415–16; Philadelphia *Christian Recorder*, June 9, 1866.

This picture of Henry M. Turner during his service as the first
black chaplain in the United States army appeared in *Harper's
Weekly*.

in Augusta in 1865, AME preacher James Lynch told a large gathering of freedmen that slavery was a violation of America's mission
and had been exterminated by the war. He insisted that continued
failure to fulfill that mission would bring down upon the nation the
wrath of an angry God: "The white man may refuse us justice. God
forbid! But it cannot be witheld long, for there will be an army mar-

shalled in the Heavens for our protection, and events will transpire by which the hand of Providence will wring from you [the white man] in wrath, that which should have been given in love." Six months later Henry M. Turner repeated the same theme at another Augusta rally. The slave-owners, who had prevented the slaves from improving themselves morally and intellectually, had failed to live up to America's mission. An angry God had chosen Lincoln to hurl the thunderbolt of emancipation.[15]

Henry Turner, by defying white opposition, encouraged black political independence. Often whites disputed the ownership of church property when blacks established an AME church independent of the Methodist Episcopal Church, South. "I did there, as I have done in all other places," Turner reported from Columbus in 1866, "had the trustees elected to assume at once the temporal responsibility, and to meet that party who would dare rob them of their church property, as is daily threatened by the malcontented rebels. I think they will have a sweet time taking it, too, be the legal decision *pro* or *con*." That same year, as Turner discussed the political situation at a Macon church, troublesome whites gathered outside the building. Young blacks in the audience rushed outside to defend the preacher, while those inside thumped their feet in his support. When the Macon whites won a victory in court over their AME opponents, they found the church burned to the ground. Speaking before a racially mixed audience in Greensboro in 1866, Turner told the blacks to keep whites from sleeping with their women, "drive these characters out of society, and treat them as brutes on the streets." His supporters, armed for the occasion, prevented disgruntled whites from drawing guns on the minister. "I never saw more fire arms among one set of people in my life," Turner remembered, "I have not seen so determined a set of colored people, South, as they are at Greensboro." Turner's example inspired one contemporary black Georgian to write: "I never saw a man travel so much, preach and speak so much and then be up so late of nights . . . drilling his official men. Surely if he continues this way, and lives the year out . . . he has nine

15. James Lynch, *The Mission of the United States Republic: An Oration Delivered by Rev. James Lynch, at the Parade Ground, Augusta, Ga., July 4, 1865* (Augusta, 1865), 2, 6, 10, 14; Augusta *Colored American*, January 13, 1866.

lives." With the advent of Radical Reconstruction, Turner vigorously worked at getting out the black vote. "I first organized the Republican Party in this state," Turner later boasted, "and have worked for its maintenance and perpetuity as no other man in the State has. I have put more men in the field, made more speeches, organized more Union Leagues, Political Associations, Clubs, and have written more campaign documents that received larger circulation than any other man in the state." Describing himself as "a minister of the gospel and a kind of politician—both," he successfully ran for the Constitutional Convention and the Georgia legislature and became the state's most powerful black politician.[16]

Equally important in the establishment of the Republican party in Georgia was the educational movement. Scarcely had Sherman left Savannah to finish his march through the Carolinas when Georgia blacks, led by their ministers, began organizing an educational movement. Northern missionaries were astonished, and later chagrined, to find that members of the city's black clergy had established by January 1, 1865, the Savannah Education Association, which staffed its schools entirely with a black teaching corps. In 1865 the *Colored American*, a black newspaper, suggested that the black educators meet in convention. The conservative-minded head of the Freedmen's Bureau, General Davis Tillson, gave the meeting his blessings, and he assured Georgia whites that the meeting's purpose was educational rather than political. On January 10, 1866, more than forty black delegates gathered in Augusta's black Springfield Baptist Church. They chose as temporary chairman James Porter, a forty-year-old freeborn minister who had come from Charleston to Savannah before the war and was preaching at a local Protestant Episcopal church. In 1865 he had attended the black ministers' meeting with Stanton, and three years later he would be elected to the Georgia legislature.[17]

16. Philadelphia *Christian Recorder*, March 24, 1866, April 14, 1866, July 21, 1866; Steward, *Fifty Years in the Gospel Ministry*, 121–22; "Ku Klux Klan Report," VII, 1034; Simmons, *Men of Mark*, 813–16. Edwin S. Redkey, *Respect Black: The Writings and Speeches of Henry McNeal Turner* (New York, 1971), 30–31.

17. Jacqueline Jones, *Soldiers of Light and Love: Northern Teachers and Georgia Blacks, 1865–1873* (Chapel Hill, 1980), 73–76; *Proceedings of the Freedmen's Convention*, 3–4. See also the Appendix and Edmund L. Drago, "Black Georgia During Reconstruction" (Ph.D. dissertation, University of California, Berkeley, 1975), 100.

In spite of Tillson's assurances, the convention took steps to politically educate the freedmen and moved in a partisan political direction. It established the Georgia Equal Rights and Educational
Association to educate the freedmen and "to secure for every citizen,
without regard to race or color, equal rights." The convention also
memorialized the Georgia legislature and passed a series of resolutions demanding protection and equal rights for blacks. Moreover, to
facilitate a black-white alliance, the black delegates named white,
Maine-born Republican John E. Bryant, a former Union captain and
Freedmen's Bureau agent, as the association's first president. In October, 1866, the association urged its members to refrain from public
political discussion at their local meetings until Congress reconstructed the South. Meanwhile, under the association, Bryant managed to bring the blacks together with the powerful white Augusta
faction that was to dominate the Republican party throughout Reconstruction. In 1866 Bryant and other white Augusta Union Lea-
guers purchased the defunct *Colored American*. Renamed the *Loyal
Georgian*, it became the official organ of the Georgia Equal Rights
and Educational Association. Several prominent white Augusta Republicans, supporters of the future Republican governor Rufus B.
Bullock, were also active in the association, serving on its state
board of education.[18]

Historians have already documented how the Republican party in
Georgia evolved from the educational movement, but they have
overlooked how important the movement was in politicizing the ex-
slaves at the grass-roots level. Chapters of the Georgia Equal Rights
and Educational Association became "schools where colored citizens learn their rights." The movement also gave Georgia's black
politicians experience and helped them overcome their own feelings
of inadequacy. It may have been because they were acutely aware of
conservative charges that blacks were incapable of self-government
and because they lacked experience at conventions that black

18. *Proceedings of the Freedmen's Convention*, 17–22, 24, 28–30; *Proceedings of
the Convention of the Equal Rights and Educational Association of Georgia, Assembled at Macon, October 29th, 1866. Containing the Annual Address of the President, Captain J. E. Bryant* (Augusta, 1866), 6, 11, 17; Drago, "Black Georgia During
Reconstruction," 104; Thompson, *Reconstruction in Georgia*, 335–36; Macon *Georgia Weekly Telegraph*, October 18, 1867.

delegates throughout the South showed an exaggerated concern for decorum at the first freedmen's conventions. Henry M. Turner, however, opposed using Cushing's *Manual* for the rules of the first freedmen's convention in Georgia "upon the ground that colored people were unaccustomed to conventions, and [he] thought a few simple rules would be preferable." There is a parallel between blacks attending these early Reconstruction conventions and the Jews at the first Zionist congress. Both groups felt the need to establish their importance to the public and to themselves. In 1897 the delegates to the first Zionist congress were required to wear formal attire, including white neckties. Zionist leader Theodor Herzl explained: "We must establish everything. People should get accustomed to seeing the Congress as a most solemn and exalted thing. The Congress was a pariah people's rudimentary form of self-determination." As Herzl's biographer noted, "Even more than to impress the outside world, Herzl wanted to impress the delegates themselves with their own importance." Although most of Georgia's black leaders did not believe they were innately inferior to whites, most agreed they were *culturally* subordinate. In a memorial to the Georgia legislature in 1866, the state's black politicians declared, "Suffering from the consequent degradation of two hundred and forty-six years of enslavement, it is not to be expected that *we* are thoroughly qualified to take our position beside those who for all ages have been rocked in the craddle [*sic*] of civilization." If the educational movement did nothing else, it bolstered the self-confidence of Georgia's budding black politicians. "The convention of colored men from all parts of the state . . . did honor to our race," boasted Henry M. Turner, "and exhibited a degree of progress intellectually, and highly commendable, in a people so recently free. There was marked ability developed in their entire proceedings. The idea that colored men could not govern themselves . . . is all a hoax." Over a quarter of Georgia's black legislators during Reconstruction had attended at least one educational convention.[19]

Since blacks were in a minority in Georgia, John E. Bryant's vision

19. *Proceedings of the Freedmen's Convention*, 4–6, 18; *Proceedings of the Equal Rights and Educational Association*, 6; Amos Elon, *Herzl* (New York, 1975), 237–38; Philadelphia *Christian Recorder*, November 24, 1866. See also the Appendix.

of a victorious Republican party rested on a black-white alliance. Economic conditions in Georgia after the war and the failure of Johnsonian Reconstruction to cope with these conditions made the Republican coalition possible. Burdened by the increasingly high prices following the war, white small farmers throughout the state, especially in northern Georgia, found themselves sinking deeper into debt. After the state supreme court struck down a debtor relief law in 1866, thousands of discontented whites joined union leagues. Republican campaign literature carefully exploited such class antagonisms. Bryant's *Loyal Georgian* argued that it was the "landed aristocracy" that brought on the war and "FORCED the poor men to fight for them." The only solution was the victory of a Republican party, "pledged to elevate labor, and to the passage of such laws as will protect the toiling masses of society in their legal rights." The Republican cause was further aided when former Confederate governor Joseph E. Brown, a favorite of small farmers before the war, joined the reconstructionists. By the fall of 1867 there were union leagues in most Georgia counties, and in April, 1868, league officials boasted a white membership of 37,000.[20]

In March, 1867, Congress cemented the alliance of black and white Republicans by passing the Congressional Reconstruction measures. Georgia's civil government was replaced by military rule. Major General John D. Pope ordered an October election to determine whether Georgia wanted to call a constitutional convention and to elect delegates to that convention. In May of 1867 Georgia's blacks organized a black Republican party and announced that they were "ready to unite with their white brethren." Soon after, the Executive Committee of the Union Republican party, headed by white Union League officials, issued a call for a state convention to be held in Atlanta on the Fourth of July. Attended mostly by black delegates, the convention nominated a state central committee dominated by white Augusta Republicans and allies of Rufus B. Bullock.[21]

20. Drago, "Black Georgia During Reconstruction," 104–106; Augusta *Loyal Georgian*, August 10, 1867; Joseph E. Brown, *Ex-Governor Brown Replies to B. H. Hill's Notes on the "Situation"* (Augusta, 1867), 15; Herbert Fielder, *A Sketch of the Life and Times and Speeches of Joseph E. Brown* (Springfield, Mass., 1882), 428–429.

21. Augusta *Loyal Georgian*, May 16, 1867; Nathans, *Losing the Peace*, 93, 32–34; John M. Matthews, "The Negro in Georgia Politics, 1865–1880" (M.A. thesis, Duke University, 1967), 30.

With the black-white alliance established, Georgia Republicans began politicking in earnest among the freedmen. Because most ex-slaves were illiterate, the Republicans used mass meetings to reach and organize the blacks. The earliest meetings were called to celebrate the passage of the Congressional Reconstruction Acts of 1867. In Macon thousands of ex-slaves marched to a rally, waving banners and singing "On Jordan's stormy banks I stand." The celebration opened with a prayer and included speeches by prominent black religious and political leaders, including Henry M. Turner and Jefferson F. Long. The freedmen passed resolutions endorsing Congressional Reconstruction and thanking Congress. Similar gatherings occurred in Augusta, Darien, and Milledgeville.[22]

The Republicans also concentrated their efforts on the cities where there were large blocs of black voters and the obstacles to voter registration were less severe, thanks to the presence of the Union army. Henry Turner urged blacks in Augusta, Savannah, Atlanta, and Columbus to establish associations that would collect funds in support of speakers to be sent throughout the state during the upcoming election campaign. At a mass meeting in Macon, he persuaded the freedmen to finance a speaker for the Fourth Congressional District. In addition, the Executive Committee of the Republican party sponsored black minister John T. Costin and Macon politician Jefferson Long to stump the state. Two thousand people attended a rally in Griffin where Long was a guest speaker. Similarly, seven hundred Sandersville blacks from all quarters of the county gathered to celebrate the Fourth of July and to hear Long and Costin urge them to support the Republican party.[23]

Most of these first rallies were politically conservative in tone. Macon blacks, for example, proclaimed that they harbored no animosity towards their former masters, and cheered a banner that read, "If we must Live and Vote in the same State, Let us be friends." Underestimating the politicization of the freedmen undertaken by the black ministers and the educational association, the conserva-

22. Macon *Georgia Journal and Messenger*, April 3, 1867; Savannah *Daily Republican*, April 18, 1867; Milledgeville *Federal Union*, May 7, 1867.

23. Matthews, "The Negro in Georgia Politics," 31–32; Griffin *American Union*, October 11, 1867; Griffin *Tri-Weekly Star*, October 8, 1867; Sandersville *Central Georgian*, July 24, 1867.

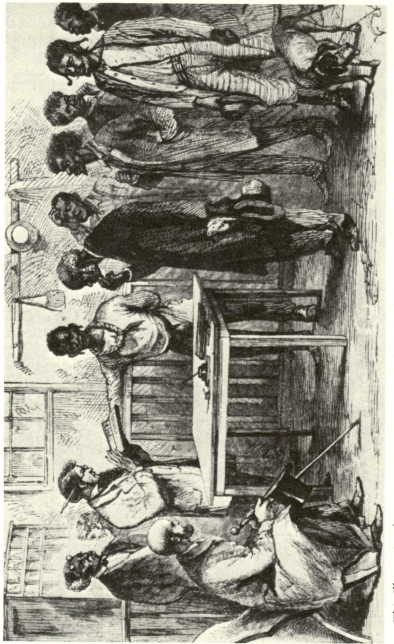

This illustration from a contemporary periodical shows the scene in September, 1867, when freedmen lined up to register in Macon, Georgia. It was the first voter registration under army rule in Georgia.

tive opposition staunchly clung to their proslavery belief that the blacks had been happy as slaves and would vote for their former masters. "The black man has now the privilege of voting for his rulers," a Milledgeville paper proclaimed. "Let us meet together, and reason together. . . . The truth is, the two races cannot live together except as they agree." Similarly, another conservative paper predicted, "If let alone, the black population would march in solid column with their former masters and present employers to the polls. . . . They know full well, that the Southern whites are their best friends."[24]

The 1867 celebration of the Congressional Reconstruction Acts in Augusta demonstrates the ability of a number of Georgia blacks to overcome in some degree the hegemony of their former owners. The meeting, sponsored by local black Republicans, was open to everybody. J. T. Shefton, the former editor of the *Colored American*, advocated black affiliation with the Republican party: "As for myself, I feel in duty bound to support that party whose principles shall make no distinction on account of race or color, in the enjoyment of civil and political rights. . . . They came to us through fire and sword; they were consecrated in the blood of fallen heroes, and must be handed down to our children." Antebellum white politicians attending the celebration were surprised by the partisan tone. Former governor Herschel V. Johnson told the two thousand freedmen present that their former master was their best friend, having lived in the same house with them and still sharing a common interest in the cotton economy. Blacks and whites were aboard the same ship, and they needed to cooperate to keep it afloat. Black Congregational preacher Lewis Carter elaborated on Johnson's analogy: "That old ship, the institution of slavery is dead, and I am glad of it. Shall I employ its captain or its manager to bear me through the ocean again? (Cheers, and voice No! No!). Is it because I am angry with the captain? No. It is because I have lost confidence in him. . . . How can we, as a people, support those that have vowed to enslave us." The Augusta freedmen voted unanimously to support the Republican

24. Macon *Georgia Journal and Messenger*, April 3, 1867; Milledgeville *Federal Union*, as quoted in Americus *Sumter Tri-Weekly Republican*, April 9, 1867; Sandersville *Central Georgian*, April 24, November 6, 1867. See also Dawson *Weekly Journal*, April 26, 1867, and Augusta *Daily Constitutionalist*, March 15, 1867.

party. After the meeting, Herschel Johnson conceded, "we wasted breath and words." Of the 106,410 votes cast in the October election, 102,283 were in favor of the constitutional convention, and of the 170 delegates elected, 37 were blacks. For better or worse, white Georgians would be confronted with some degree of Radical Reconstruction.[25]

25. Augusta *Daily Constitutionalist*, April 14, 1867; Percy S. Flippin, *Herschel V. Johnson of Georgia, State Rights Unionist* (Richmond, 1931), 279; Drago, "Black Georgia During Reconstruction," 115.

CHAPTER III

The Black-White Republican Coalition

As members of a party out of office, Georgia's black and white Republicans had been able to overlook their differences, but the Republican victory in the October elections unmasked a deep split in the party along racial lines. Most white Republicans had no desire to bring about their black colleagues' vision of a multiracial democracy in Georgia. Instead, they shared their conservative opponents' antipathy toward blacks and sought to keep the party's leadership in white hands, despite the fact that 90 percent of Republican voters were black. The Republican majority in writing the constitution would also be writing the party's platform for the April, 1868, election, but when the constitutional convention convened in December, 1867, there was a real danger that party unity would be destroyed. The Republican leaders realized that they needed an ambiguously worded constitution, vague enough for both white and black Republicans to endorse in the April election.

From the start, the constitutional convention was a white-dominated affair. Nearly 80 percent of the 165 delegates were white, and practically all of them were southern born. Less than thirteen "pure, unadulterated carpet-baggers" sat in the convention. Since federal occupation came late to Georgia and since Freedmen's Bureau chief Davis Tillson staffed his organization with native whites, Reconstruction brought few Yankee officials into the state. Although there was "quite a liberal sprinkling of good and true democrats," white Republicans controlled the convention. Their leaders came from Augusta, a center of Georgia republicanism. Of the four white Augusta Republicans who guided the activities at the gathering, only John E. Bryant could legitimately be called a carpetbagger. The others, Rufus Bullock, Benjamin Conley, and Foster Blodgett, had substantial roots in their communities. Despite the class rhetoric of the campaign, the Republican leadership adopted a conciliatory attitude toward the former slave-owners. Foster Blodgett opened the assembly with a plea that there be "no conflict between capital and labor; the landowners and the laborers should be friends; they must strive to advance the interest of each other. Let no prescriptive spirit sway our counsels or our measures." Heeding Blodgett's advice, the convention requested federal aid for planters, opposed the impeachment of Andrew Johnson, and voted down an attempt to impose disabilities on those who had supported the rebellion.[1]

The thirty-seven black convention delegates, like their thirty-two black colleagues who sat in the Georgia legislature or in Congress between 1868 and 1872, did not come from the cotton fields. As skilled artisans, house servants, and preachers, these men had enjoyed intimate contact with the planter elite. William H. Harrison of Hancock County, for example, had been body servant to the father-in-law of Linton Stephens. Harrison had learned to read and write because his owner thought every man should be able to read the Bible. After the war, he had worked on the Western and Atlantic Railroad long enough to purchase a thirteen-acre cotton farm, and in 1867 he was elected to the convention.[2]

Conservatives occasionally acknowledged that Georgia's black politicians came from a black elite. The convention's black doorkeeper, W. H. Dixon, allowed Howell Cobb's relative John C. Whitner to enter the floor because Dixon's wife had belonged to the Cobb family. "You see," wrote Whitner, "the name of 'Cobb' is an open sesame to this august body." Similarly, a Democratic newspaper, surveying the black delegates, purported to find "conservatism even among them. . . . There is a feeling of aristocracy among the black

1. Drago, "Black Georgia During Reconstruction," 115–17; "Ku Klux Klan Report," 526; Allen D. Candler (comp.), *Confederate Records of Georgia*, VI, 207, 212, 481–84, 582–84, 748–50.
2. "Ku Klux Klan Report," 922–32.

people as well as among the whites, and the 'upper ten' have as great abhorrence of leveling themselves to the common herd."[3]

Like South Carolina's black reconstructionists, Georgia's black politicians stood somewhere between the white former ruling class and the black peasantry, but they were undoubtedly much closer to the latter. Their origins were humble in comparison to those of their black colleagues in South Carolina, whom Thomas Holt described as "basically bourgeois in their origins." In Georgia there was no large, affluent community of light-skinned free blacks to dominate the politics of Reconstruction. Only 3,500 free blacks lived in Georgia before the war, most of them "on a bare subsistence level." A smaller percentage of blacks were free in Georgia in 1860 (0.8 percent) than in either Louisiana (5.3 percent) or South Carolina (2.4 percent).[4]

By all indices—status, color, literacy, occupation, and wealth—Georgia's black political elite was less well-off than its counterparts in South Carolina and Louisiana. Of the twenty black legislators whose prewar status can be determined, sixteen (80 percent) were born slaves. Not a single black politician born in Georgia was born free. Only three (15.8 percent) of the nineteen black legislators in the 1870 federal manuscript census were described as mulatto, whereas in South Carolina, Holt identified 33 percent as mulatto. Moreover, in Georgia a light skin and free status did not insure education or affluence. Representative Abram Colby of Green County, a minister and barber freed by his white father in 1851, could not read or write; he left these chores to his son William who accompanied him to the legislature in 1868. In addition, in 1870 Colby owned no property, real or personal.[5]

Like Colby, a quarter of the black politicians on whom we have data were illiterate, and probably an equal number were barely liter-

3. John C. Whitner to Howell Cobb, January 27, 1868, in Cobb Papers; Macon *Georgia Weekly Telegraph*, November 15, 1867. See also the Appendix.

4. Holt, *Black over White*, 3, 37–38; Ira Berlin, *Slaves Without Masters: The Free Negro in the Antebellum South* (New York, 1976), 136–37; Edward Forrest Sweat, "The Free Negro in Antebellum Georgia" (Ph.D. dissertation, Indiana University, 1957), 7, 141; Ralph B. Flanders, "The Free Negro in Ante-bellum Georgia," *North Carolina Historical Review*, IX (July, 1932), 259.

5. "Population," Schedule I of "Returns of the United States Census," Ninth Census, 1870 (MS in National Archives), hereinafter cited as MSS Census; "Ku Klux Klan Report," 695–707; Holt, *Black over White*, 38. See also the Appendix.

Profile of Black Legislators in Georgia

	Yes	No	No Information
Literate	24	8	37
Mulatto	3	16	50
Free before the war	8	12	49
Freeborn	4	16	49
Born in Georgia	31	24	14
Born in the South	53	2	14
Minister before the war	4	11	54
Minister after the war	24	14	31
Owned real property	8*	11	50
Owned personal property	16†	3	50

Note: These data were derived from the Appendix.

* Average value was $875.00 ($571.43 if the value of James Porter's property is excluded).

† Average value was $529.69 ($298.33 if the value of Porter's property is excluded).

ate, while in South Carolina only 10 percent were illiterate. Assemblyman Monday Floyd of Morgan County, a house carpenter, and Representative Eli Barnes of Hancock County, a mechanic, both of them ex-slaves, told a congressional committee they could read only "a little." Barnes explained, "I have not been at school. I have not had any chance, only what I picked up by the fireside, by lightwood knots." Black leaders like Henry M. Turner were painfully aware of the educational limitations of their black colleagues, "These men, who are unable to express themselves with all the clearness and dignity and force of rhetorical eloquence, laughed in derision by the Democracy of the country." Turner knew how great was the achievement of these ex-slaves, and he chided those who would mock them, "These gentlemen do not consider for a moment the dreadful hardships which these people have endured, and especially those who in any way endeavored to acquire an education."[6]

Except for Charleston-born free black James Porter, proprietor of a

6. Holt, *Black over White*, 38; "Ku Klux Klan Report," 954–59, 1060–62; Redkey, *Respect Black*, 23–24. See also the Appendix.

Savannah tailor shop, most of Georgia's black politicians amassed little wealth either before or immediately after the war. This is hardly surprising since antebellum Georgia law prohibited free blacks from owning property in their own names. According to the 1870 federal manuscript census, sixteen of the nineteen black political officials listed held personal property; eight, real property. Excluding the value of Porter's holdings (seven thousand dollars), the group owned less than four thousand dollars in personal and five thousand dollars in real property. In South Carolina, on the other hand, one-fifth of the black reconstructionists had personal property holdings in excess of a thousand dollars, and one-tenth, over a thousand dollars in real property.[7]

Sherman had prohibited blacks from enlisting in the army in Georgia, and General Tillson virtually excluded them from the Freedmen's Bureau. Lacking candidates from these two institutions, Georgia freedmen turned to their churches and ministers for leadership even though the ministers' personal experiences and religious view of the world tended to conservatize them. Twenty-five (60 percent) of the legislators and delegates whose occupations have been determined were preachers, although most were not professionals. They were barbers, servants, blacksmiths, shoemakers, and carpenters who also preached or carried out other ministerial work. Representative Romulus Moore of Columbia County was a blacksmith, for example, as well as a Baptist minister. Born a Georgia slave in 1818, he saved enough money to purchase his freedom several years before the war. In 1867 he entered politics as a federal registrar. Similarly, former slave Thomas Allen, a legislator from Jasper County, was a Baptist pastor and a shoemaker.[8]

The lack of experienced leaders hampered the black political elite throughout Reconstruction, but at the constitutional convention the black delegation was further handicapped by the absence of the state's most capable black Georgians. Long-time residents Jefferson Long, James Porter, and James M. Simms, three of the most prominent black Georgians, did not attend the convention, and the black

7. Holt, *Black over White*, 38; Flanders, "The Free Negro in Ante-bellum Georgia," 267. See also the Appendix.
8. "Ku Klux Klan Report," 607–618, 735–43.

delegation was therefore forced to turn to outsiders for leadership. Henry M. Turner, Tunis G. Campbell, Sr., and Aaron A. Bradley, with the support of a handful of white allies, including John E. Bryant, strove to write a constitution that would explicitly guarantee the freedmen political and civil rights equal to those of the whites. They were opposed not only by the Democrats but also by many white Republican delegates, especially the followers of former Confederate governor Joseph E. Brown. According to the conservatives, it was "fortunate" that Brown was present, for he helped guide "the Republican element in safe grooves." Invited to address the convention, Brown warned: "You bring both Congress and the Republican party into odium in this State when you go further than Congress has gone, and you confer upon the negroes the right to hold office or to sit in the jury box, in their present condition and you misrepresent nine-tenths of the white men who belong to the reconstruction party in the State. . . . If you are colored men, you had better be content to take what Congress has given you."[9]

Faced with such strong opposition within their own party, there was little the black delegates and their allies could do. When the Committee on the Franchise, chaired by John E. Bryant, issued a report affirming the right of all adult Georgia citizens to hold office, thirty-nine white delegates threatened to oppose the new constitution. "In many counties in the black-belt," complained Republican and future congressman William P. Edwards, "there is no one outside of *niggers* and petty United States agents to represent us." Afraid that the issue might precipitate a walkout, the Republican leadership removed the objectionable clause and assured the blacks that the provision was not necessary to protect their right to hold office. Although a black caucus expressed serious misgivings, it supported the strategy. Similarly, the controversy over the right of blacks to sit on juries was avoided by the adoption of a vague clause requiring jurors to be "upright and intelligent persons." Republican leader Amos T. Akerman explained that this phrasing would "enable the

9. Atlanta *Daily New Era*, January 11, 1868; *Daily Atlanta Intelligencer*, January 27, 1870; Isaac Wheeler Avery, *The History of the State of Georgia from 1850 to 1881, Embracing the Three Important Epochs; the Decade Before the War of 1861–5; the War; the Period of Reconstruction, with Portraits of the Leading Public Men of This Era* (1881; rpr. New York, 1972), 377.

constitution to be differently interpreted upon that subject in different parts of the State."[10]

The debate on various measures offered by blacks to end discrimination exacerbated the anti-Negro sentiments of some of the white Republicans and threatened to disrupt the leadership's strategy. The Augusta leadership responded with attempts to reassure the whites and quiet the blacks in the hope that these tactics would defuse the volatile issues of race. After Aaron A. Bradley called for an end to discrimination on public carriers, white Republican George P. Burnett introduced a resolution proclaiming that the United States and Georgia "are now and ever have been regarded by the people of this State as being a Government whose territory was secured by the white man . . . and over whose destinies the white man shall preside." Republican delegates introduced various measures "prohibiting the introduction of any Ordinance or Resolution referring to race or color" or "excluding all measures in which the distinguishing words 'white' or 'colored' occur." Although these measures died in committee, an ambiguously worded clause declaring that the "social status of the citizens shall never be the subject of legislation" was written into the new constitution. Blacks evidently felt that this clause would protect them. In 1869 they used this provision to challenge the legality of the law against intermarriage. However, Republican Joseph E. Brown, then chief justice of the state supreme court, used the same clause to uphold the law against intermarriage and the concept of segregation in general.[11]

Of all the black delegates to the convention, Aaron A. Bradley was the most militant in demanding black rights and, therefore, the most dangerous threat to the Republican leadership's attempt to write an ambiguous constitution acceptable to the various factions of the party. Born a slave in South Carolina near the turn of the century, Bradley became a shoemaker in Augusta, Georgia. At age nine-

10. Allen D. Candler (comp.), *Confederate Records of Georgia*, VI, 388, 391, 613–14, 597–99; Augusta *Loyal Georgian*, February 15, 1868; *Daily Atlanta Intelligencer*, February 16, 1868; Quattelbaum, "The Absence of Sambo in Georgia Reconstruction," 48 n 83; Constitution of 1868, Art. V, Sec. 13, No. 2; *House Miscellaneous Documents*, 40th Cong., 3rd Sess., No. 52, p. 18.

11. Allen D. Candler (comp.), *Confederate Records of Georgia*, VI, 256, 258–59; *Scott v. The State of Georgia*, 39 *Georgia Reports*, 322–28.

teen he ran away to New York City and eventually moved to Boston, where he practiced law. In late 1865 he returned to Georgia and launched a campaign for black rights that involved him in a series of battles with prominent white officials, including Davis Tillson, the conservative chief of the Freedmen's Bureau in the state. After encouraging the freedmen not to abandon lands promised them by Sherman, Bradley was sent to prison by the federal military. He was later paroled by the secretary of war.[12]

Elected as a delegate to the convention from the Savannah area, Bradley brought his uncompromising attitudes to the convention. He demanded that provisional governor Charles J. Jenkins be removed from office for not taking the test oath, and he described General John D. Pope as "weak-kneed" for not removing Jenkins. The conservative historian and journalist Isaac W. Avery described Bradley as "an incendiary negro" and accused him of "tackling with venomous and voluble impartiality the Republican and Democratic leaders." An aggressive black demanding his rights, Bradley embodied the worst fears of conservative whites. More important, his uncompromising advocacy of black rights threatened the Republican leadership's determination to avoid the race issue. The Atlanta *Daily New Era*, a Brown organ, termed Bradley a "worthless and brawling negro." He was, the newspaper said, "obnoxious to both white and black . . . a disturber of the peace, a creator of discord among his race, and an enemy to the black man, and a nuisance of which the people should be rid." Ultimately, Democrats and white Republicans united against Bradley. They claimed that he had committed a felony in New York in 1851 by seducing a black woman under the promise of marriage. When Bradley responded to these charges by accusing several white delegates, including the president of the convention, of similar transgressions, the convention, led by the Augusta Republicans, unanimously voted to expel him. Rufus B. Bullock, the party's candidate for governor in the April elections, offered a res-

12. Allen D. Candler (comp.), *Confederate Records of Georgia*, VI, 547–49; Coulter, *Negro Legislators in Georgia*, 37–38; George R. Bentley, *A History of the Freedmen's Bureau* (Philadelphia, 1955), 164; *Senate Executive Documents*, 39th Cong., 1st Sess., No. 27, pp. 92–93.

olution branding Bradley "irresponsible" and his charges "senseless mouthings."[13]

The lesson of Bradley's expulsion was not lost on the other black delegates. Henry Turner, aware that the attack on Bradley had to a large extent resulted from deep-seated anti-Negro sentiments, felt compelled to speak on his behalf. Turner, one of the most conservative black delegates, had voted for federal aid to the planters and had urged leniency for Jefferson Davis, but he was shocked by the anti-black rhetoric accompanying the debate on Bradley. Turner argued that any black man who claimed his rights and demanded that white men respect them was labeled revolutionary. "If we are inferior by nature, why fear us," he asked; "why not be willing to leave us free, unfettered, and untrammeled, why bleat over the country so much about negro rule[?]"[14]

Once Bradley was out of the way, Bullock and his lieutenants found it easier to avoid confrontations over the race issue. Most white Republicans were pleased with the new constitution. Its provisions for debtor relief and public education would appeal to the economically depressed white small farmers and artisans. Moreover, party leaders like Bullock thought it minimized "the danger of negro suffrage." Judgeships were to be appointive, eliminating the possibility that blacks could be elected to the bench in the black belt. Similarly, all state officials, except the governor, were to be elected by the General Assembly, making it unlikely that blacks would ever be voted into state offices. Even the most virulent Negrophobes among the Republicans must have found certain provisions appealing. The constitution perpetuated a host of antebellum state laws and statutes that discriminated against blacks. These laws, known as Irwin's Code, established a caste system that classified the people of Georgia as citizens, residents not citizens, aliens, and persons of

13. *Daily Atlanta Intelligencer*, December 19, 24, 1867, January 16, 1868; Avery, *The History of the State of Georgia*, 382; Atlanta *Daily New Era*, February 13, 1868; Allen D. Candler (comp.), *Confederate Records of Georgia*, VI, 577–82. For Brown's close connection with the *Daily New Era* board, see Joseph E. Brown to William D. Kelly, May 20, 1867, in Joseph E. Brown Papers, Felix Hargrett Collection, University of Georgia Library, Athens.

14. Allen D. Candler (comp.), *Confederate Records of Georgia*, 290, 480; Augusta *Daily Constitutionalist*, February 13, 1868.

color. "We got a constitution," Brown later boasted, "which soon placed the State under the permanent control of the white race." Indeed, conservative opponents eventually used the Irwin's Code provisions to deny blacks the right to hold office.[15]

Contemporary black leaders viewed the constitution as a mixed blessing. Even a shrewd white Republican like Amos T. Akerman agreed that if it were interpreted decently the constitution would guarantee the ex-slaves certain political and civil rights. Among its positive points, the constitution included a declaration of rights, sponsored by Bradley and Bryant, which pledged, "no laws shall be made or enforced which shall abridge the privileges or immunities of citizens of the United States, or deny to any person within its jurisdiction the equal protection of its laws." Other clauses provided for a system of public education, abolished whipping, and established the right of laborers to place liens against the property of their employers. Having helped choose their friend Rufus B. Bullock over more conservative candidates for the gubernatorial nomination, the blacks were optimistic about the future. They had some reason to believe that with Bullock at the helm, their rights would be respected.[16]

The black delegates had not had sufficient political power to block some of the negative features of the new constitution, but at the same time, they had misused what little political power they had. In 1874 Henry M. Turner reminded Tunis Campbell how the black delegates had mistakenly opposed John E. Bryant's efforts to insert the clause in the new constitution that would have guaranteed blacks the right to hold office: "We all joined in and struck it out. I foolishly voted for it and you foolishly voted for it. He fought us and we over-

15. Rufus B. Bullock, "Reconstruction in Georgia, 1865–70," *Independent*, LV (March 19, 1903), 672. See Constitution of 1868, Art. IV, Sec. 2, No. 8, Art. V, Sec. 9; R. H. Clark, T. R. R. Cobb, and D. Irwin (preps.), *The Code of the State of Georgia*, rev., corr., annot. David Irwin, George N. Lester, and W. B. Hill (2nd ed. rev.; Macon, 1873), 285, 296, 783, 824; *White* v. *Clements*, 39 *Georgia Reports*, 232 *et seq.*; Herbert Fielder, *A Sketch of the Life and Times and Speeches of Joseph E. Brown* (Springfield, Mass., 1883), 430.

16. *House Miscellaneous Documents*, 40th Cong., 3rd Sess., No. 52, p. 18; Allen D. Candler (comp.), *Confederate Records of Georgia*, VI, 476–78; Constitution of 1868, Art. I, Secs. 2, 22, 30; Charles G. Bloom, "The Georgia Election of April, 1868: A Re-examination of the Politics of Georgia Reconstruction" (M.A. thesis, University of Chicago, 1963), 22–25; Augusta *Daily Constitutionalist*, March 10, 1868.

powered him and struck it out." Similarly, to help finance the public school system, some black delegates supported a poll tax that conservatives later used to disfranchise thousands of freedmen who could not afford to pay it. "I was inexperienced at the time," Turner admitted; "I made a great blunder." Their inability to foresee the consequences of the poll tax derived not only from a lack of experience. The black politicians came from a southern black elite that suffered from a misplaced faith in the good intentions of their white opponents. Most of them, Turner included, refused to support a Bryant-Bullock effort to impose disabilities on high-ranking Confederate officials. When the blacks were being expelled from the legislature in 1868, the white Republican *American Union* reminded them: "So the men who were so generous to take the frozen adder to their bosom, have been stung, have they? Don't Turner want to remove some more disabilities from the Democrats. This result is deserved by Mr. Turner."[17]

Ironically, although Georgia's black politicians stood closer to the black peasantry than did the black reconstructionists in South Carolina and Louisiana, they were no more effective as representatives. South Carolina's black politicians failed because they were too bourgeois; Georgia's suffered because they lacked a certain bourgeois skill, experience, and self-confidence. As John M. Matthews noted: "slavery had not provided many opportunities for Negroes to develop a capacity for leadership, much less to be familiar with politics. One of the most serious problems facing [Georgia] Negroes was the scarcity of competent leaders. . . . Some of the most prominent Negroes, such as Bradley, Campbell, and Turner, came to Georgia from other parts of the country." Likewise, the Atlanta University scholar Ethel Maude Christler argued that the black delegation to the constitutional convention "was made up of colored men who were easily intimidated by whites."[18]

17. "A Speech Delivered in McIntire Hall-Sav-Aug 21th, 1874, by Hon. Henry M. Turner in Reply to Charges Made Against the Hon. John E. Bryant by Hon. T. G. Campbell, Previous to His Nomination to Congress" (in John E. Bryant Papers, Manuscript Department, William R. Perkins Library, Duke University, Durham, N.C.); "Ku Klux Klan Report," VII, 1041; Allen D. Candler (comp.), *Confederate Records of Georgia*, VI, 388–89, 582–84; Macon *American Union*, August 28, 1868.

18. Matthews, "The Negro in Georgia Politics," 137; Ethel Maude Christler, "Par-

The wealth, prestige, and education of the whites had bred a certain deference in Georgia's black politicians. "You have all the elements of superiority on your side," Henry Turner told the white lawmakers. "You know we have no money, no railroads, no telegraphs, no advantage of any sort. . . . You know that the black people of this country acknowledge you as their superiors, by virtue of your education and knowledge." White Republicans recognized this deference. Joseph Brown answered conservatives who charged that the Republicans were bringing black domination to Georgia with a question: "Why is it, then, if we are in danger of negro government, that they did not, when they had the power, elect a majority of their own race [to the convention] instead of about one-fifth[?]" Henry Turner confirmed Brown's assessment. He bitterly recalled how blacks in the black belt "begged" whites to run for the convention on their behalf. Had the whites responded more fully to their call, there would have been even fewer blacks at the convention.[19]

Some of the conciliatory attitudes that Georgia's black politicians exhibited had evolved from their role as preachers. As Eugene Genovese discovered, antebellum black preachers had "had to make many compromises in order to be able to do the very first thing incumbent upon them—to preach the Word." In short, they had been forced to come to some accommodation with the slave-owners. White southerners correctly perceived that the accommodationist pattern did not completely disappear after the war. "They were pleased to see that we were endeavoring to elevate the colored ministers of the South," Henry M. Turner recalled, "instead of flooding the country with Northern ministers, many of whom might be too 'radical' for the times."[20]

The message Georgia's minister-politicians expounded also had

ticipation of Negroes in the Government of Georgia, 1867–1880" (M.A. thesis, Atlanta University, 1932), 6.

19. Henry M. Turner, "Speech on the Eligibility of Colored Members to Seats in the Georgia Legislature. . . . Delivered Before That Body September 3d, 1868," in George A. Singleton, *The Romance of African Methodism: A Study of the African Methodist Episcopal Church* (New York, 1952), Appendix B, pp. 12–13; Atlanta *Daily New Era*, January 11, 1868; Macon *American Union*, October 9, 1868.

20. Genovese, *Roll, Jordan, Roll*, 263; Turner quoted in Leon Litwack, *Been in the Storm So Long: The Aftermath of Slavery* (New York, 1979), 470.

its conservative side. The messiah figure of its millennialism was Lincoln, not a black militant, and its message of Christian brotherhood glossed over racial and class differences. In 1866, for example, Henry Turner urged Augusta freedmen to "love whites," and as a result, "soon their prejudice would melt away, and with God for our father, we will all be brothers." Georgia's black minister-politicians preached a providential version of history that was rife with political fatalism. In their view, suffering and perseverance were part of the divine plan, and they counseled the freedmen to be patient. Divine Providence, they said, would ultimately intervene in their behalf as it had during the war. Some, like Turner, even pronounced slavery a part of God's plan to Christianize Africa. Moreover, clerical domination of Georgia's black politics was never greater than during the constitutional convention. Sixteen of the nineteen black delegates on whom we have occupational information were ministers, and nine of these were AME. In licensing Georgia preachers into the AME church "by the cargo," Henry Turner attracted many of them into the Republican party and probably to the convention itself. As their political mentor, the conservative Turner no doubt heavily influenced them. Recalling his philosophy at the convention, Turner claimed, "'Anything to please the white folks' [had been] my motto."[21]

Whatever its limitations, the constitution produced by the convention proved a successful platform for the April elections. White Republicans in the black belt told the ex-slaves that the constitution had granted them full political rights, while Joseph E. Brown and other Republicans assured whites elsewhere in Georgia that it did not guarantee blacks the right to hold office or sit on juries. The result was a narrow Republican victory. The constitution was ratified, Bullock was elected, and a slight Republican majority, which included some blacks, was sent to both houses of the legislature.[22]

Built on a shaky foundation, the Republican alliance was bound to shatter once the party assumed power. While the *Freemen's Stan-*

21. Genovese, *Roll, Jordan, Roll,* 272–73; Redkey, *Respect Black,* 7–8, 11–12, 30; Turner, "Speech on the Eligibility of Colored Members to Seats in the Georgia Legislature," 12–13. See also Chapter II.
22. Drago, "Black Georgia During Reconstruction," 133.

dard, edited by black minister-politician James M. Simms, was predicting that Bullock's election signaled the fall of "the Jerichoian wall of prejudice," Brown's Atlanta *Daily New Era* was advising blacks to expect no additional political or civil rights: "You must quit dabbling in politics, and go to work in order to earn an honest subsistence." The conservative *Georgia Weekly Telegraph* aptly observed, "Georgia's white radicals . . . enough of them to fill the offices . . . are quite impatient of negro interference with politics, now that the voting is over."[23]

Hardly had the Georgia legislature convened in July before the Democrats began exploiting the rift in the Republican party. Democratic state senator Milton A. Candler, citing Joseph Brown's own campaign speeches against black office-holding, moved that the eligibility of blacks to sit in the legislature be investigated. In conjunction with the Democratic move in the legislature to expel the blacks, the Democratic Atlanta *Constitution* launched a vitriolic attack on the evils of "negro government." According to the *Constitution*, only "nigger[s]" applauded Bullock's inauguration, and some of the white Republicans were "White Nigger[s]." The impact of this newspaper's campaign on white Republicans, particularly native Georgians, is impossible to measure accurately, but it undoubtedly contributed to the gnawing feeling of some that they were traitors to their race. Declining the nomination as a Grant-Colfax elector, Republican Edward R. Harden confided to a friend: "I am determined now to go with my race and section. . . . The Republican speakers I discover are inflaming the minds of the negroes and preparing them for a war of races. I cannot act with any such a party."[24]

Aware of such sentiments among some of their white Republican opponents, the Democrats couched their attempts to expel the blacks in bipartisan terms. State Senator Rufus E. Lester reminded white Republicans that Lincoln and his party wanted to exclude blacks from the territories because they competed with white laborers for jobs.

23. Savannah *Freemen's Standard*, June 13, 1868; Atlanta *Daily New Era*, April 25, 1868; Macon *Georgia Weekly Telegraph*, June 5, 1868.

24. C. Mildred Thompson, *Reconstruction in Georgia*, 211–12; Atlanta *Constitution*, July 23, 30, August 16, 1868; Edward R. Harden to his mother, August 20, 1868, in Edward R. Harden Papers, Manuscript Department, William R. Perkins Library, Duke University, Durham, N.C.

"For the good of the white race, for the good of the black race in their midst, for the preservation of law and order, for the perpetuity of constitutional government and Republican institutions," he exhorted, "the Democrats here and the Conservative Republicans here and law loving men everywhere, are unwilling that he [the black], in his present state, shall be allowed to make laws for the country." By early September, 1868, the Democrats mustered enough Republican votes to expel the blacks.[25]

Without significant Republican support, the Democrats could not have succeeded, for the Republican party held a majority in both houses of the legislature. R. L. McWhorter, Republican speaker of the house, sealed the fate of the black legislators by ruling that they could not vote on the issue of their expulsion. The final vote in the house was eighty-three to twenty-three in favor of expulsion, with thirty Republicans supporting the measure or declining to vote. More than half of the fifteen white Republicans who voted for expulsion represented counties with black majorities. "The supineness and coldness of some among the Republican members," *Nation* noted, "were what enabled the attack on the negroes to be successful. Some of the so-called carpet-baggers voted as they did in order to ingratiate themselves with the whites; of the so-called scallawags, some voted as they did for the same reason, and some doubtless from conviction." Conservative Georgians agreed. "We hope the vote . . . will open the eyes of the negroes to the real and detestable meanness of their white allies in Georgia," a Democratic newspaper gloated. "What do you think of that colored man? Without the votes of these *thirty* men . . . the movement would have failed. . . . They [white Republicans] have always declared that you were . . . plainly ineligible under the very Constitution your chosen representatives had framed in your interests."[26]

Some of Georgia's white Republicans were no doubt as detestable as the conservatives charged. Joseph E. Brown, the state's Confederate governor, changed his political colors like a chameleon and be-

25. C. Mildred Thompson, *Reconstruction in Georgia*, 214; Savannah *Morning News*, October 27, 1868.
26. *Nation*, VII (September 17, 1868), 223; Drago, "Black Georgia During Reconstruction," 179–80; Macon *Georgia Journal and Messenger*, September 8, 1868.

came Georgia's leading reconstructionist. Without scruple, he used his black allies to further his own political ends. He hoped that once the state was restored to the Union the blacks would be put in their place, and he would emerge as the savior of the white race, the state's real redeemer. Brown had apparently plotted this strategy from the very beginning. During the convention, the Atlanta *Daily New Era*, edited by Brown's close associate Samuel Bard, pointed the way: "Reconstruction does not make negro suffrage a permanency. If the white men of Georgia are unified they can secure the control of their new State Government, elect their Congressmen, and as soon as the State is once more in its place . . . they can amend their Constitution, disfranchise the negroes, and restore suffrage to the disfranchised whites."[27]

Party leaders like Brown and Bullock were not totally devoid of vision. They wanted to create a "New Era" of industrialization in Georgia. "This is . . . the kind of reconstruction that we need," intoned the Atlanta *Daily New Era* in late 1866. "Georgia wants more railroads, more rolling mills and foundries, more machine shops, more mining operations, more cotton mills. . . . We have been in the rear ranks of progress long enough." Rufus Bullock shared this view of Reconstruction. He had come to Georgia before the war as an agent for the New York–based Adams Express Company. His origins fed the suspicions of conspiracy-minded conservatives, who saw him as the tool of northern capitalists. The Augusta *Daily Constitutionalist* declared that Bullock was secretly directed by a "monster corporation" founded by "the original Carpetbagger," who had dominated the North before the war. Rufus B. Bullock was hardly an agent of northern capitalists, but he felt that northern capital was necessary to bring about industrialization. He also believed that a statewide network of railroads was essential to industrialization, and during his administration, state aid to railroads increased enormously. While he was governor, the state capital was moved from Milledgeville to Atlanta, later to become the showplace of the Republican "New Era." Unlike Brown, Bullock was genuinely concerned that the end of Radical Reconstruction would jeopardize

27. Atlanta *Daily New Era*, January 4, 1868.

black rights, but he was far more afraid that "the whole work of internal improvement carried out by Northern capital would be swept away."[28]

With the expulsion of the blacks from the legislature, conditions in Georgia rapidly deteriorated. The expulsion emboldened the Ku Klux Klan to greater acts of violence, and the legislature passed several anti-Negro measures, including one that specifically excluded blacks from the jury box. Moreover, the anti-Negro rhetoric of the conservative politicians and press fostered a climate hostile to blacks. Violence occurred in September, 1868, when several hundred Republicans, mostly blacks, approached the small town of Camilla in southwestern Georgia on their way to a political rally. As they entered the town, a drunken white shot at them. Other whites opened fire, killing seven blacks and wounding many more. Conservatives blamed the riot on the incendiary preachings of white Republicans, but the *Nation* was probably more accurate: "The truth of the matter is that the high-handed injustice of the Georgia Legislature is having its natural effect; it has put fresh heart into every young ruffian in the State, and now there is no place where the shooting of a negro by a drunken white man may not very probably lead to unprovoked murder by wholesale."[29]

The expulsion of the black legislators and its aftermath had one positive effect: the black political elite became more militant, self-sufficient, and black oriented. Black politicians began to challenge the hegemony of Georgia whites, especially that of their Republican allies. Assemblyman William A. Golden of Liberty County angrily

---

28. *Ibid.*, November 17, 1866, April 24, 1867; Wallace Putnam Reed (ed.), *History of Atlanta, Georgia, with Illustrations and Biographical Sketches of Some of Its Prominent Men and Pioneers* (Syracuse, N.Y., 1889), Pt. 2, p. 13, and Atlanta *Opinion* (as quoted in Augusta *Daily Constitutionalist*, April 17, 1868), both quoted in Bloom, "The Georgia Election of April, 1868," 27–28; Rufus Brown Bullock, *Address of Rufus B. Bullock to the People of Georgia. A Review of the Revolutionary Proceedings of the Late Repudiating Legislature. The Slanders and Misrepresentations of the Committees Exposed. A Republican Administration Contrasted with the Corrupt and Reckless Action of the Present Usurping Minority, Under the Lead of General Toombs* (n.p., 1872), 52; Nathans, *Losing the Peace*, 69.

29. Theodore Barker Fitz-Simons, Jr., "The Ku Klux Klan in Georgia, 1868–1871" (M.A. thesis, University of Georgia, 1957), 58; Macon *American Union*, October 9, 1868; Theodore Barker Fitz-Simons, Jr., "The Camilla Riot," *Georgia Historical Quarterly*, XXXV (June, 1951), 116–25; *Nation*, VII (September 24, 1868), 241.

stormed out of a committee meeting on expulsion, promising that the blacks would hold their seats at the point of a bayonet if necessary. Given one hour each to speak before being turned out of the legislature, other blacks eloquently expressed their anger. James Porter of Savannah raised the specter of war, while George Linder of Laurens warned, "*Roust* us from here [and] we will roust you." In answer to racist arguments, James M. Simms described the achievements of famous blacks in literature." Henry Turner delivered the most powerful defense of the right of blacks to sit in the legislature. Turner realized that continued deference to whites amounted to political suicide. He refused to plead with whites as some of his black colleagues had because it reminded him "of slaves begging under the lash." Instead, he threatened to "hurl thunderbolts at the men who dare cross the threshold of my manhood," and he accused the white race of treachery and cowardice. Reviewing the legal and constitutional arguments supporting his position, he declared the basic question to be "Am I a Man?" Moreover, he renounced his earlier efforts to placate the Democrats, including his support of the removal of their voting disabilities. "I will call a colored convention," he promised, "and I will say to my friends; Let us send North for carpetbaggers and Yankees."[30]

The growing disillusionment and racial awareness manifested itself in various ways among the Georgia freedmen and their political leaders. A Clarke County Union League denounced Assemblyman Madison Davis, who, because of his light skin, had been able to escape expulsion by denying that he was black. Some blacks chose flight. Minister-politician Romulus Moore and some of his Columbia County constituents made plans to migrate to Louisiana. Following the Camilla massacre of 1868, Albany blacks sent a petition to Congress in which they declared, "Protection cannot be afforded to us here, and with feelings similar to those of the Indian as he turns westward from the bones and hunting-grounds of his fathers, we ask to be removed to some other land."[31]

30. Atlanta *Constitution*, August 21, 30, September 1, 2, 1868; Turner, "Speech on the Eligibility of Colored Members to Seats in the Georgia Legislature," 1–14.
31. Atlanta *Constitution*, September 11, 1868; "Ku Klux Klan Report," VII, 739; Macon *American Union*, December 11, 1868; *House Miscellaneous Documents*, 40th Cong., 3rd Sess., No. 52, p. 97.

In October, 1868, Georgia's prominent black politicians met in Macon at a convention called by Henry M. Turner. The assembly, instigated and led entirely by blacks, was a striking contrast to earlier freedmen's conventions. Any suggestion of conciliation was tossed aside. At the first freedmen's convention in 1866, white Republican John E. Bryant had played an active role and had been elected president of the predominantly black Georgia Equal Rights and Educational Association. This time, however, Bryant only addressed the group as a visitor. Black speakers at the convention charged that in expelling the blacks from the legislature the Democrats had given support to the "murdering bands" of the Ku Klux Klan and had inaugurated anti-Negro sentiment that was "responsible for the Camilla riot." They denounced those white Republican "allies" who voted for their expulsion with the Democrats as "vipers" who had helped kill black rights. The convention created the Civil and Political Rights Association to lobby Congress for a redress of black grievances. The association, headed by Turner and with other blacks holding the remaining offices, was to organize branches throughout the state.[32]

The emergence of a politically independent black convention movement did not end the black alliance with some white Republicans. Blacks were aware that twenty-three white Republicans, mostly followers of Governor Rufus B. Bullock, had voted against expulsion and that Bullock himself had vigorously denounced it. After the expulsion, Bullock vetoed some of the more blatantly anti-Negro legislation. "While Governor Bullock had his faults," Henry Turner conceded, "he was very generous, and would listen to reason and proper appeals, and in many instances, where he knew persons had been penetentiared maliciously, he would pardon them. There are scores at liberty to-day who would have been in the penitentiary but for him." Bullock and the Republican administration pardoned roughly one in seven of the convicts admitted to the state prison between 1868 and 1871; many were black.[33]

32. Macon *American Union*, October 9, 1868.
33. Drago, "Black Georgia During Reconstruction," 184, 185; "Ku Klux Klan Report," VII, 1040; Convict Roster, 1817–1871, in Georgia Department of Archives and History, Atlanta.

For Bullock, alliance with the blacks was a necessity. He needed their support to carry forth his Reconstruction plans within the party. The dramatic drop in the Republican vote from April to November, 1868, forced him to seek federal intervention to remain in power. This alienated important white party members who wanted an end to interference from Washington. When he asked Congress to reconstruct Georgia again by reseating the blacks and purging the legislature of Democrats ineligible under the Fourteenth Amendment, Joseph Brown, John Bryant, and other party dissidents defected. In 1869 they organized themselves into a National Republican Club and opposed further Reconstruction. Georgia's black Republicans, however, came to Bullock's aid. In November, 1869, the State Republican Executive Committee held a stormy session in which a subcommittee issued a majority report recommending an end to Reconstruction. Bullock and his black allies managed to overturn it. The report finally adopted urged Congress to investigate conditions in Georgia and reseat the black legislators.[34]

The blacks themselves organized a successful campaign to pressure congressional Republicans to support Bullock's proposals. The Civil and Political Rights Association held mass rallies throughout the state to petition Congress to reconstruct Georgia again. As president of this association, Henry Turner warned United States Senator Benjamin F. Butler that blacks were leaving the party in Georgia by the thousands. "If it is a fact that the party for whom we have sacrificed everything is going to desert us in the face of all the representations made to them when you can remedy our condition in one breath," Turner declared, "it is time we knew it. . . . So we can commence to leave the State, or declare ourselves no longer members of the Republican party." Turner, James Simms, and other black leaders traveled to Washington to bolster Bullock's case and to present the grievances of the black labor convention of 1868.[35]

As part of their campaign, black Republicans countered attempts by Bullock's Republican opponents to assure Congress that Georgia

34. Nathans, *Losing the Peace*, 174–75; Atlanta *Constitution*, December 3, 1869; Avery, *The History of the State of Georgia*, 420.

35. *House Miscellaneous Documents*, 40th Cong., 3rd Sess., No. 52, pp. 88–98; H. M. Turner to Benjamin F. Butler, February 19, 1869, in Benjamin F. Butler Papers, Library of Congress; Macon *American Union*, December 4, 1868.

was a peaceful state not in need of further federal intervention. When John E. Bryant, chairman of the State Republican Executive Committee, sent a telegram to Congress claiming that conditions in Georgia were excellent for Republicans, black congressman-to-be Jefferson Long publicly challenged Bryant's assertions: "Ask those white Republicans who love their God and their country if they are satisfied with the reign of terror that now exists in Georgia; who, because they voted to retain the colored members of the Legislature in their seats, dare not return to their homes for fear they will be murdered. Ask those colored members that were driven out of the Legislature, and their constituents, if they are satisfied. Ask the wife, with her little ones in her arms, as she wails over the assassinated and mangled body of her husband, if she is satisfied." According to Long, Governor Bullock needed additional power "to speak to Georgia, as did Jackson to South Carolina." Likewise, Henry Turner criticized the Brown Republican organ, the Atlanta *Daily New Era*, for wanting to halt further Reconstruction. He maintained that the paper wanted the black man "to be a mere ass, upon whose back, any white man may ride into office, and then sink him to eternal infamy by their votes and diabolical legislation."[36]

The bitter response of the conservative Republicans indicated that the blacks' campaign for further federal intervention and Reconstruction was bearing fruit. "The allegations set forth by Messrs. Simms and Turner," charged the Atlanta *Daily New Era*, "are simply false. The poor deluded colored men are simply the tools of a few designing white Republicans who are bent on carrying out Gov. Bullock's shortsighted policy, at the risk to the future prospects of the National Republican Party." The *New Era* also reprinted an article from a northern journal that described Henry Turner as "a wandering speculator without character or influence with his race in Georgia . . . a serpent in human shape" who "contributed greatly to the present and future injury of his race."[37]

Under the Congressional Reorganization Act of 1869, the Legislature of 1868 was reconvened, the expelled blacks reseated, and a

36. Macon *American Union*, January 15, 1869, December 4, 1868.
37. Atlanta *Daily New Era*, March 6, 1869; New York *Tribune* reprinted *ibid.*, May 9, 1869.

number of Democrats purged under the terms of the Fourteenth Amendment. Angry conservatives denounced the act but gave grudging praise to the blacks, who, they conceded, had been instrumental in bringing it about. The Democratic editor of the Atlanta *Constitution* wrote: "The colored convention was an important . . . body . . . these unlettered men went to work to do their business of retribution and recovery of their privileges in an extraordinarily practical way. . . . Deeply chagrined and incensed at the deprivation of the right to hold office, the colored leaders, deserted in this valued matter by their white allies, for the first and only time in the protracted play of Reconstruction, self-reliantly took the bit in their own mouths and organized for a race victory."[38]

Despite the success of Bullock and the blacks, the Democrats and their conservative Republican allies still held considerable power in the state legislature. Conservative opposition coalesced in 1870 around the candidacy of dissident Republican John E. Bryant for speaker of the house. "Bryant is the candidate of the Democrats for speaker of the House," declared conservative Robert Toombs, "and I and Joe Brown are trying to elect him! Rather a strange conjunction, is it not? But you know my rule is to use the devil if I can do better to save the country." Bryant explained his conversion to conservatism in a letter to Alexander H. Stephens in 1870: "I was taught to regard the Southern people as *rebels* who should be punished. . . . As I became acquainted with the Southern people, I was satisfied that they were honest, and, although they might be technically guilty of treason, they were not morally guilty. . . . At first I favored disfranchisement. Now I favor Universal amnesty." Bryant concluded: "Men change asses don't. Your writings have done much to change my views."[39]

In Bryant the Democrats and their Republican friends thought they had a candidate for speaker who would attract black votes. The Democratic Atlanta *Intelligencer* published a letter from a conservative Republican urging blacks in the house to support Bryant's

38. Avery, *The History of the State of Georgia*, 423–32, 405–406.
39. Ulrich B. Phillips (ed.), *The Correspondence of Robert Toombs, Alexander H. Stephens, and Howell Cobb*, Annual Report of the American Historical Association, for the Year 1911 (Washington, D.C., 1913), II, 707; J. E. Bryant to Alexander H. Stephens, June 17, 1870, in Alexander H. Stephens Papers, Library of Congress.

candidacy: "Col. Bryant fought in the Union Army to emancipate you. . . . he was the first white man in Georgia who demanded for you equal political rights with white men. . . . In the General Assembly when the attempt was made to expel you, he was one of the white men who had nerve enough to make speeches against your expulsion." Bryant's opponent, R. L. McWhorter, was hardly problack; as speaker in 1868 he had ruled that the black legislators could not vote on their expulsion. The contest illustrated the dilemma in which Georgia's black politicians repeatedly found themselves. In this instance, none of them supported Bryant, and McWhorter was victorious.[40]

The Congressional Reorganization Act of 1869 only delayed Bullock's ultimate defeat. The Democrats, with the support of the Ku Klux Klan, had reduced the Republican vote to the point where a Democratic victory in the December, 1870, elections was a foregone conclusion. As a desperate ploy to remain in power, Bullock turned to prolongation. Because Congress had not yet admitted Georgia's congressional representatives, Bullock contended that the state was still governed by the military under the Reconstruction Acts of 1867. Therefore, he urged the legislature to suspend the scheduled elections and prolong its sitting.[41]

Most blacks supported prolongation in the state legislature and defended it before Congress. They maintained it was absolutely necessary for the passage of vitally needed legislation and to ensure the physical safety of the freedmen. In a dramatic speech before the assembly, Henry Turner declared that Georgia had forfeited its claim to independence by expelling the black legislators in 1868. Prolongation was retribution for the suffering Georgia blacks had incurred at the hands of the 1868 legislature in their absence. He asked the Democrats:

> Have you paid my constituents for the losses they have sustained? Have you paid them for keeping them off the jury for nearly three years, and for the hundreds you have convicted through white juries, poison[ed] with prejudice, and sent to the Penitentiary in perfect caravans, or hung

40. *Daily Atlanta Intelligencer*, January 27, 1870; Drago, "Black Georgia During Reconstruction," 190.
41. Avery, *The History of the State of Georgia*, 438–40.

for the most trivial charges and false allegations? Have you paid the damages done to the rising youths of our State for not enacting a school bill, as the Constitution . . . required? . . . Have you paid for that abominable decision which the Supreme Court made under your affairs, which allows white men to generate their species with colored women, and however much they may love each other . . . force [sic] them to live a life of adulterous conjugality, and thereby bastard their children[?] . . . Have you paid for murdering my bill, offered in 1868, after expelling me, providing a regulation to govern common carriers, thereby compelling colored passengers to pay as much as the whites, then to be thrust into Jim-Crow cars, for white men to insult their wives, and blackguard our daughters, and smoke them to death?

Have you paid for not legislating upon the provision of our Constitution which gives the laborer a lien upon the property of the employer, and subjecting him to be driven away penniless[?] . . . Have you paid for inflaming the public mind, as you did when you expelled the colored members, and for arousing worse passions that [sic] were ever touched by the batteries of hell . . . disarming the negro of his civil and political rights . . . ?

Turner predicted that the fall elections would bring violence and ultimately the impeachment of Governor Bullock. To emphasize the gravity of the situation, Georgia's black legislators presented a petition to the black United States senator from Mississippi, Hiram R. Revels, in which they declared: "If elections take place this fall. . . . Violence and bloodshed will mark the course of such elections, and a fair expression of the will of the people cannot be had. We shall be driven from the polls, as in the Presidential election by armed and organized bands of rebels, and our State given over to the guidance and control of the most extreme men of the Democratic party."[42]

The blacks' nearly unanimous support of Bullock's schemes for further Reconstruction did not preclude serious problems between white and black Republicans in the Bullock coalition. Officeholding was the most devisive issue. The white Republicans had initially refused blacks all but a token share of elective offices. Georgia's sole black congressman, Jefferson Long, filled only a short term. All of the state officials in the Bullock administration were white. Similarly, no blacks sat on the Georgia delegation to the Republican Na-

42. Drago, "Black Georgia During Reconstruction," 191; Atlanta *Daily New Era,* August 14, 1870; Atlanta *Constitution,* March 16, 1870.

tional Convention in 1868, and throughout Reconstruction, black office-holding on the county and municipal level was minimal.[43]

Even before their expulsion from the legislature, some of Georgia's black politicians were critical of their exclusion from both the party's leadership and a fair share of elective offices. In July, 1868, black assemblyman James Simms denounced the white Republicans' monopoly on the pursuit of office. He demanded that blacks be given half the elective offices, and expulsion only increased the blacks' demand for offices. "We are told," Henry M. Turner pointed out, "that if black men want to speak, they must speak through white trumpets; if black men want their sentiments expressed, they must be adulterated and sent through white messengers, who will quibble, and equivocate, and evade as rapidly as the pendulum of the clock." In April, 1869, Edwin Belcher angrily asked United States Senator Benjamin Butler: "Do you think it would be just . . . to appoint all white men in Georgia when ninety thousand of the 120,000 republicans in Georgia are colored men?" Similarly, before a meeting of Savannah Republicans in 1870, black state senator Aaron A. Bradley argued: "Why should we seek to elevate a third-class white man over a *first-class* colored man. I do not believe there are 1,000 white Republican voters in the First Congressional District. Then, why should the colored voters, over 20,000, be cheated out of three hundred offices by persons no way their mental superiors?"[44]

After the expulsion, blacks attending Republican rallies and conventions were increasingly assertive. When Savannah blacks met in 1869 to protest the support of white Republicans for expulsion, black speakers demanded an all-black ticket for county offices on the grounds that whites could no longer be trusted. At a mass meeting in Augusta the blacks demanded two black candidates for the assembly seats. Bullock supporter Ephraim Tweedy withdrew his candidacy for assembly rather than risk losing to a black. In 1870 after a heated contest, De Kalb County Republicans nominated a black over a white for the county's assembly seat. The same year black assem-

43. Drago, "Black Georgia During Reconstruction," 193–96.
44. Macon *American Union*, July 10, 1868; Turner, "Speech on the Eligibility of Colored Members to Seats in the Georgia Legislature," 3; Edwin Belcher to Butler, April 5, 1869, in Butler Papers; Americus *Weekly Sumter Republican*, December 16, 1870.

blyman Thomas P. Beard bolted the Bullock faction of the party and voted against prolongation; he was rewarded with the party's nomination for Congress from the Fifth Congressional District, a Bryant stronghold. In 1870 Aaron Bradley joined Bullock's opposition and persuaded a convention of fifteen hundred Savannah blacks to nominate a predominantly black ticket to oppose the party regulars.[45]

Governor Bullock was well aware, even before the expulsion, of the growing dissatisfaction among the blacks over their exclusion from a fair share of the offices. Congressman C. H. Prince warned him in July, 1868, about the potential damage this discontent could do to the party: "Our colored friends feel that they were not treated well by the Gen. Ass[embly] in its election of officers, and as they compose the main body of our party, it is for our interest to do all for them possible." With Georgia reconstructed again in 1869 through significant black support, Bullock and the party conceded the freedmen a larger share of the offices. "Bullock appears to have a decided fancy for the color opposite his own," the Atlanta *Constitution* noted in December, 1868. "All the election managers of his . . . for Brooks county are negroes." In 1870 the governor appointed loyal black supporter James Simms judge of the Superior Court of Chatham County. Blacks also began receiving a larger share of the federal patronage. Henry Turner was nominated for postmaster in Macon, while Edwin Belcher was appointed a United States revenue assessor. In 1871 black politician Jefferson F. Long was elected to Congress, and the following year nine blacks sat on the Georgia delegation to the Republican National Convention.[46]

Most white Republicans saw the blacks' desire for office not as a healthy sign of their growing independence, but as an indication of their ingratitude and selfishness. When James Simms suggested that the blacks might not continue to vote Republican unless they shared

45. Savannah *Daily Advertiser*, July 6, 1869; Augusta *Daily Constitutionalist*, December 4, 1870, January 31, February 12, 1871; Atlanta *Constitution*, December 4, 1870, August 13, 1870, Savannah *Morning News*, October 6, 1870.

46. C. H. Prince to R. B. Bullock, July 27, 1868, in Executive Department, Correspondence of Rufus B. Bullock, July 4, 1868, to October 29, 1871, Georgia Department of Archives and History, Atlanta; Atlanta *Constitution*, December 20, 1868; Paul Laurence Sanford, "The Negro in the Political Reconstruction of Georgia, 1865–1872" (M.A. thesis, Atlanta University, 1947), 55; Drago, "Black Georgia During Reconstruction," 195–96.

the offices, the staunch Republican *American Union* responded: "Did Mr. Simms take his musket, and with his own blood purchase the freedom he boasts of? We think not. . . . Mr. Simms should look back a few years, and he will comprehend the fact that even now he is supported upon the shoulders of patriotic white Republicans, who, should *they* do as he threatens the blacks will do, would make the black man worse than a slave." Furthermore, the *Union* editor, along with other white Republicans, argued that the blacks were not qualified to hold office or, at the very least, were less qualified than whites. The *Union* claimed that black politician John F. Quarles, who was demanding more offices for blacks, "would send a cornfield negro to the United States Senate simply because he was black. He [Quarles] cares not about the salvation of the country; it is the fat salary . . . he is after."[47]

In answer to these charges, Quarles maintained that blacks had been more than generous in putting white Republicans into office. "When the editor of the *Union* asserts that the colored man has but one object—self,—I say a more consummate libel was never committed to paper. They [the blacks] constitute nine-tenths of the Republicans of Georgia yet they do not fill one in fifty of the offices in the State." Moreover, the blacks warned that unless they received a significant share of the offices disillusionment would set in and the party would be doomed to defeat.[48]

Opportunism on all sides obscured the dispute. The conservatives were undoubtedly correct in charging that some white Republicans opposed black officeholding because they wanted the offices for themselves. "The trouble among us," admitted a white Republican in 1869, "is that too many white Republicans seek office to the exclusion of worthy and intelligent colored men, thus impairing the confidence of thousands of colored voters." However, some blacks like Edwin Belcher, who denounced "hungry miserable unscrupulous white politicians" seeking office, were equally hungry themselves. Belcher used both sides of the color issue to his own advantage. He won his federal appointment as a revenue assessor by arguing that

47. Macon *American Union*, July 10, 1868, August 10, 1871.
48. *Ibid.*, August 10, February 2, 1871; Atlanta *Daily New Era*, October 1, 1870; Macon *American Union*, quoted in Atlanta *Constitution*, December 3, 1870.

blacks like himself deserved a share in the offices because the party in Georgia was predominantly black. Yet, once in office and facing conservative opposition, the light-skinned Belcher sought Alexander Stephens' support for his appointment on the grounds that the Democrats could expect nothing better under the circumstances. Similarly, Aaron Bradley raised the race issue to his advantage. Incensed over his loss of the regular party's 1870 congressional nomination to Richard W. White, Bradley attacked White, who was part Indian, for not being black enough. He cautioned blacks not to throw away their votes on "this ineligible Indian."[49]

In this dispute on officeholding, the blacks were, if anything, too deferential to whites. John Quarles was probably correct when he noted that "the unselfishness they have shown in holding themselves back and supporting their white friends for all the prominent positions had no parallel in the history of American politics." Moreover, the blacks were acutely aware of the problem of qualifications and usually went out of their way to find able candidates. Superior Court Judge James Simms of Savannah nominated for the position of Chatham County district attorney the son of a prominent white Savannah family. Edwin Belcher refused to staff his office with persons white or black whom he considered incompetent. In fact, the blacks were not as ambitious to hold office as the white Republicans charged. They showed amazing restraint until white Republicans joined with the Democrats to expel them from the legislature. Even after the expulsion, most black politicians wanted an equal share of the offices, not a majority of them.[50]

Increasingly, Georgia's black reconstructionists came to realize that the Bullock administration had neither the will nor the power to help the freedmen. Few articulated this disenchantment more eloquently than Aaron Bradley. Bullock had earned Bradley's enmity at the constitutional convention after he had sponsored a resolution critical of the black delegate. The split between the two men wid-

49. John Henry Foy to Butler, April 15, 1869, Belcher to Butler, April 5, 1869, both in Butler Papers; Coulter, *Negro Legislators in Georgia*, 95–96.

50. Macon *American Union*, August 10, 1871; Savannah *Morning News*, February 9, 1871; Belcher to Stephens, May 5, 1869, in Stephens Papers, Library of Congress. I have not found a single instance of a black's demanding a majority of state and federal offices for blacks.

ened in 1868 when Bradley lost the party's nomination for Congress to Bullock supporter and incumbent Joseph W. Clift. Bradley ran as an independent in the elections, thereby endangering Clift's chances. In 1870 Bradley opposed prolongation on the grounds that the Bullock administration had not done enough for blacks. He attacked the Bullock administration for not rewriting Irwin's Code, accused Bullock of appointing "rebel" judges, and called the governor a "murderer" for allowing the leasing of black convicts to the railroads. With a petition ten feet long, signed by his black supporters, Bradley demanded Bullock's impeachment. "If our own party will not give ear," he threatened, "and come to our assistance, we in a body will go to the Democracy, who are now anxious to do for us all we require. When the time arrives then good-bye to Georgia's 'carpet-baggers' and 'scalawags.'"[51]

Bradley's course of action was not typical of most black politicians. In 1870, while he was denouncing Bullock, other black politicians were still praising the governor as "an advocate of equal rights." Nonetheless, Bradley's position was eventually shared by the other black politicians, even the most conservative of them. In the early days of Radical Reconstruction, Henry M. Turner was regarded as conservative. During the constitutional convention he had pleaded leniency for Jefferson Davis, and at the first session of the 1868 legislature, he had been instrumental in removing some of the voting disabilities of Democratic members. But after his expulsion, Turner became increasingly radical and disenchanted with Bullock. Although he still supported Bullock, his speech in 1870 backing prolongation betrayed a severe disillusionment with the Republican party:

But for all, what have we got in Georgia, simply the right to vote and sit in the General Assembly. . . . Not a colored juror or a colored police in all the State. Two colored magistrates, one colored clerk of the court, and one or two colored bailiffs make up the compliment [sic] for Georgia. . . . If we get on the cars we have to pay first-class fare, and to two exceptions, go into any old dirty box they choose to put you. . . . If a colored man even picks up the filthiest white wench in the streets, and attempts to relieve her necessities by marriage, he is sent to the penitentiary for

51. Drago, "Black Georgia During Reconstruction," Chap. III and pp. 199–200; Savannah *Morning News*, May 26, October 6, 1870.

twenty years. But on the other hand, great God, *What a tale I could tell.* We are forced to pay taxes to keep up schools and municipalities, and not a dollar is ever extended for the benefit of colored children. We are tried and condemned by the courts, with laws enacted thirty years ago. Our statute books are as proscriptive now as they were in slave times to the exception of whipping and selling. . . . not a single law has ever been passed by the Georgia Legislature or by any city municipality in the whole State, that was intended, or even contemplated the bettering of the colored man's situation.

Like Bradley, Turner predicted that Georgia blacks would be forced to seek an accomodation with the conservatives. "I am now prepared," Turner announced, "to send a colored delegation to the Democratic Convention . . . to capitulate terms for a union."[52]

Prolongation was soundly defeated, as Turner had predicted, and Congressional Reconstruction virtually ended after Republicans and Democrats in the legislature agreed to lease the state-owned Western and Atlantic Railroad to private capitalists. According to the Democrats, the Republicans, facing certain defeat in the 1870 elections, had planned to lease the railroad to friends and thereby retain a degree of political power. A company headed by Joseph Brown and involving Bullock aide Hannibal Kimball, as well as the Republican-supported Georgia Railroad, nearly secured the lease. In response, the Democratic-backed Central Railroad organized a rival company to compete for the lease. Hard pressed by financial problems, Benjamin H. Hill, Sr., joined the company's efforts. In a shrewd political move, Hill's group appealed directly to prominent officials in Washington, enlisting the support of President Grant's friends, including U.S. Senator Simon B. Cameron, Andrew Carnegie's mentor Thomas Scott of the Pennsylvania Railroad, and John S. Delano, son of Grant's secretary of the interior.

To avoid a ruinous political battle, the contending companies merged. The sight of Benjamin Hill and Joseph Brown, bitter political foes, successfully joining hands in a business venture alarmed conservatives, especially after Hill abruptly ended his opposition to Reconstruction and urged Georgians to accept it. Speaking to the

52. Savannah *Morning News*, October 6, 1870; Turner, "Speech on the Eligibility of Colored Members to Seats in the Georgia Legislature," 12; Atlanta *Daily New Era*, August 14, 1870.

alumni of the University of Georgia in 1871, Hill echoed Brown's rhetoric, professing the need for a "New South." In retrospect the Brown-Hill affair appears to have been a case of crass opportunism, but most Republicans, like Brown, were only marginally interested in helping blacks. By accepting the deal, Hill and the legislature seemed to be endorsing the "New Era." For some Republicans, the Brown-Hill endeavor was a national victory. "We whipped Toombs & co," wrote Republican William C. Morrill to Simon Cameron in 1871. "The Legislature has conducted itself with great caution and moderation. The people do not care to fight the U.S. anymore."[53]

While Morrill was hailing the great Republican victory, Georgia's black politicians were meeting in a convention called by Henry M. Turner. Although the gathering supported the reelection of Grant, there was widespread disillusionment with the Republican party. Black assemblyman W. H. Harrison bitterly denounced Grant for failing to help the freedmen, and Turner concluded, "We must evidently either dispense with the ballot, and quit the political arena in toto, or leave the country, or waste out of existence." After the convention, nine black legislators testified before a congressional committee investigating the Ku Klux Klan. The investigation led to the passing of anti-Klan legislation by Congress. But with the Democratic return to power, followed by Bullock's resignation and departure from the state in October, 1871, to escape certain impeachment, Congressional Reconstruction, what little there was, came to an abrupt end.[54]

53. Drago, "Black Georgia During Reconstruction," 135–39; C. Mildred Thompson, *Reconstruction in Georgia*, 238–39, 245–50; Benjamin Hill to Simon Cameron, John S. Delano, and Thomas Scott, February 27, 1871, W. C. Morrill to Cameron, November 20, 1871, both in Simon Cameron Papers, Library of Congress; E. Merton Coulter, "The New South: Benjamin H. Hill's Speech Before the Alumni Society of the University of Georgia, 1871," *Georgia Historical Quarterly*, LVII (Summer, 1973), 179.
54. Drago, "Black Georgia During Reconstruction," 202.

CHAPTER IV

The Black Politicos as Black Leaders

"I wish the whole newspaper fraternity were dead, or would let me alone," Henry M. Turner complained; "they have no more regard for truth than the devil does for holy water." Most of Turner's black colleagues would have concurred—they, too, were being defamed by the white press—and even conservative newspapers, if they were fair minded, would have had to agree with this assessment. When a newspaper in a neighboring county described black representative William Guilford as an escaped horse thief, the Thomaston *Georgia Herald* warned, "The Courier should be careful how it slanders a whole county in one breath." Denouncing the *Courier*'s calumny, it printed Guilford's reply: "It is no wonder that there are so many assassinations and so much bloodshed and crime in Southwest Georgia, when they have an Editor . . . who will stoop so low as to publish a lie on a black man, just because he advocates what he thinks is right."[1]

Henry Turner had ample reason for disliking the press; it had highlighted charges made by white Republican J. Clarke Swayze, editor of the *American Union*, that Turner had passed counterfeit money. Actually, the charges were politically motivated; Swayze had coveted a federal appointment that was awarded Turner. The black preacher was acquitted of all charges, and even his bitter foe, the

1. Macon *Daily Telegraph*, May 15, 1869; Allen D. Candler (comp.), *Confederate Records of Georgia*, VI, 428; Macon *American Union*, October 29, 1869; Atlanta *Daily New Era*, February 2, 1871; Thomaston *Georgia Herald*, June 18, 1870.

Macon *Daily Telegraph*, had to admit that "in all probability Turner is entirely innocent of complicity with counterfeiting."[2]

Turner's case illustrates the difficulty of assessing the integrity of Georgia's black politicians, who were under the scrutiny of a hostile white press. Turner was also accused of being profane and sexually immoral. The charges were unsubstantiated, but one of his detractors conceded, in any case, that these "were faults common to most 'great' men in Georgia." The black politicians were probably no more and no less ethical than their white counterparts. Some were courageous. Representative Abram Colby of Greene County was beaten because he refused conservative bribes. Others were disreputable. Moses H. Bentley, delegate to the constitutional convention, shot and killed black representative Malcolm Claiborne after a heated argument over the pay of house pages. A few were egotistical and abrasive. Aaron A. Bradley alienated everybody, including his black senate colleagues George Wallace and Tunis G. Campbell, Sr. Campbell, Bradley's staunch defender at the constitutional convention, became his bitter political foe after Bradley invaded his political turf in McIntosh County. Campbell's supporters reportedly ran Bradley out of the county because they claimed he had sold out to the Democrats. In truth, Bradley was *sui generis*; he attacked Republican and Democratic leaders alike.[3]

There is no evidence that Georgia's black politicians shared in any Reconstruction graft, although this is probably no tribute to their honesty. It may simply be another example of white Republicans' determination to keep the booty and spoils of office for themselves. The blacks were generally silent about the seaminess of some Republican schemes, particularly when party loyalty was reinforced by racial self-interest. For example, few of them denounced the purchase of the Atlanta Opera House as the new state capitol. Bullock's adviser Hannibal I. Kimball, whose family profited mightily from the transaction, had employed black laborers in building the opera house and, therefore, enjoyed a measure of popularity among the

2. Macon *Daily Telegraph*, July 17, 18, 21, 23, 1869.
3. Coulter, *Negro Legislators in Georgia*, 16–26, 131–32, 137–38, 70–71, 84, 67–68, 138; Macon *American Union*, July 30, 1869; "Ku Klux Klan Report," VII, 702, 704–705, 935–36, 1059–60; Christler, "Participation of Negroes in the Government of Georgia," 62–63, 68; Avery, *The History of the State of Georgia*, 382.

freedmen. As one popular Negro song went, "H. I. Kimball's on de floor, 'Taint gwine ter rain no more." One black politician, State Senator George Wallace, was an outspoken critic of the purchase. He proposed that the issue be put to a vote of the people. However, since Wallace represented the Milledgeville area and his constituency wanted Milledgeville to remain the state capital, his moral indignation was good politics.[4]

The only black politician to be officially charged with taking graft was Assemblyman Alexander Stone. He was accused of accepting bribes from conservatives to oppose further Reconstruction measures. Although several of his black colleagues voted against him, the house overwhelmingly cleared him of the accusations. At the same time, the house exonerated white Republican James Atkins, who was charged with accepting a bribe from a black man to support Joseph E. Brown's candidacy for the United States Senate. The debate on Atkins' case reflected the tensions between black and white Republicans. At one point, James Simms sarcastically noted that if the charges were correct, then it was the first time in Georgia a black man ever bought a white man. Simms also demanded and received an apology from Brown for referring to the black man alleged to have been involved in the affair as "boy."[5]

A survey of Georgia's sixty-nine black legislators during the period (see the Appendix) indicates that most black politicians were consciously aware of their blackness, publicly committed to their race's well-being, and able to influence large numbers of freedmen. In postwar Georgia, where a caste system prevailed, few blacks had any racial identity problems. The state legal code arbitrarily defined *free persons of color* as "all negroes, mulattoes, and mestizoes, and their descendants, having one-eighth negro, or African blood, in their veins." Henry Turner and other black leaders discouraged such

4. Avery, *The History of the State of Georgia*, 412–13, 418, 444–46; C. Mildred Thompson, *Reconstruction in Georgia*, 321, 218; *Georgia House Journal*, 1870, pp. 381–82; Clarence Albert Bacote, "William Finch, Negro Councilman, and Political Activities in Atlanta During Early Reconstruction," *Journal of Negro History*, XL (October, 1955), 346; Atlanta *Constitution*, August 6, 1870; Allen D. Candler (comp.), *Confederate Records of Georgia*, VI, 734–36.

5. *Georgia House Journal*, 1870, pp. 509–523; *Daily Atlanta Intelligencer*, September 1, 2, 3, 1870.

distinctions. "We want representative men," Turner told Augusta blacks, "without regard to color, as long as they carry the brand of negro oppression. We need power and intellectual equality with the whites. It does not matter whether he be a pretty or ugly negro; a black negro or a mulatto, whether he were a slave or a free negro; the question is, is he a negro at all?" Robert Perdue, in his study of Savannah blacks, noted that the light-skinned black elite was responsive to the needs of the entire black community. Only Edwin Belcher and Madison Davis appear to have had serious racial identity problems. These two light-skinned assemblymen escaped expulsion in 1868 because the legislature could not prove that they were sufficiently black to fit the state's definition. Their racial identity problems, however, were quickly resolved for them.[6]

Edwin Belcher, born in South Carolina, was sent as a youngster to Pennsylvania where he attended white schools. As a captain in the Union army, he was assigned to Georgia, where after the war he secured a job as an agent in the Freedmen's Bureau. Apparently he tried to pass for white, but in 1867 local whites discovered his ancestry. "My blood has died [*sic*] the soil of the Sunny South as deep a red as any other Soldier's," he complained to Georgia Bureau Chief Caleb O. Sibley. "It is very annoying to me to have it continually thrown in my face that I am a negroe [*sic*] when I do not know whether it is a fact or not. My services during the war was just as acceptable as any other man's and they was appreciated." Belcher soon learned that in race-conscious Georgia even the slightest trace of black blood, much less than the legally stated one-eighth, was enough to define a man as black. The Democratic press branded him "black vomit." Eventually, he not only acquiesced in his blackness, but used it to further his political ambitions. He won appointment as a federal official by reminding United States Senator Benjamin F.

6. *Acts of the General Assembly of the State of Georgia,* 1865–1866, p. 239; C. Mildred Thompson, *Reconstruction in Georgia,* 213; Philadelphia *Christian Recorder,* January 20, 1866; Robert E. Perdue, *The Negro in Savannah, 1865–1900* (New York, 1973), 92–93. For discussions of the term *leader* on which I relied for my implied definition of a black leader, see Andrew Stuart McFarland, *Power and Leadership in Pluralist Systems* (Stanford, 1969), Chap. III, and Nancy G. Hassler, "A Dream Deferred: The Nature of Black Leadership During Reconstruction" (unpublished research paper, University of California, Berkeley, 1969), 3–5.

Butler that the Georgia Republican party was predominantly black and that blacks like himself deserved a share of the offices.[7]

Representative Madison Davis of Clarke County escaped expulsion from the legislature in 1868 by denying that he was black, whereupon a black Clarke County Union League denounced him "for treason to his color" and declared him no longer a representative of the black race. Nevertheless, Clarke County whites considered him black, and in 1870 he was reelected to the house on the strength of black votes.[8]

The black politicians' attitudes towards "New Era" legislation manifested how racially oriented most of them were. They gave their support to legislation that would benefit their black constituents. Several black legislators sponsored measures giving state aid to railroads crossing their districts. Thomas Allen of Jasper County sought state aid for a railroad going through Monticello, home of his chief political support, a five-hundred-man Union League. Similarly, Madison Davis of Clarke County introduced a bill allowing Athens to help the Georgia Railroad build a new line through the city. The ambitious black assemblyman persuaded some of his more affluent black constituents to purchase 150 shares of stock in the new railroad. Unlike these black legislators, Edwin Belcher was harshly critical of railroad aid. With tongue in cheek, he proposed, since there was no more available territory in Georgia, that "we ask the United States Government for permission to construct railroads in Alaska, and that we be allowed to extend State aid to the same."[9]

Although most black legislators acquiesced in the railroad-building mania of the times, they split on various roll-call votes involving railroads. The pattern of their voting suggests that they carefully

7. Edwin Belcher to Caleb O. Sibley, May 14, 1867, in Records of the Bureau of Refugees, Freedmen, and Abandoned Lands, Record Group 105, National Archives; Belcher to Alexander H. Stephens, March 5, 1869, in Stephens Papers, Library of Congress; Washington (Ga.) *Gazette*, April 23, 1869; Belcher to Benjamin F. Butler, April 5, 1869, in Butler Papers.

8. Atlanta *Constitution*, September 11, 1868; *Georgia House Journal*, 1872, p. 226, 1871, p. 110.

9. *Georgia House Journal*, 1870, pp. 170, 502, 307; Robert S. Gamble, "Athens: The Study of a Georgia Town During Reconstruction, 1865–1872" (M.A. thesis, University of Georgia, 1967), 133; "Ku Klux Klan Report," VII, 607; Atlanta *Constitution*, September 1, 1870, quoted in Edward Barham Young, "The Negro in Georgia Politics, 1867–1877" (M.S. thesis, Emory University, 1955), 51.

weighed the impact of each bill on their own constituencies. For example, they evenly divided over the hottest issue of the period, the lease of the state-owned Western and Atlantic Railroad. James Simms of Chatham County preferred keeping the line in state hands because this had benefited blacks. Edwin Belcher, on the other hand, maintained that under the Bullock administration, the road had discriminated against blacks, offering them only menial jobs.[10]

Sometimes the "New Era" ideology threatened the welfare of the freedmen. In a move to financially retrench and provide railroads with cheap labor, the Bullock administration leased state convicts to Grant, Alexander, and Company, which used them to build railroads, including lines managed by Bullock's close friend and political right-hand man, Hannibal Kimball. In 1870 a Republican-dominated joint committee of the legislature, including blacks James Simms, Henry Turner, and George Wallace, uncovered serious abuse in the leasing procedures. Prison officials had failed to keep an accurate account of the convicts assigned to them. Apparently some were going straight from the courtroom to construction sites. Both male and female convicts were whipped and worked at night on Sundays, and one black man had died after a guard beat him. The blacks on the committee faced a dilemma: they could either criticize the report and aid the conservatives, whose criticism of convict abuse was more political than humanitarian, or suffer in silence and allow the continued abuse of black prisoners.[11]

The joint committee submitted a report that whitewashed the whole sordid affair, and James Simms and Henry Turner endorsed it. They had second thoughts when the report reached the floor of the legislature, however. Turner wanted it amended, and Simms, who denied signing it, charged that the chairman had been bribed. Other blacks were more critical. Edwin Belcher demanded that the lease be terminated. Aaron A. Bradley condemned both the administration

10. *Georgia House Journal*, 1870, pp. 752–53, 278–81; Atlanta *Constitution*, October 13, 1870.

11. A. Elizabeth Taylor, "The Origin and Development of the Convict Lease System in Georgia," *Georgia Historical Quarterly*, XXVI (June, 1942), 114; Blake McKelvey, "Penal Slavery and Southern Reconstruction," *Journal of Negro History*, XX (April, 1935), 156; *Proceedings of the Joint Committee Appointed to Investigate the Condition of the Georgia Penitentiary* [1870].

and the company, concluding that, since convicts were being used on railroads financed by Henry Clews, a New York banker and Bullock ally, the whole scheme must have been concocted on Wall Street.[12]

Most black politicians, if Henry Turner was representative, were only superficially committed to the "New Era." Turner supported Republican spending schemes not only out of party loyalty. He expected in return to receive support for his racially oriented proposals. At the same time, he did not believe the "New Era" ideology to be incompatible with black rights. When Joseph Brown and his newspaper, the Atlanta *Daily New Era*, refused to support Turner's efforts to persuade Congress to reseat the blacks expelled from the legislature in 1868, Turner renounced his earlier support for some of the "New Era" programs. He denounced white Republicans like Brown for saddling the state with "a worthless debt of hundreds of thousands of dollars." They "have done the State more harm than they will ever do it good; besides, have helped ruin the Republican party, and crush out the living hopes of the black man."[13]

Like Henry Turner, many of Georgia's black politicians derived much of their influence over the freedmen from their role as religious leaders. Even Aaron Bradley, although he was not a preacher, launched his political career in Savannah churches, and the black church remained the focal point of black political activity throughout Reconstruction. It provided both the political leadership and the organization necessary to mobilize black voters. According to conservatives, the black preachers "control them [the blacks], and their preaching is often political in character." White Republicans, on the other hand, thought that the preachers retained such popularity among the freedmen because "they are to some extent representative men; there is no doubt about that. They are generally a little better educated than the mass of the negro race."[14]

The relationship between the pulpit and politics was not always

12. Taylor, "Origin and Development of the Convict Lease System," 115; *Proceedings of the Joint Committee Appointed to Investigate the Condition of the Georgia Penitentiary*, 200; *Daily Atlanta Intelligencer*, July 28, 30, August 3, 1870.
13. Macon *American Union*, December 4, 1868.
14. "Ku Klux Klan Report," VII, 1184, 1133; Coulter, *Negro Legislators in Georgia*, 39, 41.

harmonious. Some blacks resented their ministers' involvement in politics. After Bryan County Baptist minister Ulysses L. Houston won a seat in the assembly in 1868, his parishioners became angry over his absence from church affairs, as well as apprehensive at the hostility his political activity was engendering among local whites. Capitalizing on this discontent, Alexander Harris, the church deacon, got himself named pastor in Houston's place. When Houston lost his bid for reelection in 1870, he opened a rival church. Two years later, he and his supporters, including Baptist minister-politician James Simms, physically occupied Harris' church. Harris called on the intervention of white Savannah city officials and had Houston and Simms arrested. For this he incurred the wrath of his congregation. Houston and Simms became heroes, and Harris lost his pastorship to Houston.[15]

Georgia's black politicians also looked to other than religious sources for their political ideology. The Declaration of Independence was especially favored, and black conventions rang with the rhetoric of the American Revolution. In terms reminiscent of Jefferson's indictment of George III, a black gathering in 1868 castigated its political enemies:

> They have expelled our colored legislators in violation to the Constitution and laws. . . .
> They then refused to allow their protests to go on [sic] the Journals of the House.
> They have robbed us of the right to be Jurors. . . .
> They have inaugurated strife and discord between white and colored citizens.
> They have demoralized society. . . .
> They have refused to require common carriers to give us respectable accommodations, when we pay equal rates. . . .
> They have voted down every measure for the establishment of schools for the education of our children. . . .
> They have not only invaded our political rights, but nullified by prejudicial legislation, our civil rights.
> They have given indirect countenance to the murdering bands of the KKK. . . .

15. James Meriles Simms, *The First Colored Baptist Church in North America. Constituted at Savannah, Georgia, January 20, A.D. 1788* (Philadelphia, 1888), 150–84.

Ulysses L. Houston, whose political activities lost him his
church.

Similarly, Albany blacks justified federal intervention in Georgia on
the grounds that "the State government does not answer for the purpose for which it was established, protection and justice for all."[16]

16. *Proceedings of the Council of the Georgia Equal Rights Association, Assembled at Augusta, Ga., April 4th, 1866. Containing the Address of the President,
Captain J. E. Bryant, and Resolutions Adopted by the Council* (Augusta, 1866),

Houston's First Bryan Baptist Church, built in 1873.

Most black politicians also adopted the "free soil, free speech, free labor, and free men" ideology of the northern Republicans. "This is

12–13; *Proceedings of the Freedmen's Convention*, 17, 20, 28–29, 30; *Proceedings of the Convention of the Equal Rights and Educational Association*, 15, 17; Macon *American Union*, October 9, 1868; *House Miscellaneous Documents*, 40th Cong., 3rd Sess., No. 52, pp. 96–97.

the day of gratitude for the freedom of labor," Henry Turner told Augusta blacks celebrating the Emancipation Proclamation in January, 1866. "Heretofore, our chief study was how to do the least work possible and escape punishment. Labor was not sweetened by reward—it was forced from us then." Three years later, a black labor convention proclaimed "its unqualified admiration of the doctrine which asserts the dignity of labor and holds up an honest laborer as the noblest work of God." It likewise declared that "the laborer is the life of the country" and extolled "the men whose brawny arms and skilled hands feed and clothe humanity."[17]

As Radical Reconstruction progressed, black political leaders from other institutions, including the army, the Freedmen's Bureau, and the Union League began to come into prominence. Edwin Belcher, for example, came to Georgia as an officer in the Union army and later became a bureau agent. In 1868 he developed a sufficient following among Wilkes County blacks to get himself elected to the assembly. Lacking the pulpit, some black leaders used the Union League for their entry into politics. George Wallace, for example, joined the Macon league in 1868 and proceeded to organize similar associations throughout the state. That year he was one of a handful of blacks elected to the state senate. Jefferson Long, the state's only black congressman, was president of the Macon league.[18]

The first Union League was established in Cleveland, Ohio, in November, 1862, by about a dozen men who were disturbed by the growing opposition to the war. Its purpose was to promote "uncompromising and unconditional loyalty to the Union." The league spread south with the victorious northern armies, as white southerners who had become disenchanted with the war began organizing their own local leagues. Economically hard pressed and unsympathetic to the war, thousands of Georgia whites, particularly in the northern counties, had joined by 1865. The league was also strong in

17. Redkey, *Respect Black*, 11; Macon *American Union*, October 22, 29, 1869. For an exposition of this ideology, see Eric Foner, *Free Soil, Free Labor, Free Men: The Ideology of the Republican Party Before the Civil War* (New York, 1970).

18. Belcher to Sibley, May 14, 1867, in Records of the Bureau of Refugees, Freedmen, and Abandoned Lands, "Ku Klux Klan Report," VII, 613–17; Matthews, "The Negro in Georgia Politics," 53.

Congressman Jefferson Long.
Library of Congress

Augusta, headquarters for the Freedmen's Bureau and a center of Republicanism.

In 1865 Georgia blacks were permitted to join the leagues, although at first they were segregated. Despite this discriminatory policy, large numbers had become members by 1866, particularly in the major cities of Macon, Savannah, Atlanta, and Augusta, where they were protected by the presence of the Union army. Black political leaders also effectively used the leagues to reach plantation blacks. Wherever nine interested freedmen were found, a club was organized. Every county was headed by a president, and each militia district had a vice-president.[19]

Contrary to traditional interpretations, the leagues were not simply vehicles used by opportunistic white radicals to organize superstitious blacks. Many of the local black league leaders enjoyed considerable grass-roots support among the freedmen. The ritual and secrecy of the meetings were means of protecting league members from the planters' wrath. In preparation for the 1868 presidential election, Webster County blacks organized a league meeting "in their own peculiar way, without the knowledge of the white citizens, except their white skin allies—the preparations have been made with the strictest secrecy." It was a prudent secrecy, for black speakers at the rally denounced the Democrats and condemned the white Republicans for not allowing the freedmen a fair share of the offices. Two of the most militant acts by freedmen during Radical Reconstruction involved local black league officials. The so-called Ogeechee uprising was touched off when a Savannah sheriff arrested the black president of a rice plantation union league. In 1870 Cudjo Fye, the president of a Louisville league, led a group of fifty blacks who stormed the city jail to free a fellow union league member.[20]

While black local union league officials and other black leaders may have exerted considerable influence over the freedmen, few blacks were elected to office on the county or municipal level. Nothing alarmed white southerners more than the thought that blacks might control their county or city governments. "I am very conservative as to the Legislature—which sits in Atlanta and can tolerate my driver voting for his own color then," planter Democrat

19. "Ku Klux Klan Report," VII, 613–17; Drago, "Black Georgia During Reconstruction," 105; Roberta F. Cason, "The Loyal League in Georgia," *Georgia Historical Quarterly*, XX (June, 1936), 125–53.

20. Savannah *Daily News and Herald*, August 15, 1868, reprinted the account of the rally in a letter from the Americus *Sumter Republican*; E. Merton Coulter, "Cudjo Fye's Insurrection," *Georgia Historical Quarterly*, XXXVIII (September, 1954), 213–16.

Howell Cobb, Jr., told his wife in 1870, "but when it comes to the home municipal-government—all the blacks who vote against my ticket shall walk the plank." Despite the fears of southerners like Cobb, nearly all of Georgia's counties and cities were controlled by the Democrats. Even in Clarke County, where Republicans elected two black assemblymen in 1868, all county offices, except tax collector, remained in Democratic hands. Similarly, Democratic control of the cities was virtually complete. In August, a center of republicanism, the Democratic mayor swept every ward in 1870. That year Macon also reelected its Democratic mayor, and Savannah stayed "under Democratic rule" throughout the period. Urban Republicans could affect the outcome of an election only by delivering their votes to sympathetic Democratic candidates, but the tactic was not always successful. In 1870 Atlanta Republicans supported the winning candidate for mayor, Dennis F. Hammond, a Democratic reformer who promised an administration of equal justice. One year later he was defeated in a landslide.[21]

Throughout Reconstruction, black officeholding on the county and municipal level remained minimal. Only seventeen blacks were elected to county offices in Georgia in November, 1868; nine of them were coroners, the least important county officers. In subsequent elections, a handful of black law enforcement officials were elected. These officials came from a middle-class black elite. They were under the close scrutiny of whites, and they enforced the letter of the law among the ex-slaves. Savannah's black magistrate King S. Thomas, for example, ordered white police into the city's black community to arrest two drunken black men for disturbing the peace. When blacks attempted to free the prisoners, the police shot into the crowd. Thomas testified that they were acting in the line of duty. Thomas, a devout Baptist, also ordered the arrest of a black man for swearing in front of a black woman. Had they failed to strictly enforce the law among the freedmen, local black officials might have

21. Howell Cobb, Jr., to his wife, December 27, 1870, in Cobb-Irwin-Lamar Papers, University of Georgia Library, Athens; C. Mildred Thompson, *Reconstruction in Georgia*, 187, 354; Gamble, "Athens," 141; Augusta *Daily Constitutionalist*, December 8, 1870; "Ku Klux Klan Report," VI, 177; Macon *Georgia Weekly Telegraph*, December 20, 1870; Bacote, "William Finch, Negro Councilman," 341–64; Atlanta *Daily Sun*, December 3, 1870; Drago, "Black Georgia During Reconstruction," 211–13.

found themselves its victims. Magistrate Tunis G. Campbell, Sr., nearly landed himself in jail for presiding over an interracial marriage, a violation of state law.[22]

The white press sometimes praised these elected black officials for their strict enforcement of law and order. The Democratic Savannah *Morning News* described black constable Austin Jones as a "terror to evil doers in and around the Isle of Hope. His merits as an able detective should be noted and rewarded as they deserve to be." It also lauded Lewis J. Moody, a black magistrate in the Ogeechee district who prevented rice plantation blacks from hanging two white constables. "We take great pleasure," another white Savannah newspaper commented, "in according praise to all persons without regard to color, race or previous condition, when they justly earn the right to claim it, but we take especial pleasure in praising officials, who, under trying circumstances, and in the face of an infuriated mob, have the moral courage to uphold the majesty of the law, and to bring evil doers to justice. The action of Lewis J. Moody . . . merits the hearty approbation of all law-abiding citizens."[23]

Although they were proponents of law and order, these black law enforcement officers were hardly tools of the conservative establishment. A black officer who applied the letter of the law to blacks and whites alike sometimes proved embarrassing to conservative officials. For instance, less than six months after receiving the accolades of the white Savannah newspapers, Magistrate Moody ordered the arrest of several prominent Democrats, including a city alderman, for committing fraud in the congressional elections of 1872. Moreover, a strict law-and-order stance was not necessarily detrimental to blacks. When Savannah officials proposed sending an army to Ogeechee, Moody went instead. By stopping the Ogeechee blacks from killing the two white constables, he prevented a harsh white reprisal.[24]

22. Americus *Tri-Weekly Republican*, December 15, 1868; Simms, *The First Colored Baptist Church*, 141; Savannah *Morning News*, October 11, December 28, 1869; Coulter, *Negro Legislators in Georgia*, 155.
23. Savannah *Morning News*, August 14, 16, 1872, August 24, 1871; Savannah *Daily Republican*, August 16, 1872.
24. Edward Clifford Anderson Diary (MS in Edward Clifford Anderson Papers, Southern Historical Collection, Library of the University of North Carolina at Chapel Hill), VIII, August 13, 1872; Savannah *Daily Republican*, November 10, 1872.

Although blacks ran for city council in most of Georgia's major municipalities, less than a dozen black candidates were elected. Since most cities had white majorities, conservatives succeeded in keeping blacks off the council by electing their municipal officials on a city-wide, rather than a district or ward, basis. However, in 1870 the Republican-dominated legislature rewrote the city election laws for Macon and Altanta to allow for ward representation. Subsequently, several black aldermen were elected, to the dismay of conservatives. "Our city election for Mayor and Aldermen this week," an Atlanta merchant wrote in his diary, "resulted in getting two *niggers* in as aldermen!" The Republican *American Union* pronounced the election of a black Macon alderman "a most complete revolution in our city government. Heretofore the negro has not even been allowed to vote for any office, much less be voted for."[25]

Unfortunately, little is known about these black aldermen, except for Atlanta's William Finch. Born a slave, Finch lived with Justice J. H. Lumpkin of the Georgia Supreme Court. After the war Finch opened a tailor shop in Atlanta, where he was elected alderman from the city's black Fourth Ward in 1870. An ordained African Methodist Episcopal minister, Finch preached hard work, thrift, and frugality. He also displayed the same concern for morality and law and order that other black local officials exhibited.

As alderman, Finch urged police to attend to the problems of "certain females" who were on the streets late at night and demanded that the council refuse to grant an extension of the closing time of a local bar. He also urged the police to patrol the city's suburbs to insure law and order. However, except for his successful effort to keep the city from extending Mitchell Street through Atlanta University, Finch failed in most of his efforts to aid his black constituents. With his support, Mayor D. F. Hammond named a Radical to head the police commission, but after a local Democratic newspaper charged that the appointment would bring "negro policemen stalking the streets of Atlanta," the city council overturned the mayor's decision. In December, 1871, Finch lost his bid for reelection after the method

25. Drago, "Black Georgia During Reconstruction," 211; S. P. Richard Diary (MS in S. P. Richard Papers, Atlanta Historical Society), December 10, 1870; Macon *American Union*, December 15, 1870.

of choosing aldermen was changed from district-based representation to city-wide voting.[26]

The only significant enclave of black power during Reconstruction centered around Darien, a McIntosh County lumber town down the coast from Savannah. The boss of this black political machine was Tunis G. Campbell, Sr., who came to symbolize for white conservatives the essence of "nigger-rule." His political career demonstrates how black leaders who effectively challenged white hegemony were removed from power. Trained as a missionary for Africa by the African Methodist Episcopal Zion church, the New Jersey–born preacher found his calling in postwar Georgia, where he was appointed a Freedmen's Bureau agent for the Sea Islands in 1864. A year later he was fired by the conservative new chief of the Georgia bureau, General Davis Tillson. In 1867 Campbell, with his family and friends, migrated to Darien in McIntosh County.[27]

Darien was fertile soil for the establishment and growth of Campbell's political machine. The city and surrounding counties were mostly black. Moreover, Campbell had those characteristics that produced successful black leaders during Reconstruction. He was intelligent, ambitious, charismatic, and a minister of the Gospel. Campbell had also brought with him from the Sea Islands a group of devoted followers and relatives who served as the nucleus of his political machine. Toby Maxwell, one of Darien's four black aldermen, had followed Campbell from the Sea Islands. Campbell's own son, Tunis G. Campbell, Jr., sat with his father in the state legislature, and an adopted son, Edward E. Howard, became clerk of the superior court. Campbell himself, besides serving in the constitutional convention and state senate, was also elected justice of the peace.[28]

It was as justice of the peace of McIntosh County that Campbell proved most troublesome. He exercised his powers arbitrarily and totally to the benefit of blacks. In 1871 when the British bark *Grace* arrived at a port near Darien, black crew members jumped ship, charging that the captain had impressed them into service against

---

26. Bacote, "William Finch, Negro Councilman," 341–45, 352, 358–60; Atlanta *Daily Sun*, December 3, 1870; Drago, "Black Georgia During Reconstruction," 211–13.
27. Drago, "Black Georgia During Reconstruction," 213–15.
28. *Ibid.*, 215.

their will. Ignoring the question of whether or not he had legal jurisdiction over a foreign vessel, Campbell arrested the captain and ordered him to pay court costs and the sailors' wages. Even his adopted
son Edward Howard had to admit that his father sometimes acted
arbitrarily. Campbell ordered Howard to tamper with the jury box in
order to get more blacks on juries. Such tampering would have been
illegal, and Howard refused to comply.[29]

Predictably, Campbell's actions provoked the wrath of conservative whites. In 1870 Darien's four white aldermen refused to serve
on the city council, and irate white townspeople threatened to with-
hold their taxes. The spectacle of a black magistrate arbitrarily exer-
cising the law in favor of blacks, a turnabout of one hundred years of
Georgia justice, especially infuriated white employers. One planter-
lawyer claimed his former slaves, having attended Campbell's meetings, showed "a distrust, a disposition to refuse to enter into contracts, or if already made to violate them." Sea Islands plantation
mistress Frances Butler Leigh agreed: "There seemed to be no remedy for this evil, the negroes throwing all our authority to the wind,
and following Campbell wherever he chose to lead them . . . we had
no proper authorities to appeal to, should our negroes misbehave
themselves."[30]

Conservatives attempted to bribe Campbell, but he refused to accept their money. They then tried to terminate home rule in McIntosh County, even though the need for home rule had been their
rallying cry against Congressional Reconstruction. The Democratic
legislature responded in 1872 by establishing a board of commissioners to govern McIntosh County; its powers included the judicial
functions formerly exercised by Campbell. A Fulton County judge
had issued a warrant for Campbell's arrest on the grounds that

29. Charles Wilson, Robert Wing, W. J. Dunwoody, Francis Lee, and James Cala-
more, affidavits and testimony, John Irvine, "Protest of John Irvine, Master of the British [?] *Grace*" (all MSS in Tunis G. Campbell, Sr., Papers, Georgia Department of
Archives and History, Atlanta); Augusta *Daily Constitutionalist*, August 10, 1871;
Coulter, *Negro Legislators in Georgia*, 147–50; E. E. Howard, affidavit (MS in Campbell, Sr., Papers).
30. James H. Bradley to J. H. Taylor, June 13, 1870, in Campbell, Sr., Papers; Atlanta *Constitution*, April 7, 1870; W. R. Gigniliat, affidavit (MS in Campbell, Sr., Papers); Frances Butler Leigh, *Ten Years on a Georgia Plantation Since the War* (New
York, 1969), 135–37.

he falsely imprisoned the captain of the *Grace*. In 1871 the matter reached a federal commissioner in Savannah, who charged Campbell with violating the congressional Ku Klux Klan Act. Four years later the conservatives finally succeeded in eliminating the black magistrate. They sent him to prison for the false arrest of a white man who had appeared before his court. Commenting on Campbell's fate, a contributor to the Savannah *Colored Tribune* wrote, "I don't suppose there is a white Justice of the Peace in the State but that has committed ten times worse crimes, if it was a crime at all, and this is the first instance in a hundred years, where an officer of the law has been so disposed of."[31]

On the state level, blacks were more successful in electing their own officials. However, during Reconstruction, blacks composed less than 20 percent of the membership of the state legislature. Some of these legislators established remarkable rapport with their constituents. During a recess in the constitutional convention, delegate Philip Joiner of Dougherty County and several other black leaders went to Albany to address a gathering of black laborers who were holding out for higher wages. "You suppose I'd let my wife and children starve when there was plenty close by [the planters' stock and crops]," Joiner exhorted, "No, never. (Several voices no never.) You stand firm for good wages . . . and money besides, and if you hold out to the end, you will get it."[32]

Because the overwhelming majority of their black constituents were illiterate, Joiner and his legislative colleagues used mass rallies to reach them. These meetings were festive occasions when the black community would celebrate national events, picnic, and listen to black orators describing the blessings of their new freedom. In 1870 four thousand attended a political rally in Augusta to celebrate the passage of the Fifteenth Amendment. According to a local newspaper, "there must have been a general suspension of farm and other

31. Leigh, *Ten Years on a Georgia Plantation*, 135–36; A. W. Corker, affidavit, Benjamin Conley to T. G. Campbell, December 19, 1871, both in Campbell, Sr., Papers; Drago, "Black Georgia During Reconstruction," 218; Savannah *Colored Tribune*, January 22, 1876.
32. Unidentified Albany newspaper clipping dated January 4, 1868, in Eliza Frances Andrews Scrapbook, Garnett Andrews Papers, #1839, Southern Historical Collection, Library of the University of North Carolina at Chapel Hill. See also the Appendix.

labor within a radius of ten miles square from the city." Several thousand gathered in Macon to celebrate the same event.[33]

The three most popular black legislators were Tunis Campbell, Sr., Henry Turner, and Aaron Bradley, all of whom had spent time in the North. Like Campbell, Turner was a minister-politician. A relentless campaigner, Turner drew thousands of blacks into the AME church and the Republican party. As the organizing force behind most of the black conventions, he became Georgia's leading black reconstructionist. Aaron Bradley was never popular with Turner, Campbell, and the rest of the black political elite, but he established a strong and loyal following among the ex-slaves living on the river plantations outside Savannah. Once, when authorities arrested him, a local newspaper correctly predicted that his imprisonment would only add "the eclat of a successful knight militant to his previous reputation among his followers for serene saintship." In 1870 this "knight militant" split with the regular Republicans of Chatham County; he encouraged fifteen hundred of his supporters to nominate a predominantly black ticket to oppose the regulars.[34]

All three of these charismatic leaders used the church as a rallying point. "Mr. Campbell's influence is great with the majority of the colored people," a federal army officer observed. "They gaze upon him as . . . a demigod . . . and they almost worship him and follow him withersoever he leads." Given the turmoil of the war, emancipation, and Reconstruction, times were ripe for the emergence of such men. Georgia blacks were a good deal like the Jews of the Old Testament, who "broke from a subordinate social and political status, only to find themselves wandering, for though they felt themselves to be a chosen people, they had yet to establish their promised land." The Jews turned to a charismatic leader, Moses, who made critical decisions and set up a paradigm (the Ten Commandments) for the new society. In similar circumstances, Georgia freedmen turned to charismatic leaders like Henry M. Turner, who compared them to the Jews of the Old Testament and envisioned a promised

33. Atlanta *Daily New Era*, May 4, 1870; Augusta *Daily Constitutionalist*, April 28, 1870.

34. Savannah *Morning News*, October 6, 1870; Savannah *Daily News and Herald*, January 4, 7, 1868.

land. The paradigm these leaders offered was the Protestant ethic, with its emphasis on hard work, thrift, frugality, and morality.[35]

The freedmen and their political spokesmen shared the same general vision; they wanted full and equal participation in every aspect of Georgia society. Although they compared themselves to the Jews of the Old Testament, their providential version of history was not exclusive or separatist. Their evangelicalism, derived from the Great Awakenings of the eighteenth century, stressed the brotherhood of all mankind. This sense of brotherhood was reinforced by their interpretation of the Declaration of Independence. They saw themselves as the catalyst in God's plan to remake the United States as the land of universal freedom and unbiased justice. The blacks believed that freeing the slaves and extending to them an equal share and role in society would fulfill the country's mission as delineated in the Declaration of Independence, and they were certain that failure to follow the ideals of that document would provoke the wrath of God. Once freed, the blacks wanted and expected equal political, civil, and economic rights as Americans.

When it came to establishing priorities for implementing this vision, however, differences emerged. Most freedmen were concerned about the economic problems of day-to-day existence. They wanted to own or rent land, and if they had to work as sharecroppers or wage earners, they wanted fair wages and decent working conditions. The black political elite, on the other hand, placed the highest priority on attaining political and civil rights. In 1870 at the peak of Radical Reconstruction, Georgia's black legislators introduced fewer than a dozen bills directly dealing with the economic well-being of black laborers. Their expulsion from the legislature did not shake their belief in the efficacy of the ballot. "We still have that potent weapon, the Ballot," they declared at an 1868 convention, "and if allowed to wield it without molestation . . . we can remedy all evils."[36]

Some black leaders, such as Edwin Belcher, Tunis Campbell, Sr., and Henry Turner, fully understood the economic hardships facing

35. James H. Bradley to J. H. Taylor, June 13, 1870, Alonzo Grayton, affidavit, both in Campbell, Sr., Papers; Coulter, *Negro Legislators in Georgia*, 39; McFarland, *Power and Leadership in Pluralist Systems*, 164–69.

36. *Georgia House Journal*, 1870, *passim*; Macon *American Union*, October 9, 1868.

the freedmen and sought to ameliorate them. Freedmen's Bureau agent Belcher and Justice of the Peace Campbell vigorously used their offices to protect black laborers. Likewise, recognizing how some planters manipulated contracts to keep their workers in a kind of peonage, Henry Turner offered legislation to regulate wages. He and Aaron Bradley advocated an eight-hour workday. Turner also joined with James Porter of Savannah in persuading the legislature to charter black stock companies (cooperatives). Moreover, Georgia's black legislators were united in their efforts to block some of the more odious planter-oriented economic legislation, something historians have tended to overlook. For example, when the blacks were reseated in the legislature in 1870, they succeeded in repealing legislation that had been passed in their absence to prohibit the sale or purchase of agricultural products at night in several counties. The planters had supported this piece of legislation because they suspected their workers of selling part of the employer's share of the crop under cover of darkness. The blacks argued that the law penalized honest men who had no other free time in which to sell the produce of their own gardens. Two years later, over the bitter protest of black state senators James B. Deveaux and George Wallace, the legislature extended the original bill to other black-belt counties.[37]

Nevertheless, most black politicians balked at any thoroughgoing economic reform, including land redistribution and unionization. In 1869 Jefferson Long and Henry Turner called a convention of black legislators to discuss labor problems. The Macon gathering denounced the unfair treatment of laborers and urged that black women be taken from the fields. It proposed the formation of black stock companies and even suggested that the freedmen organize themselves into a labor association. But these associations were not to be trade unions. Conservatives praised the delegates for their "good sense" and "moderation."[38]

37. *Georgia House Journal*, 1868, pp. 218, 212, 1871, p. 143, 1872, pp. 41–42; *Acts of the General Assembly of the State of Georgia*, 1870, pp. 118–21, 458, 1869, p. 178, 1872, pp. 484–85; Coulter, *Negro Legislators in Georgia*, 85; *Georgia Senate Journal*, 1872, pp. 494–95; Atlanta *Constitution*, August 17, 1872. For an account of a black labor convention, see Macon *American Union*, October 22, 29, 1869.

38. *Proceedings of the Freedmen's Convention*, 28–30; Macon, *Georgia Weekly Telegraph*, October 29, 1868; Macon *American Union*, October 29, 1869.

The political situation accounted for some of the black legislators' reluctance to press for real economic reform. Unionization probably would have provoked instant planter retaliation. On the eve of the Macon labor convention, a conservative local newspaper denounced unions, predicting "those who employ the negroes, and without whose employment they cannot exist, will combine against them, and they must go to the wall." Moreover, the blacks' white Republican allies were themselves ardent believers in the sanctity of private property and strongly opposed to both land reform and unionization. "The interest of the laborer and that of the planter are identical," the Republican Atlanta *Daily New Era* proclaimed. "Strikes and long settlements should be avoided." Likewise, the Macon *American Union*, a supporter of the Bullock administration, declared that unions were the offshoots of European tyranny. "If you are industrious, and honest," the paper advised blacks, "you can thrive by buying land and working it."[39]

Georgia's black politicians would doubtless have agreed with this advice. Like most nineteenth-century politicians and the abolitionists before the war, they preached and believed in the American dream of success. Given certain political and civil rights, all men, even former slaves, could achieve success through hard work, thrift, and frugality. The black politicians were more prosperous than most freedmen; many of them owned land. They saw no need for radical economic reforms because their own lives seemed to confirm the truth of the Protestant ethic. Asked by a white man how he could afford horses, Atlanta's black alderman and AME preacher William Finch moralized: "Do you drink beer, etc., smoke, chew tobacco; and if so, how much does the use of them cost you. . . . I *do* neither. This is why I am able to keep horses to ride. The money you spend foolishly for such things, I save. Do likewise and you too can ride."[40]

Some minister-politicians were more concerned about the spiritual

39. Manuel Gottlieb, "The Land Question in Georgia During Reconstruction," *Science and Society*, III (1939), 373–75; Macon *Georgia Journal and Messenger*, October 5, 1869; Atlanta *Daily New Era*, October 23, 1869; Macon *American Union*, October 1, 1869.
40. Theodore Maxwell Lawe, "The Black Reconstructionists in Georgia, 1865–1877" (M.A. thesis, Atlanta University, 1966), 53; Carter, *The Black Side*, 76–77.

than the earthly well-being of their constituents. Minister Romulus Moore offered no economic-oriented legislation, but he did sponsor a bill "to enforce the Bible in schools, academies, and universities." His black colleagues introduced legislation forbidding hunting on the Sabbath, condemning public immorality, regulating the sale of liquor, and prohibiting the sale of lottery tickets. According to their providential version of history, Divine Providence would ultimately intervene on the freedmen's behalf as it had during the war. Conservatives had to concede that this kind of counsel inclined the freedmen to be less militant and to accept suffering as part of God's plan. Democrats in Jones County attributed the fact that there had been "no serious collision" of the races during Reconstruction to the influence of black assemblyman Jacob P. Hutchings, while Clarke County conservatives praised black assemblyman Madison Davis for "always being on the side of law and order." Clarke County's other black assemblyman Alfred Richardson, himself a target of Klan violence, told his black constituents, "never create any difficulties with the white people. I would come up sometimes where there would be a fuss with white men, round the bar-rooms and places, and I would tell the colored men to break it up and quit fussing. I could control almost all of them, and make them quit fusses, whenever I came across them." Even after Klan activity reached its peak in 1868, a convention of black politicians declared, "*Far be it from us to recommend violence, rather, let us suffer the outrage longer,* and hope for the deliverance through milder means."[41]

Although they continued to counsel nonviolence, most black politicians came to endorse the right of self-defense. Their expulsion from the legislature and the concomitant increase in Klan terrorism prompted them to accompany their customary plea for nonviolence with equally strong affirmations of the fundamental right of Americans to defend their homes and families when attacked. A Macon meeting of blacks held in 1870 decided "to avoid all breaches of the

41. Augusta *Colored American*, January 13, 1866; *Georgia House Journal*, 1870, pp. 387, 615, 255, 391, 1868, p. 190; "Ku Klux Klan Report," VII, 1133, VI, 5; Hull (ed.), *Annals of Athens*, 321; Richard Henry Hutchings, *Hutchings Bonner Wyatt: An Intimate Family History* (Utica, N.Y., 1937), 198; Macon *American Union*, October 9, 1868.

peace—and use their utmost discretion to prevent collisions with intractable white men" but "to be always ready, in self-defense, to protect their own at whatever cost to others." For some, self-defense did not exclude retaliation. When Macon whites threatened the lives of Henry Turner and Jefferson Long, the blacks put a guard of 150 men around their two leaders' homes and banned all whites from the area, including local police. An alarmed city council called a meeting of conciliation after the freedmen threatened to burn the city if another black man was killed.[42]

Two of the most vocal black proponents of retaliation had a history of defiance as slaves. When black assemblyman William H. Harrison of Hancock County was threatened by the Klan, he promised *"burning* will be done if any harm comes to Radicals in his county." As a slave, Harrison had been "troublesome," and in 1863 he had been implicated in a slave insurrection. James Simms, who had escaped to freedom during the war, reprinted in his Savannah *Freemen's Standard* a broadside warning the Klan "And all BAD MEN" who threatened the lives of Republicans that "the house in which he or they takes shelter, will be burned to the ground." Simms termed the broadside "a notice of the spirit and determination of the loyalist" to enforce "the law of retaliation." He continued, "Let no man or set of men think that the loyal citizens BUT MORE PARTICULARLY THE COLORED, will tamely submit to be attacked and murdered in Savannah as at Memphis and New Orleans."[43]

From the point of view of the twentieth century, the black politicians may seem subservient. It is true that their religion and their class influenced them toward conservatism. Nevertheless, to proclaim the right of self-defense and demand racial equality with whites (even if only with regard to political and civil rights) were radical and courageous acts in postwar Georgia. Furthermore, there is a danger in making too sharp a dichotomy between political and economic priorities; the two were interrelated. Although the black elite's legislative program lacked sufficient economic content, it was not irrel-

42. Macon *American Union*, June 30, 1870; "Ku Klux Klan Report," VII, 1036–37.
43. "Ku Klux Klan Report," VII, 979–80; Macon *American Union*, April 2, 1869; Savannah *Freemen's Standard*, April 4, 1868.

The Reverend James M. Simms.

evant to the economic needs of the ex-slaves. If implemented, it would have constituted a modest assault on the hegemony Georgia whites held over the freedmen. In an 1870 letter to Chatham County's black assemblyman James Porter, Richard W. White, black clerk of the superior court of that county, summed up the legislative pri-

Freemen's Standard.

"LABOR, ITSELF, IS PLEASURE.....LABOR CONQUERS EVERYTHING."

VOL. 1.   SAVANNAH, GA., SATURDAY, FEBRUARY 15, 1868.   NO. 1.

The front page of the *Freemen's Standard*, February 15, 1868. The paper was edited by James M. Simms.

orities of most black leaders: "give us the *Militia Law*, the *Jury Law*, the *Common School Law*, & the *Common Carrier Law*, and all will be well in this portion of the State."[44]

In placing the militia law at the top of the list, Richard White was expressing the deep concern all Georgia blacks felt for their physical safety. The black politicians were the special targets of Klan violence and intimidation. Their need for protection and that of their constituents demonstrated how closely political and civil rights were related to the economic well-being of the freedmen. Part of the rationale behind the Klan was to keep the black laborer in his place. Angry whites drove black landowners off their property and harassed any blacks who showed signs of prosperity. As one former slave put it, "Jus' as de Neggers was branchin' out and startin' to live lak free folks, dem nightriders com' long beatin', and cuttin', and slashin' 'em up."[45]

Throughout Reconstruction, Georgia's black politicians organized meetings to demand federal protection. In 1868 Savannah blacks pleaded, "unless the power of the federal government is brought to bear in our favor our last estate must prove worse than our first, our freedom only another form of slavery." That same year, freedmen in southwestern Georgia, responding to the killing and wounding of scores of blacks during the Camilla riot, declared: "At this time the colored people are under a species of oppression before unknown to any country professing to be civilized. . . . We are no revolutionists, but . . . we say that the present State government does not answer for the purpose for which it was established, protection and justice for all." In 1871 nine black legislators told a congressional committee investigating the Klan that their constituents had no safety and needed federal protection. "You ask any one of my people out there," assemblyman Thomas Allen implored, "even the most ignorant of them, and they will tell you so."[46]

Despite their pleas, the federal government offered the blacks lit-

44. R. W. White to James Porter, July 16, 1870, in Executive Department, Bullock Correspondence; *White* v. *Clements*, 39 *Georgia Reports*, 232 *et seq.*

45. "Slave Narratives, Georgia," No. 3, p. 102; "Ku Klux Klan Report," VII, 861.

46. *House Miscellaneous Documents*, 40th Cong., 3rd Sess., No. 52, pp. 88–90, 96–97; "Ku Klux Klan Report," VI, 1–9, VII, 607–619, 1057–60, 845–64, 695–707, 1060–62, 923–32, 735–43, 1031–42.

tle protection. Fewer than two thousand northern soldiers were expected to police 133 counties, and few of these troops were abolitionists. Most of them had fought the war to save the Union, not to end slavery. Their behavior during the elections of 1868 and 1870 indicated that many of them were anti-Negro or sympathetic to the opponents of Congressional Reconstruction or both. In April, 1868, a Republican candidate for the legislature from Talbot County found the troops more of a hindrance than a help. "They not only attempt openly in the streets to dissuade the colored man from voting as he wishes, but hesitate not to grossly insult myself and others who are willing to assist the freedmen in maintaining their rights." The soldiers continued this same kind of misconduct in subsequent elections. They felt a natural sympathy towards the white opponents of Reconstruction, and some, hoping to make their military stay in Georgia more bearable, sought to ingratiate themselves with local whites. In December, 1870, following an election when several blacks were badly beaten, members of the 18th United States Infantry thanked the people of Augusta in a letter for "the kindness and gentlemanly treatment we received. . . . So much so that it would please us greatly to be quartered here altogether. . . . we say hurrah for Augusta; may she have a Democratic majority, and be so well represented by so worthy a mayor."[47]

Responding to this serious lack of federal protection, Georgia's blacks and their leaders attempted to create a state militia loyal to the Republican governor. In 1868 one hundred Savannah blacks, all Union veterans, pledged their services to Governor Bullock. Black legislators repeatedly raised the issue and were always defeated. "We tried to raise colored militia," recalled black representative Abram Colby, "but the white Republicans were too weak for us, every time it was brought to a vote we would lose it." Democratic assemblyman John Cobb of Sumter County wrote in 1870, "There are good Radicals, who live & own property in their counties, & they are compelled to live here, can't take their carpet bags & carry their all in it,

<hr>

47. Drago, "Black Georgia During Reconstruction," 12–21, 280–82; Willard W. Wight (ed.), "Reconstruction in Georgia: Three Letters by Edwin G. Higbee," *Georgia Historical Quarterly*, XLI (March, 1957), 87; Atlanta *Constitution*, December 10, 1870; Augusta *Daily Constitutionalist*, December 8, 11, 1870.

and they are afraid to vote for this measure & then face their people at home."[48]

The jury bill, second on Richard White's list of legislative priorities, reflected the black reconstructionists' resolve to overhaul Georgia's antebellum-oriented judicial and legal system. The constitutional convention had adopted almost all of Irwin's Code, the state's antebellum collection of laws. Georgia's code, in the words of Aaron A. Bradley, was "formed when negroes had no rights that a white man was bound to respect." White judges and juries used it to send hundreds of freedmen for minor offenses to chain gangs or to the state prison, where they were leased to Grant, Alexander, and Company for work on the railroads. Bradley and several other black legislators endeavored, without much success, to revise Irwin's Code and reform the convict-lease system. The 1870 legislature, with the blacks reseated, renewed the lease with Grant, Alexander, and Company, but it did forbid courts and judges to send convicts guilty of misdemeanors to work on chain gangs.[49]

Georgia's black politicians were also frustrated in their efforts to get blacks on juries. The constitution of 1868 required only that jurors be upright, honest, and intelligent, but most white county officials equated these attributes with being white. After expelling the blacks, the legislature of 1868 specifically prohibited freedmen from serving as jurors, and even after the black legislators were restored, few ex-slaves ever sat on juries. In 1870 a meeting of Macon blacks charged that most juries were composed of prejudiced whites. T. G. Steward, their spokesman, contended that the former slaves were at a further disadvantage before the law because "the influence of the almighty dollar is generally on the side of the white man against the black. . . . We want a jury on every case where whites and blacks are litigants composed equally of white and black men." Federal officials privately concurred with the blacks' assessments. "There is no distinction of colour authorized by law," wrote General Alfred H. Terry,

48. J. F. Wilson to R. B. Bullock, August 13, 1868, in Executive Department, Bullock Correspondence; "Ku Klux Klan Report," VI, 700; John A. Cobb to his wife, July 20, 1870, in Cobb Papers.
49. Drago, "Black Georgia During Reconstruction," Chap. III, 171, 167; Atlanta Constitution, February 15, 1868.

the military commander of Georgia, in 1870, "but in practice until now the name of no negro had been put in the box. . . . I have no doubt that before exclusively white juries it is very easy to convict a negro of a crime [but] *extremely difficult* to convict a white man of a crime against the person or property of a negro & that in civil cases between parties of the opposite colour Sambo generally goes to the wall."[50]

The need for an equitable jury system emphasized the extent to which economic and political priorities were interrelated. Without police willing to arrest and juries willing to convict whites who maimed or murdered blacks, the freedmen had little protection from violence. A meeting of Albany blacks complained to Congress in 1868 that it was impossible to convict and punish a white man in the courts of Southwest Georgia for the murder of a Negro. Moreover, planters used the judicial system to retain their economic domination over the freedmen. This, in turn, engendered resentment among the blacks and created potentially explosive situations. In 1867 Edwin Belcher reported that freedmen in Wilkes County were being jailed on trumped-up charges, "sustained by the most prejudiced Jury in the Country." Belcher predicted that the ex-slaves would be "forced to take the law into their own hands and entail the most dreadful consequences upon themselves and their oppressors." Blacks in a nearby county reached that point in 1870. Led by their union league president Cudjo Fye, they broke into a Louisville jail to free a fellow league member. All of them were subsequently arrested, jailed, and tried for insurrection.[51]

In 1870 the black politicians achieved a limited victory in their campaign for jury reform when the legislature passed a measure that required commissioners revising the jury boxes to take an oath promising to discharge their duty with impartiality and without regard to color or previous condition. The act, however, availed the freedmen little. "The negroes say that even putting a fair proportion

50. C. Mildred Thompson, *Reconstruction in Georgia*, 354; Macon *American Union*, October 9, 1868, June 23, 30, 1870; Alfred H. Terry to William T. Sherman, June 20, 1870, in William T. Sherman Papers, Library of Congress.

51. *House Miscellaneous Documents*, 40th Cong., 3rd Sess., No. 52, p. 93; Belcher to Col. Lewis, June 8, 1868, in Records of the Bureau of Refugees, Freedmen, and Abandoned Lands; Coulter, "Cudjo Fye's Insurrection," 212–25.

of their names in the box would not remedy this evil," General Terry wrote, "for the liberty to challenge is so great that they would by it be gotten rid of in case their names should be drawn." Terry refused the blacks' request that three freedmen be placed on juries involving civil trials between whites and blacks. Conceding that it would provide "a much needed" protection for the blacks, he nevertheless concluded: "I don't like to be always sort of wet-nurse to the negroes. . . . if with a majority in each branch of the Legislature favorable to them, they cannot pass measures for their protection they had better suffer for a time."[52]

Although next to last on Richard White's list of priorities, the education bill was an issue that appealed to nearly all of the freedmen. Long before W. E. B. Du Bois advanced the notion of a "talented tenth," Georgia's black political elite was stressing the need for a professional class of blacks to provide leadership for the race. In 1869 a black labor convention urged parents to encourage their young men to enter the professions. It suggested that blacks in every county select "the most promising men in their midst" and "defray the expenses of such persons at some college, where they may receive a thorough education to fit them for such professions as may be selected by such persons." Blacks in the 1870 legislature pressed for state subsidies for black higher education. Henry M. Turner wanted the state to use the abandoned capitol at Milledgeville for educational purposes. Philip Joiner of Dougherty County suggested that Turner's bill be amended to include a $100,000 appropriation for the funding of a black college. James Porter thought that the money should be spent on Atlanta University or for the establishment of a college in the black belt.[53]

The movement for a public school system began immediately after the war when blacks and their white allies established schools throughout the state and organized the Georgia Equal Rights and Educational Association. The blacks' chief proponent of public education was James Porter of Savannah. Porter had been born a free

52. *Acts of the General Assembly of the State of Georgia*, 1870, pp. 414–15; Alfred H. Terry to Sherman, June 20, 1870, in Sherman Papers.
53. Macon *American Union*, October 29, 1869; Sanford, "The Negro in the Political Reconstruction of Georgia," 46–47.

black in Charleston, South Carolina, and had come to Savannah before the war, where he preached at a local Protestant Episcopal church. In 1865 he attended the black ministers' meeting with Stanton and Sherman, and one year later, he became vice-president of the Georgia Equal Rights and Educational Association. Elected to the legislature from Chatham County, he attempted to implement the provision in the constitution of 1868 that called for a public school system. The legislature, purged of its black members, failed to fulfill this requirement. When he was reinstated in 1870, Porter introduced a bill that finally led to the creation of Georgia's first public school system.[54]

The legislative debates on the public education bill revealed the low priority most black politicians placed on integration. The bill originally allowed local school districts to decide whether or not to integrate their schools. White legislators viewed even so mild a provision with alarm, as the first step towards race mixing. Although Edwin Belcher and black representative Thomas P. Beard of Richmond County demanded that the world *color* be struck from the measure, most black legislators acquiesced in a separate-but-equal clause. In 1872 a Democratic legislature amended the act to provide separate systems that were to be equal "as far as practicable."[55]

Despite their acceptance of a segregated school system, Georgia's black politicians protested against racial segregation when it meant inequality. Richard White had included on his list of priorities a request for a public accommodations bill. After the war, public accommodations, entertainment, and transportation all remained segregated, and the treatment blacks received on railroads and streetcars was especially demeaning. Before the war, blacks had paid half fare to ride in substandard "Jim Crow" cars that were often used by whites as a smoking car. The same practice continued after the war, with one exception—the freedmen were required to pay the full fare.[56]

54. Drago, "Black Georgia During Reconstruction," 172, 100–101.
55. Savannah *Morning News*, August 27, 1870; Sanford, "The Negro in the Political Reconstruction of Georgia," 47; *Acts of the General Assembly of the State of Georgia*, 1872, p. 69, 1870, p. 57.
56. Drago, "Black Georgia During Reconstruction," 174–75.

Mrs. Henry M. Turner, who, like many of her fellow blacks, was forced to ride in a Jim Crow car.

Throughout Reconstruction, black conventions protested such mistreatment. Blacks at the constitutional convention unsuccessfully tried to insert into the new constitution a clause requiring equal facilities for all races on public carriers. In 1870 black representative Ulysses L. Houston of Savannah wrote such a bill and succeeded in having it passed. The act did not require integration, but attempts to specifically include a separate-but-equal clause had failed. In 1891 the act was finally amended to include the segregation of the races.[57]

It may be because the issue touched them personally that Georgia's black political leaders were so sensitive to discrimination on public carriers. Henry Turner's wife was once forcibly removed from a white-only car and made to sit in a Jim Crow car, for example. However, this sensitivity was not confined to the black elite. In July, 1872, a Savannah streetcar company segregated its passengers but failed to provide black commuters with sufficient cars. After unidentified persons sent a letter threatening to bring suit against the company if it did not abandon segregation, the company stopped enforcing its Jim Crow policies. In late July blacks began sitting in white-only cars, only to be expelled by irate whites. Retaliating, angry freedmen halted a streetcar on one of its trips around the city and pelted it with bottles. At one stop, a crowd of a thousand blacks and whites confronted each other. As the car came to a halt, a black man boarded it and was expelled. A shot was fired, and an ugly race riot began. Three blacks were killed, and a number of people of both races were wounded. Several days later, a United States commissioner ruled that, although the company could segregate the races, it had to supply more cars for blacks.[58]

The streetcar riot suggests that it is wrong to make too sharp a dichotomy between the priorities of Georgia's black politicians and their constituents. While they failed to sufficiently stress the economic priorities of their black followers, their program of political and civil rights was relevant to the day-to-day existence of the ex-slaves, including those out in the fields.

57. *Ibid.*
58. Macon *Telegraph*, quoted in the Savannah *Morning News*, August 17, 1869; Savannah *Morning News*, August 3, 5, 1872; Augusta *Daily Constitutionalist*, July 30, 31, August 6, 1872.

CHAPTER V

The Development of the
Postbellum Labor System

Slavery officially died in 1865, but the racial attitudes that made it possible lived on. "Most of the white citizens believe that the institution of slavery was right, and the best condition for colored men and women," a Georgia newspaper acknowledged in 1866. "Believing that slavery was right . . . they will believe that the condition, which comes nearest to slavery, that can now be established will be the best."[1] Among most Georgia whites there was a consensus that blacks were racially inferior and therefore deserving of only the lowest place in society. Many blacks, on the other hand, refused to accept this restricted concept of their freedom, and their "place" in society. They viewed any remnants of slavery as infringements upon their newly won freedom. The northerners, for their part, found themselves caught between these contending attitudes and forces. Some were sympathetic to the freedmen, but most shared in varying degrees the racial attitudes of Georgia's white community. Out of the struggle emerged a new labor system that never entirely satisfied either white or black Georgians. While the planters retained much of their power, they were no longer able to exercise the nearly complete hegemony they once held as slave-owners.

Some white Georgians felt a sense of moral relief at the demise of slavery; it had made them uneasy and unable to relate to the Christian world outside the South. In 1865 an Augusta newspaper argued

1. Augusta *Loyal Georgian*, March 3, 1866.

that the abolition of slavery had removed "a mark of difference between our own peculiar civilization and the established Civilization of Christendom." Nevertheless, racism pervaded all classes of white Georgians. Poor whites in Savannah, a northerner reported, regarded "the negroes as still a servile race, who must always be inferior by virtue of their black skins." However, black minister Robert Kent of Augusta informed federal officials in 1866, "It was not the low-down ignorant class that treated the negro the worst, or from whom he had the most to fear; it was the middle class."[2]

Georgia planters were the most adamant and vocal in proclaiming the verities of the old proslavery argument. "Custom in civilized countries," stated the Dawson *Weekly Journal* in 1866, "has rendered it necessary to have a *class* to take the place of 'hewers of wood and drawers of water'—or servants. African slavery—or the basis of natural inferiority—is the only system that ever worked harmoniously, and the only one that ever will. While the social status of the negro has been altered . . . his relationship to the white race, remains virtually the same . . . our people will embrace and act upon the idea that the negro is still to raise cotton, corn, etc. though under a different system of labor." Attempts to uplift the blacks were considered useless since the race was "by nature indolent and careless, and will only work under compulsion and to gratify temporal wants." To northerners, this attitude suggested an eventual return to slavery in some form. "The people express an external submission to its Abolition," observed a Union general in 1865, "but there is an evident desire on the part of some to . . . substitute a gradual system of emancipation, or a modified condition of Slavery."[3]

The legislation enacted in Georgia between 1865 and 1866 reflected how deeply entrenched were the old antebellum attitudes toward the blacks. "I have looked into some of the laws passed in 1866,

2. Matthews, "The Negro in Georgia Politics," 4; Elizabeth Hyde Botume, *First Days Amongst the Contrabands* (New York, 1968), 169; Augusta *Daily Constitutionalist*, June 5, 1866.

3. Eliza Frances Andrews, *The War-Time Journal of a Georgia Girl*, 340; *House Executive Documents*, 39th Cong., 1st Sess., No. 34, Pt. 2, p. 2; Dawson (Ga.) *Weekly Journal*, December 7, 1866; Macon *Journal and Messenger*, May 31, 1865; J. H. Wilson to W. D. Whipple, June 15, 1865, quoted in C. Mildred Thompson, *Reconstruction in Georgia*, 53.

when the old ruling class had full sway," wrote Republican politician and former Confederate officer Amos T. Akerman in 1875. "It is curious to see how closely they stuck to Confederate ideas." Although hostile criticism from the North forced Georgia to modify the eleven laws of its black code, the state was nevertheless able to create a caste system that denied blacks the right to vote, to sit on juries, to intermarry with whites, or to give testimony in court when whites were involved. "Why require a *special* code of laws to regulate them?" asked a black Georgia newspaper. "If he [the ex-slave] stood to you as you now stood to him, and he was to enact a special code of laws to regulate your conduct . . . would you not growl about it[?]" Ironically, white Georgians considered the codes "a positive tangible demonstration, in the form of *law*, of her [Georgia's] interest in the black population, and her intention that they shall be protected against oppression and made secure in all their rights."[4]

The black population was evolving a far different concept of freedom. More than likely, each ex-slave perceived freedom in his or her own peculiar way. Few, however, would have disagreed with the definition of slavery presented in a memorial to Congress in 1868 by blacks from Southwest Georgia. Quoting Webster, the memorial defined slavery as "the state of entire subjection to another." Freedom, then, meant for the blacks an independence from the white man and the abolition of the restraints of slavery. Georgia blacks also envisioned a society that provided them equal opportunities with whites and the concomitant material well-being. Freedom to them, wrote a disgruntled white, was "plenty to eat,—equality with whites."[5] Specifically, it meant owning land, establishing more permanent family ties, and getting an education.

4. Amos T. Akerman Diary (typewritten copy in Amos T. Akerman Papers, Georgia Department of Archives and History, Atlanta), March 17, 1875; Augusta *Colored American*, January 13, 1866; *Acts of the General Assembly of the State of Georgia*, 1865–1866, p. 239; R. H. Clark, T. R. R. Cobb, and D. Irwin (preps.), *The Code of the State of Georgia*, rev. and corr. David Irwin (Atlanta, 1867), 15, 334–35, 735, 251, 344, xi; Macon *Daily Telegraph*, March 4, 1866, quoted in Cason, "The Loyal League in Georgia," 128.
5. *House Miscellaneous Documents*, 40th Cong., 3rd Sess., No. 52, p. 97; John Floyd King to Lin Caperton, July 31, 1865, in Thomas Butler King Papers, #1252, Southern Historical Collection, Library of the University of North Carolina at Chapel Hill.

Rural blacks, according to all observers, were nearly unanimous in their desire to own land. General Davis Tillson, head of the Freedmen's Bureau in 1866, found them "impelled by their almost universal desire to possess land." "We shall still be slaves . . . until ebr'y man can raise him own bale of cotton and say, '*Dis is mine,*'" reasoned one ex-slave. Anything short of owning land meant that the freedman would be working for someone else, usually his former master. "But they will almost starve and go naked before they will work for a white man," noted a planter, "if they can get a patch of ground to live on, and get from under his control."[6]

Freedom, further, meant the opportunity to create a more tightly knit and secure family life. Many slaves had been separated from family members, and when they were freed, some immediately sought out their lost relatives. Many tried to legalize their conjugal relationships and to develop a more independent family life. Mass wedding ceremonies were not unusual. Asserting their familial independence, blacks adopted surnames different from those of their former masters. Many also chose economic arrangements that fostered a more meaningful family life. Despite financial hardships, black men demanded that their women stay home, away from the white man's house and field labor. "There are a great many negro women taken from the field to the shanty," a Southerner observed, "to live the lady: poor fellows [husbands], they'll catch it when they come to foot the bill." However, as Noralee Frankel has suggested, most black women who remained at home with their families were not simply acquiescing in their husbands' demands; they were reasserting some control over their own lives. In 1871 the editor of a Georgia agricultural journal complained, "Negro women . . . will not, to a great extent, pick cotton, which is a woman's work; they have the idea, that, since their emancipation they should live very much like ladies, and consequently they will merely take care of their own households and do but little work out of doors."[7]

Black efforts to tighten family ties during Reconstruction suggest

6. *Senate Executive Documents*, 39th Cong., 2nd Sess., No. 6, p. 57; Athens *Southern Cultivator*, XXV (March, 1867), 69; Thomas Wentworth Higginson, "Fair Play the Best Policy," *Atlantic Monthly*, XV (May, 1865), 626.
7. Augusta *Colored American*, December 30, 1865; Eliza Frances Andrews, *The*

that slavery had had a detrimental effect on Negro family life, but most black families survived slavery intact. On Frances Butler Leigh's Sea Islands plantations, there was no black matriarchy; the men ruled their families with an iron hand. Moreover, the general stability of Negro family life continued during Reconstruction. According to a Congressman investigating the Ku Klux Klan in 1871, "very many of the raids upon colored people by these disguised bands have disclosed the fact that their victims were found in bed with their wives and their little children around them, where they lived in organized and regular families." By 1880 a planter in Middle Georgia had to concede that it "was commonly thought that the negroes when freed, would care very little for their children, and would let them die for want of attention, but experience has proved this surmise unfounded."[8]

Most ex-slaves, particularly the black political elite, perceived education, which they had long been denied, as a necessary vehicle for success. They believed that education would narrow the gap between the races and provide black leaders. Thus, Georgia's blacks, both urban and rural, shared their leaders' enthusiasm for education. In Macon a northern traveler found a night school attended by two hundred children and some adults. "The eagerness of the older ones to learn," the school superintendent remarked, "is a continual wonder to me. The men and women say, 'We work all day, but we'll come to you in the evening for learning, and we want you to make us learn; we're dull, but we want you to beat it into us!'" After Sherman evacuated Savannah, local blacks organized an educational association that schooled nearly one-quarter of the city's black children. In Augusta a black man who had taught an underground school during the war continued teaching in a store below some tenements, and in 1865 missionary Frederick Ayer encountered two ex-slaves conducting a school for freedmen in an old Atlanta church.[9]

War-Time Journal of a Georgia Girl, 321, 346–47; Macon *Daily Telegraph*, April 7, 1866; Noralee Frankel, "Rural Black Women in Mississippi: Their Withdrawal from the Work Force, 1865–1868" (paper read at the Organization of American Historians Convention, April, 1980); "Ku Klux Klan Report," VII, 829.

8. Leigh, *Ten Years on a Georgia Plantation,* 164; "Ku Klux Klan Report," VII, 836; "A Georgia Plantation," 835.

9. *Proceedings of the Freedmen's Convention,* 18–19; Trowbridge, *The South,*

Like their urban brethren, plantation blacks flocked to schools. "Other hands from the neighboring plantations come in," observed Columbia County planter Charles Stearns, "so that our Sunday school now numbers over one hundred pupils, mostly adults; seventy-five of them have already purchased the National Primer, and all are anxious to learn. . . . Most of them spend their two hours' nooning which I give them, in learning their lessons, and it is a pleasant sight . . . every noon and every night, to see on the door step of every negro cabin, a knot of darkies trying to pry into the mysteries of the spelling books." Northern reporter Sidney Andrews saw "common plantation negroes, and day laborers in the towns and villages . . . supporting little schools themselves. Everywhere . . . [he] found among them a disposition to get their children into schools if possible." By late 1866, over one hundred schools for blacks existed throughout the state, many of them self-supporting.[10]

The blacks had been raised in an American society that lionized education as the key to success. For this reason, it is not surprising that the freedmen wanted to emulate the whites they had observed going to school. "It wasn't so long after the surrender before schools for Negroes were opened," recalled an ex-slave. "It looked like they went wild trying to do just like their white folks had done." Their reasons for wanting education were also pragmatic. In the postbellum society, their livelihood was going to be based on contractual agreements, and they realized the necessity of a basic education. "Negroes had to go to school fust and get larnin'," reasoned one ex-slave, "so they would know how to keep some of them white folks from gittin' land 'way from 'em if they did buy it."[11]

The rapid influx of ex-slaves into the cities at the conclusion of the war dramatized what their newly won freedom meant to them.

465–66, 509–510, 490; Clarence Albert Bacote, *The Story of Atlanta University: A Century of Service, 1865–1965* (Atlanta, 1969), 3–4.

10. Charles Stearns, *The Black Man of the South, and the Rebels; or, The Characteristics of the Former, and the Recent Outrages of the Latter* (1872; reprint ed. New York, 1969), 162; "House of Representatives, Report No. 30. Report of the Joint Committee on Reconstruction, Part III. Georgia, Alabama, Mississippi, Arkansas," *Reports of the Committees of the House of Representatives*, 39th Cong., 1st Sess., Vol. II, 174; John Watson Alvord, *Third Semi-Annual Report on Schools for Freedmen*, January 1, 1867 (Washington, D.C., 1867), 14.

11. "Slave Narratives, Georgia," No. 1, p. 223, No. 2, p. 191.

Almost every city experienced an increase in its black population. The war itself had brought phenomenal urban growth, as the cities expanded to meet the needs of the Confederate war machine. Many of the slave-owners who were made refugees by the war took their slaves along when they fled to the cities. Other slaves were sent to town to work in the emerging war-related industries. The black migration to the cities after the war, however, was substantially larger. White Georgians viewed this migration as proof of the blacks' innate irresponsibility. They believed that the freed slaves, hell-bent on testing their new freedom, had simply run pell-mell into the cities, where, lacking the "wholesome" restraints of slavery, they had sunk into sloth and idleness. These interpretations, however, ignore the many and varied reasons why blacks fled the plantations. Some blacks were forced to leave because planters refused to pay their just wages once the crops were gathered. In addition, because urban slaves had been afforded greater freedom of movement and economic opportunity than rural and plantation blacks, rumors of a better life in the cities had spread among plantation blacks even during the antebellum period. "Many of our people who have never had the opportunity of leaving their homes, and having heard such fabulous stories about the splendor of our cities," declared a memorial by blacks to the Georgia legislature in 1866, "have left their homes to lounge, in several instances around our towns and villages, with false ideas concerning the benefits thereby to be realized." In the eyes of these migrants, the cities promised a greater degree of autonomy than the plantations. Many blacks were anxious to escape the cotton fields. They went to work in lumberyards, built railroads, or became cooks, stevedores, deckhands, teamsters, and waiters.[12]

A number of blacks thought they could best realize their American dream of success in the cities, where they had greater economic and educational opportunities, the protection of federal troops, and

12. C. Mildred Thompson, *Reconstruction in Georgia*, 43–45, 55; Eliza Frances Andrews, *The War-Time Journal of a Georgia Girl*, 340, 344, 365; Macon *Journal and Messenger*, May 31, 1865; Mohr, "Georgia Blacks During Secession and Civil War," Chap. IV; Philadelphia *Christian Recorder*, July 1, 1865; *Proceedings of the Freedmen's Convention*, 17, 20; Richard C. Wade, *Slavery in the Cities: The South, 1820–1860* (New York, 1964), Chaps. V and VI; Drago, "Black Georgia During Reconstruction," 36–37.

the aid of the Freedmen's Bureau. Imbued with the Protestant-capitalistic work ethic, some of them became small businessmen. Southerners complained that their servants were disappearing and "setting up their own establishments." One ex-slave explained to her employer, "you see, mammy wants to open up a laundry and she want[s] me to help her . . . as a partner." In Augusta black iron-workers, in the best tradition of Benjamin Franklin's Poor Richard, advertised: "Work wanted. . . . We have not turned fools because we are free, but we know we have to work for our living, and are determined to do it. We mean to be sober, industrious, honest, respectful to white folks, and so we depend on them to give us work." Gradually a homogeneous urban black middle class of doctors, lawyers, druggists, and businessmen of all sorts emerged. "In all of the towns and cities," a black minister noted in 1865, "colored men of enterprise, means and intelligence may be found who have risen in spite of opposing forces."[13]

The cities also witnessed a sharp conflict between the black man's aspirations and the white man's resolve to keep him in his place. Everywhere whites complained of blacks asserting themselves, sassing back, or loitering in the streets. "I'll clean no streets for poor white folks' uses" was a common response of blacks to offers of menial jobs. At a government stock auction held in Augusta during the summer of 1865, thousands of whites and blacks mingled. According to the liberal journal *Nation*, this resulted in "numerous conflicts between the two races. . . . The former slave begins to assert himself in some cases too much."[14]

To keep the black man in his place, urban whites exerted a number of economic, social, and political pressures. Economically, they made it difficult for the freedman to get a good job. "The whites are crowding us out of employment," complained an Augusta black preacher. "The whites and the Irish are getting all the drays and the

13. Drago "Black Georgia During Reconstruction," 36–37, 38–39; Fannie Atkisson to Marion Blackshear, May 27, 1865, in Baber-Blackshear Papers, University of Georgia Library, Athens; Mary Ann Harris Gay, *Life in Dixie During the War, 1861, 1862, 1863, 1864, 1865* (Atlanta, 1897), 286, Augusta *Daily Chronicle and Sentinel*, January 31, 1866, quoted in C. Mildred Thompson, *Reconstruction in Georgia*, 56, Philadelphia *Christian Recorder*, September 9, 1865.

14. Drago, "Black Georgia During Reconstruction," 39; *Nation*, I (September 21, 1865), 354; Quattelbaum, "The Absence of Sambo in Georgia Reconstruction," 14.

negro is nowhere." A large part of the Savannah fire department had always been black, but after the war, a local newspaper launched a campaign to replace black firefighters with Confederate veterans.[15]

Bolstered by years of custom, social segregation prevailed everywhere. "We accept the death of slavery," said one white Georgian, but he added, "Our people have not been brought up to associate with negroes. They don't think it decent; and the negroes will be none the better for being thrust into the places of white men's sons." An Augusta newspaper maintained that "there should be some distinct line" between blacks and whites "in all social and mercantile connections." In nearly every city, blacks lived in ghettos: "Shermantown" in Atlanta, "Canaan" in Augusta, "Blackfriars" in Athens, and "darktown" elsewhere. Moreover, most public places and transportation facilities were segregated. In Athens at circuses and horse races there were "Separate seats for the colored persons." The Savannah city council closed down the local park in 1865, rather than integrate it. Atlanta, however, was more flexible in its attitude towards integration. It allowed blacks to be buried in the same cemeteries with whites until 1877, when the city council ordered the black bodies exhumed and buried elsewhere.[16]

Politically, city officials used the courts to control the black population. The ex-slave was often arrested on negligible evidence, fined, jailed, or put to work on street gangs for minor offenses. Faced with an influx of freedmen, the cities beefed up their police forces. "With a vagabond freed element in our midst, and constantly pouring into the city . . . it is a matter of necessity to keep up at any cost an efficient Police Force for our protection," said the mayor of Savannah in 1866. There was no doubt where the sympathy of most of the policemen lay. Many were Confederate veterans not predisposed to deal fairly with the ex-slaves, some of whom had fought them as Yankees. Conflict was inevitable. The mayor's court of Savannah regularly tried blacks for resisting arrest or assaulting officers. In Macon an

---

15. Augusta *Daily Constitutionalist*, June 1, 1865, June 5, 1866; Savannah *Daily Advertiser*, May 16, 1866.

16. Whitelaw Reid, *After the War: A Tour of the Southern States, 1865–1866*, ed. C. Vann Woodward (New York, 1965), 152; Augusta *Daily Constitutionalist*, October 15, 1865; Drago, "Black Georgia During Reconstruction," 41; Gamble, "Athens," 67; Savannah *Daily Advertiser*, June 12, 13, 1866; Minutes of the City Council of Atlanta (MS in Atlanta Historical Society), April 4, 1877.

exchange of insults between a policeman and a discharged Union soldier in January, 1866, attracted a crowd of allies for each side. In the battle that ensued one Negro was shot.[17]

Regardless of what had initially attracted them to the cities, most black refugees found urban life difficult. A black mother in Atlanta who supported her family by taking in washing commented, "Sometimes I gits along tolerable, sometimes right slim; but dat's de way wid everybody; times is powerful hard right now." Lacking any means of support, many became vagrants. In addition, the refugees were particularly susceptible to the various epidemics sweeping postwar Georgia, especially cholera and smallpox. The black mortality rate soared in almost every large city.[18]

Harassed southern city officials turned to the federal military for help. In Athens, federal troops assisted the city council in collecting overdue taxes, paving roads, and fighting fires. Besides fully cooperating with such requests, the military was supportive of southern city officials, particularly after the mustering out of the last black troops in 1865. Yankees genuinely interested in the welfare of the freedmen were few in number. Sympathetic commanders who tried to help the ex-slaves were hampered by inadequate forces and the hostility of the white community. Besides, many Union officers shared the southerners' racial attitudes. They were openly hostile or indifferent to the freedmen. A northern traveler found the bias strongest among western troops, whose commanders, "utterly unfit to deal with the blacks," were "only less proslavery than the natives themselves." Such officers zealously cooperated with city officials in controlling the blacks. They prohibited the freedmen from leaving the plantations without passes, thrashed and returned runaways, and disciplined ex-slaves disrespectful to their former owners. Federal officials in Athens even won the praise of local whites for their disciplinary actions against blacks caught stealing. Some of the culprits,

17. Savannah *Daily Advertiser*, December 25, 1865, May 5, 6, 10, 1866; Augusta *Loyal Georgian*, October 13, 1866; Drago, "Black Georgia During Reconstruction," 41–42, 43, 45–46; *Report of Edward C. Anderson, Mayor of the City of Savannah, for the Year Ending September 30, 1866* (Savannah, 1866), 5; Macon *Daily Telegraph*, January 25, 1866.

18. Augusta *Daily Constitutionalist*, May 10, 1866; Albany (Ga.) *Patriot*, June 24, July 1, 1865; Trowbridge, *The South*, 453–54; Drago, "Black Georgia During Reconstruction," 44–45.

their heads shaved, were tied up by their thumbs and forced to wear signs that said "I am a thief." Others, decked with similar placards, were paraded through the streets.[19]

Such harsh treatment by federal and local officials, as well as unemployment, disease, and starvation, took its toll. By the summer of 1865, most of the black refugees had returned to the plantations. "All the negroe[s] are here now," a Decatur County planter wrote in August, 1865. "They seemed penitent & looked like they had been starved." According to a planter living near Macon, "Most of our people have come back to us & seem to be willing to go to work." A Liberty County woman, visiting Atlanta, found her former slaves "really in distressing circumstances . . . without means & wish to return home where they can obtain an honest livelihood." Some freedmen were willing to accept even the most pitiful wages. "Our country is full of negroes," a Gordon County overseer noted, "going from house to house begging to get work just for something to eat."[20]

As dramatic as the migration to and from the cities was, most blacks never left the plantations. "If us had left," recalled an ex-slave, "it would have been jus' lak swappin' places from de fryin' pan to de fire, 'cause Niggers didn't have no money." More often than not, the news of freedom was calmly received. "Pa called the negroes together," the daughter of one planter remembered. "They were all standing in the back yard. He stood on the steps and talked to them. . . . He told them they were all free now to go where they would and do the best they could for themselves; but that those who wanted to stay could do so and that he would do the best he could for them." The disruption of plantation life was often minimal. On the Burge plantation near Covington, the freedmen continued to work as they had before the war for a one-sixth share of the crop.[21]

19. Drago, "Black Georgia During Reconstruction," 45–49; Sidney Andrews, *The South Since the War*, 382; C. Mildred Thompson, *Reconstruction in Georgia*, 49–50; Eliza Frances Andrews, *The War-Time Journal of a Georgia Girl*, 287, 340; Hull, *Annals of Athens*, 302–303.

20. Thomas Barrow to his father, August 30, 1865, in Barrow Papers; Eugenius Aristides Nisbet to Reuben, January 19, 1866, in Eugenius Aristides Nisbet Papers, Manuscript Department, William R. Perkins Library, Duke University, Durham, N.C.; Mary Jones to her daughter, October 3, 1865, in Charles Colcock Jones, Jr., Papers, University of Georgia Library, Athens; E. Lowrey to John S. Dobbins, January 12, 1866, in John S. Dobbins Papers, Emory University, Atlanta.

21. "Slave Narratives, Georgia," No. 3, p. 64; Myrtle Long Candler, "Reminis-

On the plantations, as in the cities, freedom was interpreted differently by the blacks and whites. Many whites continued to act as if slavery had never ended. As one ex-slave stated, "Negroes was free but they weren't 'lowed to act lak free people." Some planters still required their ex-slaves to obtain passes before leaving the plantations. Others even refused to pay them for their labor. A few kept their employees in virtual bondage by abusing the Apprentice Act of 1866, which was ostensibly designed to provide an orphan with a guardian and a good home until he reached the age of twenty-one. Northern journals were quick to record this abuse. They were joined in their criticism by an unlikely ally, the Georgia Supreme Court, which warned "public functionaries" to be "vigilant in preventing anyone under the name of master, from getting the control of the labor and services of such minor apprentice, as if he were still a slave."[22]

With the legal abolishment of slavery, violence against blacks increased. In Henry County, for example, "Jayhawkers" whipped, robbed, killed, and drove blacks from the plantations where they had labored for the past year. Conservative newspapers, growing apprehensive over the violence, conceded that "crimes of this kind *do* exist in some portions of the country, to the mortification of candid and honorable men throughout the State." Although the violence was partly a product of the bitterness engendered by the war, it had its roots in the labor problem. In the last quarter of 1865, terrorism against the freedmen coincided with their receiving pay for past work and the contracting of laborers for the new year. While most planters never personally engaged in violence, they failed to condemn a situation from which they benefited. Near Columbia County, where whites went on a rampage, stealing from blacks, beating and killing them, only one planter, a transplanted Yankee, had the courage and conviction to condemn the lawlessness.[23]

cences of Life in Georgia During the 1850s and 1860s, Part V," *Georgia Historical Quarterly*, XXXIV (March, 1950), 11; James I. Robertson, Jr. (ed.), *The Diary of Dolly Lunt Burge* (Athens, 1962), 113.

22. "Slave Narratives, Georgia," No. 2, p. 191; *Proceedings of the Freedmen's Convention*, 17; *Nation*, II (February 1, 1866), 142; *Comas* v. *Reddish*, 35 Georgia Reports, 235–38; *Alfred* v. *McKay*, 36 Georgia Reports, 441–42.

23. Stearns, *The Black Man of the South*, 163; David Tillson to the citizens of Henry County, Elijah Foster, chairman, October 16, 1866, in Negroes File, Georgia De-

Out of this atmosphere of violence and uncertainty emerged the Freedmen's Bureau, established by an act of Congress in March, 1865. Several months later Major General Oliver O. Howard was appointed commissioner with his headquarters in Washington, D.C. He was empowered to appoint only ten assistant commissioners, several of whom had to be assigned more than one state. Howard delegated Georgia and South Carolina to Major General Rufus B. Saxton, who in turn placed General Edward A. Wild in charge of Georgia. In September, 1865, Wild was relieved from his command and the Office of Assistant Commissioner for Georgia was established. Brigadier General Davis Tillson became acting assistant commissioner, responsible for bureau affairs in Georgia. He reported to Saxton in South Carolina until December, 1865, and after that, directly to Howard.[24]

Even if Davis Tillson had been an abolitionist, dedicated to improving the lot of the freedmen, he would still have faced a number of other serious obstacles. Because there were never more than 250 officials, it was impossible for the bureau to adequately supervise Georgia's 133 counties. Davis Tillson, however, was no abolitionist. He was chosen to conciliate President Andrew Johnson and Georgia's planters. His predecessor, General Wild, had apparently sided too often with the freedmen, thereby alienating white public opinion. Andrew Johnson ordered an investigation of the entire bureau, and the investigators were scheduled to reach Georgia in the summer of 1866. In appointing the conservative Tillson, Howard managed to mute much of their criticism. When the investigation was concluded, Johnson's men had warm praise for Tillson.[25]

Tillson's first task in assuming command of the Georgia bureau was to end the violence against the blacks and to get them back to

partment of Archives and History, Atlanta; Augusta *Loyal Georgian*, October 13, 1866; Reid, *After the War*, 150; Philadelphia *Christian Recorder*, July 28, 1866; Augusta *Daily Constitutionalist*, October 19, 1866. Trowbridge noted the large number of fines levied against planters in late 1865. Trowbridge, *The South*, 463, 499–500.

24. National Archives and Records Service, General Services Administration, *Records of the Superintendent of Education for the State of Georgia Bureau of Refugees, Freedmen, and Abandoned Lands, 1865–1870. National Archives Microfilm Publications Pamphlet Accompanying Microcopy No. 799* (Washington, D.C., 1969), 1.

25. *Senate Executive Documents*, 39th Cong., 3rd Sess., No. 6, p. 49; O. O. Howard to R. Saxton, September 12, 1865, in Records of the Bureau of Refugees, Freedmen, and Abandoned Lands; C. Mildred Thompson, *Reconstruction in Georgia*, 64–65.

work. To achieve his goals and stabilize the labor system, he forbade planters to discharge their employees without paying them, and he made them responsible for the well-being of their aging slaves. Moreover, Tillson threatened to use force to halt the violence. He moved quickly to dispel the planters' greatest fear—that the blacks would not return to work—by reducing rations to the freedmen and ordering them back to the plantations.[26]

While he began to implement his program to end violence against the ex-slaves and compel them to work, Tillson also embarked on a program of upgrading the monthly wages of the freedmen. His two-pronged approach included transporting enough willing blacks to western states, where wages were higher, thus forcing Georgia planters to raise their wages. In addition, he introduced a minimum wage of twelve dollars per month or one-quarter share of the crop for first-class male hands. Initially, Tillson's action brought praise from established black leaders, but hostility from planters protesting the minimum wage and chafing at his making them responsible for their aging ex-slaves. However, most of their criticism and apprehension subsided with Tillson's subsequent decisions. He limited the jurisdiction of bureau courts to minor matters, and by March, 1866, he had turned most disputes over to the civil courts. More important he replaced radically inclined agents with native-white Georgians. In December, 1865, the Georgia constitutional convention agreed to his request that justices of the peace and ordinaries of the various counties be made bureau agents. General Howard concurred in these measures. "He directs me," wrote Howard's adjutant to Tillson, "to assure you that your action meets with his approval, and the appointment of civilians as Agents of the Bureau, perfectly satisfactory. . . . They will need careful watching and prompt removal in case they do not perform their duty. Genl Howard directs me to caution you not to alienate the negro by apparent endorsement of the wishes of their former masters."[27]

26. *Senate Executive Documents*, 39th Cong., 2nd Sess., No. 6, pp. 57, 49–53; Trowbridge, *The South*, 462; *Proceedings of the Freedmen's Convention*, 13–14.

27. *Proceedings of the Freedmen's Convention*, 13; Davis Tillson to Benjamin C. Yancey, December 17, 1866, in Benjamin C. Yancey Papers, #2594, Southern Historical Collection, Library of the University of North Carolina at Chapel Hill; *Senate Executive Documents*, 39th Cong., 2nd Sess., No. 27, pp. 88–89, 93–94; Trowbridge, *The South*, 498, 492; Athens *Southern Cultivator*, XXIV (January, 1866), 3–4; Drago,

Planters quickly noted the conservatism of the new bureau agents. In May, 1866, Baldwin County planters thanked the local agent "for the enlightened, moderate and useful administration of his office among us." Not surprisingly, planters used the bureau to control their laborers. When blacks on a Liberty County plantation called a work stoppage because they felt they had been cheated in the contract, the bureau agent threatened to put the ring leaders in chains if the protest continued. Similarly, Columbia County planter Charles Stearns found the bureau a valuable ally in helping him "govern my hands." Soon Georgia whites began praising Tillson and the bureau. So complete was the shift in sentiment that a northern traveler reported, "all the better class of planters recognized the sincere efforts of the Freedmen's Bureau to aid them." When Tillson left the bureau in January, 1867, to become a Georgia planter himself, a state newspaper lamented, "we think it unfortunate that General Tillson, who has become so familiar with our people and learned to appreciate our character as well as that of the negroes, has been removed from a position where he could have done so much good."[28]

More radically inclined whites and blacks failed to appreciate the moderation in Davis Tillson's tenure as Georgia's bureau chief, a moderation historians would later applaud. The increasingly conservative and proplanter tilt of the bureau under his command alarmed them. In June, 1866, Augusta freedmen gathered in a black Baptist church to meet with Andrew Johnson's emissaries, Generals Joseph S. Fullerton and James B. Steedman. The Reverend Samuel Drayton told the generals: "There is no regulation for wages. No system. The colored people have not the means. Some of them are working for very low wages and even the payment of that is denied them on the most trivial plea." The freedmen could not get work, another black speaker charged, "and when they get work, they have to work cheaper

"Black Georgia During Reconstruction," 59; Tillson to James Johnson, October 25, 1865, in Davis Tillson Papers, Georgia Department of Archives and History, Atlanta; Sidney Andrews, *The South Since the War*, 258–59; Gottlieb, "The Land Question in Georgia during Reconstruction," 369; Max Woodhull to Tillson, November 21, 1865, in Records of the Bureau of Refugees, Freedmen, and Abandoned Lands.

28. Milledgeville *Federal Union*, May 1, 1866, quoted in C. Mildred Thompson, *Reconstruction in Georgia*, 64; Mary Jones to C. C. Jones, Jr. May 28, 1866, in Jones Papers, University of Georgia Library; Stearns, *The Black Man of the South*, 108; Trowbridge, *The South*, 464; Dawson (Ga.) *Weekly Journal*, February 1, 1867.

than a white man; even the Government officers who were sent out here for their protection made them work for less. A poor nigger had no work, and if he was found on the streets he was arrested and made to work in the chain gang for nothing. (A voice—Yes, for nothing, and there is no white man there)." Five months later, a group of black educators and politicians reversed their earlier support of Tillson. They claimed most of the bureau agents were "Southern men who will not take notice of outrages perpetrated upon our people." They asked the bureau to "give us Northern Agents or allow colored men to hold these offices." General Howard himself later admitted, "General Tillson was conservative and a harmonizer, leaning possibly to the side of the white employers."[29]

In criticizing Tillson, the black leaders were simply reflecting a growing disenchantment among rural blacks. In January, 1865, their hopes were stirred when General William T. Sherman issued Field Order No. 15, which set aside the Sea Islands and certain coastal regions of South Carolina and Georgia for black settlement. Some black families received forty acres of land and were given possessory titles until Congress could confirm the ownership. Barely one year later, Tillson aggressively implemented pro-Johnson directives allowing the planters to regain their confiscated lands. In February, 1866, he permitted planters to return, advising them to settle all labor disputes with their local agent. On the Sea Islands of Georgia he consolidated all valid land claims by blacks to one part of an island; he ordered the remaining ex-slaves to contract with the returning planters or be forcibly removed.[30]

The reaction among the coastal blacks was immediate and predictable. When federal officials explained the new policy to the freedmen at meetings, they were shouted down. "Dat's no Yank," exclaimed an unbelieving freedman at one such gathering; "dat just some reb dressed in blue clothes and brought him here to lie to us."

29. Augusta *Daily Constitutionalist*, June 5, 1866; *Proceedings of the Convention of the Equal Rights and Educational Association*, 18; C. Mildred Thompson, *Reconstruction in Georgia*, 61; Nathans, *Losing the Peace*, 25; Oliver Otis Howard, *Autobiography of Oliver Otis Howard, Major General, United States Army* (2 vols; Freeport, N.Y., 1971), II, 286.

30. Drago, "How Sherman's March Through Georgia Affected the Slaves," 372–73; *Senate Executive Documents*, 39th Cong., 1st Sess., No. 27, pp. 102–103, 105–106.

Another ex-slave commented, "Me tort when de Yanks come, dey gib us all dis country. An now dat man say we git nuffin', 'cept we work." Surprise turned to resentment. "If the General don't tell them cuffees that they're to have their share of the land and horses and everything else," a white observed, "you'll see a hell of a row today." In 1867 a Union force confronted a hundred determined blacks, some armed, on a rice plantation near Savannah. The blacks insisted that the land belonged to them. Rather than argue the point, the Union commander chose a hasty retreat.[31]

Spectacular as these confrontations between Yankee and freedman or planter and freedman were, they were exceptional. The shape of the new labor system was being hammered out on plantations far from the cities, the bureau, and the Union army. Contemporary blacks saw more continuity than change in the transition from slavery to the postbellum labor system. They pointed to the widespread abuse of the Apprentice Act of 1866 as a revival of slavery. Edwin Belcher, bureau agent and black politician, reported that one-third of the black children in Monroe County had been bound out to planters by 1867. "It would first be proper for me to denominate it a system of slavery analogius [sic] to the old Russian serfdom," Belcher wrote to his superiors. "In some instances the parties . . . drive off the father and then go to the ordinary and make affidavit that the father is out of the County and the mother unable to support the Child. . . . This system is slavery revived only for a term of years— their condition is precisely the same as if they were slaves."[32]

Articulate blacks also reasoned that laborers deprived of the fruits of their labor were not really free. They argued that the contract system was being manipulated by the planters. Employers read freedmen only selected portions of their contract, Henry M. Turner explained, and later the freedmen found themselves bound by all sorts of restrictive clauses. "They have another method of swindling the Freed people," Belcher wrote in 1867, "that is by charging to them things at fabulous prices which they have never received they being

31. See citations in Gottlieb, "The Land Question in Georgia During Reconstruction," 360, 363–364; Savannah *Daily Republican*, January 21, 1867.
32. Edwin Belcher to Caleb C. Sibley, September 23, 1867, in Records of the Bureau of Refugees, Freedmen, and Abandoned Lands.

unable to read cannot keep their own [account]." In 1868 a black politician won the applause of Albany blacks when he explained how planters were exploiting them: "The planter writes it all down mighty nice, and promises to give good wages, and the officers approves it; the negro comes to work and thinks he will have a heap of money. When the settling day comes the agent comes on with another paper, and pulls it out, and it 'counteracts' the contract. So much for jumping over the fence at the [ends] of the rowe [sic]—sixty days loss time with rations, when nigger was sick six days, tobacco more than nigger ever heard of, and all sorts of mean charges, when added up it out multiplies the contract and the year's work, and nig's in debt. Is that freedom, or is it slavery."[33]

According to some freedmen, a good number of planters simply refused to pay them. In 1868 a sharecropper told a visitor how his employer cheated him. The planter "let on as if I'd eat up all my sheer in de 'visions he sole me, I wasn't gwine to be pumfoozled . . . so I jest straddled de bales, but he got de Sheriff, and drug me off, and tuk de cotton." Black educator William S. Scarborough maintained that written contracts were "often useless. . . . On the eve of the harvest just before the laborer receives any compensation whatever for his service, the farmer comes to him and accuses him of unfaithfulness, negligence or theft, etc., for which a dispute arises which terminates in a dismissal. The unfortunate man is forced to leave the plantation regardless of contracts or anything else."[34]

Henry M. Turner felt there was a conspiracy among the planters to keep their laborers in debt. "Whenever there is much fear that the laborer will go to work with some one else the following year," Turner testified, "he is mighty apt to come out twenty-five or thirty dollars in debt, and his employer calls upon him to work it out." Turner termed this condition peonage. In 1869 a black labor convention reported counties where freedmen "generally come out in debt," "don't know they are free," or were "getting along very badly." This kind of situation led Albany blacks to question whether they were really

33. "Ku Klux Klan Report," VII, 1042; Belcher to J. R. Lewis, September 11, 1867, in Records of the Bureau of Refugees, Freedmen, and Abandoned Lands; clipping dated January 4, 1868, from an unidentified Albany newspaper, in E. F. Andrews Scrapbook.
34. Powers, Afoot and Alone, 55–56; Philadelphia Christian Recorder, May 4, 1876.

free, since "now, as when they were 'slaves,' they receive nothing for their labor."[35]

The blacks were correct in perceiving the continuity between slavery and the newly evolving labor system, especially immediately following emancipation. On some Georgia plantations, the method of work seemed unchanged from antebellum days. Travelers continued to describe gangs of fifty or sixty laborers, including women, plowing cotton fields, living in quarters, and being supervised by overseers. Although deprived of their once nearly absolute control over the blacks, the former slave-owners were not powerless. Most contracts contained clauses that gave them broad powers to fine the freedmen. Charles Stearns devised a scale of fines for various infractions, ranging from twenty-five cents for abusing animals and fifty cents for refusing to work, to five dollars for stealing. James A. Spratlin, manager of a Clarke County mill, kept a detailed account of the time lost by the various hands. His decisions revealed the arbitrary nature of fining. "Marche was Behinde tim this morning and I charg to him a half a day According to contracte this the 30 may 1866," read one entry. On another day Spratlin wrote, "I charge March with half of the day for not going to work untile the sun was up August the 16th." He fined another freedman half a day for being half an hour late. A freed woman named Ann was penalized because "on the 21 and on the 1 and 2 of may 1866 She was over 15 mineuits Behinde the time that the contract Say they must be at Worke." Surveying the first two years of freedom, one ex-slave concluded, "Freedom didn't make so many changes on our place right at fust, 'cause most of de slaves stayed right on dar, and things went on jus' lak dey had 'fore dere was any war."[36]

The black critics were also correct in pointing out how little remuneration the ex-slaves received at first. Few became landowners, for in a society where land was power, Georgia planters were "doubly reluctant to sell land to Negroes." Most freedmen were, in any

35. "Ku Klux Klan Report," VII, 1041; Macon *American Union*, October 29, 1869; *House Miscellaneous Documents*, 40th Cong., 3rd Sess., No. 52, p. 97.

36. Trowbridge, *The South*, 483–84; Freedmen's Contract, State of Georgia, Dougherty County, July 22, 1865, in Yancey Papers; Stearns, *The Black Man of the South*, 363; James A. Spratlin Accounts (typescript in Barrow Papers); "Slave Narratives, Georgia," No. 2, p. 263.

case, too poor to purchase land, and the federal government did little to encourage them. Under Sherman's field order, less than five hundred blacks received land. Nor could most freedmen afford transportation to the lands designated under the various homestead acts. Those who did succeed in purchasing property usually had to content themselves with marginal land. Most blacks were wage earners or share-croppers. The former struggled along on eight to ten dollars a month, and the latter usually worked for only a one-fifth share before 1868. As a former slave observed: "Times warn't no better after de war wuz over and dey warn't no wuss. We wuz po before de war and we wuz po after de war."[37]

Slowly, however, conditions improved. The rise in the price of cotton and pressure from the Freedmen's Bureau, which mandated a one-quarter share, brought an increase in the size of the shares the freedmen received. By 1867 most were receiving one-third shares, and some began making more than a subsistence living. Growing numbers were able to save enough money to buy their own farming implements. In 1869 an Augusta newspaper congratulated six black farmers from Burke County who drew enough money on their crops to purchase six new horses and buggies, "an illustration of what industry, good behavior and thrift will accomplish for the colored man as well as the white man." That same year, a black labor convention cited counties where the ex-slaves were "getting along very well," "doing quite well," and receiving "very liberal contracts." The few financial ledgers that survive from this period also suggest that growing numbers of black sharecroppers were beginning to show a modest return. In 1871 and 1872 planter George W. Bryan began to plant Waverly and Scotland plantations, located near Albany. Most of his thirty-two sharecroppers showed a profit after two years' work.[38]

37. Haygood, *Our Brother in Black*, 10; Register of Land Titles Issued to Freedmen, April–September, 1865 (MS in Records of the Bureau of Refugees, Freedmen, and Abandoned Lands); *House Miscellaneous Documents*, 40th Cong., 3rd Sess., No. 52, pp. 96–97; "Slave Narratives, Georgia," No. 3, p. 117; Drago, "Black Georgia During Reconstruction," Chaps. II, VI.

38. Drago, "Black Georgia During Reconstruction," Chaps. II, VI; Augusta *Daily Constitutionalist*, August 6, 1869; Macon *American Union*, October 29, 1869; George W. Bryan Papers, Volume VI, in Southern Historical Collection, Library of the University of North Carolina at Chapel Hill.

Despite obstacles, by 1874 blacks throughout the state had accumulated 300,000 acres of land. In at least one county there was widespread prosperity among the black farmers. Liberty County had been settled by Puritan Congregationalists, who practiced a milder form of slavery than the rest of Georgia. Slaves had been allowed to accumulate modest amounts of livestock and crops. As a consequence, Henry M. Turner argued, they possessed "a higher sense of manhood and citizenship, than is to be found in our race elsewhere in the state." In 1874 Turner toured the county, finding "plantation, after plantation, owned, stocked and cultivated by colored men. These plantations were well fenced in, with houses . . . and everything [a] heart could desire." Turner even encountered white men plowing the fields for black planters.[39]

Although many of the externals of slavery survived the war, there was a significant change. Planters everywhere noticed how the former slave had shed his docility. "He [the ex-slave] wished to be sole arbiter," exclaimed an exasperated Savannah doctor, "and to work when he chooses and to stop when he chooses." Substantial numbers of household servants changed employers, often with little notice over the slightest provocation. In December, 1866, an alarmed Atlanta city council recommended that citizens hire only servants who presented references from their most recent employer. One black cook, indignant over the way the wife of a northern planter treated her, asked: "Now, missus . . . does ye suppose I gwine to give up all my rights to ye, just cause youse a Yankee white woman? Does ye know missus that we's free now? Yes, free we is, and us ant gwine to get down to *ye*, any more than to them rebs." Much to their chagrin, rich white women, some for the first time, had to do their own housework, "while scores of lazy negroes . . . are lying around idle."[40]

Field hands were equally assertive. The once privileged planter

39. W. E. B. Du Bois, "The Negro Landholder of Georgia," *Bulletin of the Department of Labor*, No. 35 (July, 1901) (Washington, D.C., 1901), 665–66; Philadelphia *Christian Recorder*, June 18, 1874.

40. Richard Dennis Arnold, *Letters of Richard D. Arnold, M.D., 1808–1876*, Papers of the Trinity College Historical Society, Double Series XVIII–XIX (Durham, N.C., 1929), 122; Minutes of the City Council of Atlanta, December 14, 1866; Drago, "Black Georgia During Reconstruction," 74–75; Stearns, *The Black Man of the South*, 45; Eliza Frances Andrews, *The War-Time Journal of a Georgia Girl*, 374.

found himself reduced to negotiating with his ex-slaves for their labor. A Liberty County plantation mistress complained that the majority of planters had "*invited* the negroes to come to their places. . . . the negro is virtually master of the soil. . . . Some planters have crowds whilst others of our most worthy & reliable *citizens*—have not one under contract simply because they insist upon controlling the laborer & binding him by a just and firm contract." Georgia planters were learning their first lessons in the economics of a free labor system. "Why is it," asked a perplexed employer in 1871, "that the planter with all the land and all the capital is dependent upon an independent negro, who has neither the land nor the money?" In some instances, the freedmen understood the nature of the new economic system better than their former owners. They were quick to exploit the economic competition between planters and city merchants for their credit. By directly securing credit from the merchants, they could strike better deals with the planters, and were less susceptible to the planters' demands. However, such competition was short-lived. The Georgia legislature, with the conservatives again in power, passed a law in 1873 granting first liens on crops to landlords. Subsequent legislation insured the primacy of landlords' liens over both merchants' and laborers'.[41]

The freedmen's new assertiveness rested on the fact that they could select their employers at a time when labor was scarce. The abolition of slavery had significantly reduced the size of the labor force. By 1866 thousands of blacks had left Georgia to seek higher wages in the western states. The labor force was further reduced by the migration of plantation blacks to the cities and by the successful efforts of black men to take their women out of the cotton fields. "The rising generation of negroes [are] as far as possible, shunning labor in the field," a southerner wrote. "The female portion have almost entirely abandoned labor in the field." According to planter and agricultural expert David Dickson, "The present system of labor does not exceed sixty per cent of the slave labor, involving fully a

41. Mary Jones to C. C. Jones, Jr., January 19, 1866, in Jones Papers, University of Georgia Library; Athens *Southern Cultivator*, XXIX (February, 1871), 45–46; Du Bois, "The Negro Landholder of Georgia," 668. Joseph P. Reidy, "The Unfinished Revolution: White Planters and Black Laborers in the Georgia Black Belt, 1865–1910" (a paper read at the Organization of American Historians Convention, April, 1980), 10.

loss of one-third of the labor by men going to villages, railroads, mining, and other enterprises. One-half of the women and children are absent, housekeeping, idling, and other things."[42]

Planters could not cling too tenaciously to the old ways because they now had a labor force that could disrupt the plantations. The areas most plagued by labor difficulties were the Sea Islands and the rice plantations near Savannah, where the cultivation of the great staples required a large and rigidly supervised labor force. According to Sea Islands plantation mistress Frances Butler Leigh, work in these two areas "went on just as it did in the old times." Her force of nearly three hundred men was divided into gangs, each working under a "head man—the old negro drivers." But this arrangement caused numerous problems. Her workers cheated her by outright theft or malingering; many left her plantations over the actions of a hot-tempered overseer; in 1873 one of them burned down her mill and several other buildings, causing damages of more than fifteen thousand dollars.[43]

The rice plantations near Savannah were in constant turmoil throughout Reconstruction. In 1866 and 1867 federal troops were needed to drive off reluctant freedmen after President Johnson ordered that the lands be returned to their original owners. Racial tensions continued during the presidential election of 1868. Several weeks after Grant's victory, violence erupted on an Ogeechee plantation located several miles outside of Savannah. According to a neighboring planter, "when Mr. Middleton rented those places, the blacks became dissatisfied with anyone having possession of those places, they having had them pretty much to themselves. I heard them say that they had a right to the lands. They didn't think Mr. Middleton had any right to come over there and hire lands." In addition, a dispute had risen over both the method and the amount of work. Middleton called in federal troops to drive the discontented workers off the plantation, and he also ordered the union league on the premises disbanded. Middleton next charged several of his former em-

42. Drago, "Black Georgia During Reconstruction," 77, 75, 245; Athens *Southern Cultivator*, XXVII (March, 1869), 90; David Dickson, *A Practical Treatise on Agriculture; to Which Is Added the Author's Published Letters*, ed. J. Dickson Smith (Macon, Ga., 1870), 86.

43. Leigh, *Ten Years on a Georgia Plantation*, 175–76, 200–201, 138, 56–57.

ployees with stealing several thousand bushels of rice. He had the Savannah sheriff arrest several blacks, including the president of the local union league. While waiting at the depot for the train to Savannah, the sheriff and his deputies were surrounded by a throng of angry blacks who demanded and obtained the release of the prisoners. Concurrently, several whites, including overseers, were beaten. When the panic-stricken sheriff and his deputies reached Savannah, a wave of hysteria swept the city. A hastily gathered "posse" of 120 men returned with the sheriff to the depot and managed to shoot an innocent black teenager. Fortunately, the local federal commander remained calm. He and black politician James Porter rode out to the area and found a frightened group of freedmen eager to surrender to the northern authorities. In January, 1869, more than two dozen of them were indicted for insurrection.[44]

Elsewhere in the state, blacks protested low wages and unfair working conditions. In 1868 freedmen near Albany struck for higher wages; their spokesmen urged them to eat the planters' mules before consenting to inadequate wages. One year later, half of John Cobb's employees left the plantation when he refused to grant what he considered an "outrageous demand" concerning the "mule question." In 1870 blacks along the coast struck for a minimum wage of $1.50 per day. In the face of such group protests, planters found themselves "powerless and had to submit. We could only discharge them, and that would leave us without hands." "It has been a terrible struggle for me," wrote Cobb in 1867, "but I have at last come to the conclusion that we are in the power of the negroes & will have to submit to their ideas on some subjects if we want to work them."[45]

Pressed for laborers, planters found themselves faced with the necessity of conceding some changes in the old method of working them or losing potential employees. "Let any man offer them some little thing of no real benefit to them, but which looks like a little

44. Savannah *Morning News,* November 4, 1868, January 28, 1869, December 31, 1868, January 11, 1869, January 16–February 1, 1869 (account of the Court of Examination).

45. Clipping dated January 4, 1868, from an unidentified Albany newspaper, in E. F. Andrews Scrapbook; John A. Cobb to his wife, January 4, 1869, John A. Cobb to Mrs. Howell Cobb, February 14, 1867, both in Cobb Papers; Milledgeville *Federal Union,* December 27, 1870; Stearns, *The Black Man of the South,* 364.

more freedom," moaned one planter, "and they catch at it with avidity and would sacrifice their best friend without hesitation and without regret." Younger planters, more willing than older ones to compromise, had greater success in procuring hands, and Yankee planters with liberal attitudes were more successful than native whites. Although many freedmen still worked under overseers, they resented it. Planters like Charles C. Jones, Jr., of Liberty County recognized that the blacks' "great desire seems to be to get away from all overseers—to hire or purchase land and work for themselves." An influential planter journal even predicted that the day of the overseer was past. This was an exaggeration, but most postwar overseers had to be more cautious in ordering the freedmen about, and planters no longer called the "head man" overseer or driver, but rather "foreman," "captain," or "superintender."[46]

Many southerners felt that both the quality and quantity of work suffered with the demise of slavery. "I always kept two women just to weave," said a planter's wife. "The same women are with me now. Before they were declared free, they could weave six and eight yards of cloth a day, easy. Now the most they do is about one yard." Frances Butler Leigh claimed, "The negroes talked a great deal about their desire and intention to work for us, but their idea of work unaided by stern necessity, is very vague, some of them working only half a day and some even less." In 1866 a planter from Houston County concluded: "I have this year been living on the plantation endeavoring to make cotton with free negro labor. It has been a failure. . . . The negroes are idle, slothful, dishonest and every way unreliable." Such assessments might have been overly pessimistic or unduly biased, for the same year another Houston County planter reported, "everything has gone on pleasantly. . . . the negroes, mainly, are conducting themselves in an orderly and becoming manner." Similarly, a Monroe County planter observed that his laborers were "doing much better than . . . expected. The greater portion

46. Ulrich B. Phillips (ed.), *The Correspondence of Robert Toombs, Alexander H. Stephens, and Howell Cobb*, 684; Trowbridge, *The South*, 485; Stearns, *The Black Man of the South*, 164; C. C. Jones to Eva Jones, November 7, 1865, in Jones Papers, University of Georgia Library; Athens *Southern Cultivator*, XXIII (December, 1865), 181; Leigh, *Ten Years on a Georgia Plantation*, 56, 194–95; "A Georgia Plantation," 831.

of them get a part of the crop, work well, are obedient, respectful, and stick to their contract." Perhaps the fairest assessment came from prominent planter Charles C. Jones, Jr., "Some of the negroes work pretty well, some very well, and some again very indifferently." Northerner Sidney Andrews divided the black workers into similar categories.[47]

The incentive offered the ex-slave usually determined whether he worked more or less in freedom. Few wanted to work as hard as they had as slaves for little or no reward. "If ole massa want to grow cotton," declared an ex-slave to fellow blacks, "let him plant it himself. I'se work for him dese twenty year, and done got nothin' but food and clothes, and dem mighty mean; now, I'se freedman, and I tell you I ain't going to work cotton *nohow*." Given little incentive to work, some responded as they had as slaves. They deceived their employer, malingered, carelessly used his tools, killed or abused his animals, sold his crops at night, and stole. But with sufficient economic opportunity, most blacks worked diligently. Lem Bryant had been a severe disciplinary problem as a slave. "Since he been freed," his former master observed, "he has grown honest, quiet, and industrious; he educates his children and pays his debts." Charles Stearns allowed one ambitious employee to rent twenty acres of land; the freedman produced three times as much cotton as Stearns did on a similar amount of land worked by sharecroppers. According to Frances Butler Leigh, the older ex-slaves feigned sickness or old age to avoid work, but "let them get a bit of ground of their own given to them, and they become quite young again."[48]

The most substantial change in the newly evolving labor system concerned the method of payment. Despite the myriad of different arrangements the planters and their employees agreed upon, most planters preferred paying monthly wages as "the best method of con-

47. Trowbridge, The South, 485–86; Leigh, Ten Years on a Georgia Plantation, 24–25; S. C. Edgeworth to his uncle, October 18, 1866, in Georgia Papers, Manuscript Department, William R. Perkins Library, Duke University, Durham, N.C.; Macon Georgia Journal and Messenger, March 14, 1866; Macon Daily Telegraph, April 7, 1866; C. C. Jones, Jr., to Mary Jones, June 4, 1866, in Jones Papers, University of Georgia Library; Sidney Andrews, The South Since the War, 398–99.
48. Nation, I (October 5, 1865), 426; Drago, "Black Georgia During Reconstruction," 81; "A Georgia Plantation," 836; Stearns, The Black Man of the South, 517; Leigh, Ten Years on a Georgia Plantation, 57–58.

trolling their workers." They could work them in gangs and assign them to whatever tasks they saw fit under strict supervision. But since cash was scarce, and money earners had little incentive to remain until the crops were gathered (some ran away), planters increasingly turned to the collective share. In July, 1865, for example, Benjamin Yancey of Dougherty County contracted with one hundred freedmen to work "as they have heretofore done, whilst slaves under the superintendence & direction of his present managers." Yancey furnished house and room, firewood, meal, and syrup as he had done before the war, plus an additional one-sixth share of the crop to be collectively divided among his workers according to a hand system. First-class male hands received the largest share; first-class female hands, two-thirds of that share. The bulk of workers, male and female, fell between ages of twenty-one and forty. Males under twenty and not yet at the peak of their physical ability were paid as second-class hands. Men and women over forty whose output had declined were third-class hands. The young, aged, disabled, and women "suckling" children were named half-hands and worked for room and board.[49]

Between 1867 and 1880, Georgia planters abandoned wages and collective shares. They divided their plantations into small "one-horse" farms on which black families lived and raised a cotton crop, a portion of which they returned to the landlord. Planters made this transition to sharecropping as we know it today because they found that this system provided better motivation for their workers and because it obviated the sticky problem of dispersing a collective share among the freedmen. Likewise, the blacks themselves exerted pressure towards a true sharecropping system. Once the ex-slave had secured the vote, a Wilkinson County planter reported, "notions of political greatness and personal aggrandizement had almost destroyed his usefulness. He did not want to work for wages this year, but wanted to be furnished with land, mules, implements and provisions, and receive half of the products of the land."[50]

49. Drago, "Black Georgia During Reconstruction," Chaps. II, VI; Contract dated July 22, 1865, in Yancey Papers.
50. Drago, "Black Georgia During Reconstruction," Chaps. II, VI; Macon *Georgia Weekly Telegraph*, June 26, 1868; Athens *Southern Cultivator*, XXIV (December, 1871), 444, 451–52.

To the majority of planters, the new sharecropping arrangement represented an erosion of their power. "When a man agrees to give half interest in a crop," complained an Oglethorpe County planter in 1872, "he gives the laborer an equal right to dictate whether it shall be plowed deep or shallow, or whether it shall be plowed at all or not." Another planter argued that sharecroppers "claim rights, and often assert them in the mode of cultivation, & it leads to contentions and troubles." Still another employer reasoned that sharecroppers become "co-partners, and they have the right to say so in everything." According to one unhappy planter who tried shares: "I have not found it advantageous to hire laborers . . . to crop on shares, to manage them successfully, and this you can hardly do, when your laborers are partners. . . . It is better and cheaper to pay $10 per month, and provision them. You have their services for the year, and can employ them at any work you see proper." However, in 1872 after the "Redeemers" gained control of the state, the Georgia Supreme Court did much to allay the fears of planters. It ruled that the sharecropper was a day laborer and not a real tenant, that he had no exclusive right to the premises or title to the crop he produced. Later court rulings reinforced this decision.[51]

A small number of freedmen, certainly less than one in ten, became renters during Reconstruction. Renting gave them more independence than sharecropping, for as sharecroppers, they received from the planter all the supplies necessary to make the crop and were therefore legally subject to his supervision. Once they paid the rent, however, the landlord had no legal right to dictate how they managed their farms. While most planters opposed renting because it gave the ex-slaves too much autonomy, some employers, like David C. Barrow of Oglethorpe County, found it to their advantage. After the war, Barrow worked his 160-man labor force on shares and in gangs under overseers, but he found his crops neglected and his animals abused. To better motivate his workers, he agreed to rent

51. Drago, "Black Georgia During Reconstruction," Chaps. II, VI; Athens *Southern Cultivator*, XXX (February, 1872), 58; Washington (Ga.) *Gazette*, January 29, 1869; Athens *Southern Cultivator*, XXVI (May, 1868), quoted in Robert Preston Brooks, "The Agrarian Revolution in Georgia, 1865–1912," *Bulletin of the University of Wisconsin* No. 639, History Series, Vol. III, No. 3 (Madison, 1914), 50, and for laws governing sharecropping, see pp. 67–68.

each of them twenty-five to thirty acres of land. The renters eventually abandoned their centrally located quarters and erected houses on their rented lands. By 1880 Barrow seldom interfered with them, except to collect his rent.[52]

Nearly all observers agree that postwar economic conditions gave the blacks some collective power in shaping the new labor system. Relying almost exclusively on planter accounts, especially the experience of David C. Barrow in Oglethorpe County, earlier scholars have argued that the plantation system evolved from a centrally controlled and strictly supervised wage system into a tenant system in which black renters enjoyed considerable autonomy. Unfortunately, the traditional interpretation relies too heavily on the accounts of the planters themselves, who tended to regard any concession to the blacks as a sharp break with the past and a serious threat to their authority. It is a one-sided view that ignores what the blacks themselves felt. In any case, during Reconstruction, most Georgia blacks were sharecroppers or wage earners rather than renters, and many continued to work under overseers. Black demands supported by economic pressures led to a modification of the old labor system, not an immediate abandonment.[53]

The Indianola plantation of Charles Colcock Jones, Jr., was more representative of the transition from slavery to freedom than the Barrow plantation. The Jones plantation was located in the black-belt county of Burke. Jones employed two dozen workers in 1867 and 1868 and paid a one-quarter collective share. He managed to maintain most of the trappings of the antebellum plantation, including both overseers and drivers, but he also encountered financial and labor difficulties that greatly reduced his control over the plantation. Like most postwar planters, he resisted the temptation to sell or rent his land to blacks, preferring to keep his entire plantation intact. Although renowned for his Christian paternalism toward the slaves, Jones regarded planting as primarily a money-making enterprise. In April, 1867, he cautioned his overseer not to extend rations and

52. Drago, "Black Georgia During Reconstruction," 244, 256; "A Georgia Plantation," 830–36.
53. Brooks, "The Agrarian Revolution in Georgia," 24, 53; Drago, "Black Georgia During Reconstruction," 248.

credit to black women and children because their debts might ultimately have to be paid by Jones himself. Jones also employed an overseer of the old school and underpaid his workers. As a result, his crops were neglected and his animals abused.[54]

The shaky financial prospects of Indianola created a dilemma for Jones. On one hand, he needed a steady and strict supervision of his laborers to insure a profit; yet on the other hand, too much supervision could alienate the freedmen and bring financial ruin. A dispute between Jones's overseer and his black driver illustrated the limits of his power and the subtle change in the plantation system after the war. Jones attributed the dispute to the fact that the overseer was from the antebellum school of overseers, who expected "the old regime to be still in vogue." Rather than support his overseer, Jones attempted to conciliate both parties. Fearing that a disruption of the crop would result if the feud continued, he ordered his overseer to end his dispute with the black driver in the interest of raising the best possible crop. Similarly, he urged the driver to cooperate with the overseer, suggesting a possible promotion. The overseer died shortly thereafter, but Jones's problems did not end. Black informants told him that the new overseer and the black driver were colluding in an attempt to cheat him. Although he rewarded the informants, Jones probably never knew for sure who was really representing his interests in Indianola. Like many postwar Georgia planters, he was more mediator than disciplinarian.[55]

Other factors were at work in upgrading the condition of the exslaves. Those planters who continually cheated their laborers ultimately reaped the ill will of the freedmen, and their planting opera-

54. C. C. Jones, Jr., to Eli Sconyers, February 28, 1866, in Letter Press Copybook, 1864–1867, pp. 62–63, C. C. Jones to Careless Dawson, September 30, 1867, C. C. Jones, Jr., to MacPherson Berrien Eve, November 11, 1868, both in Letter Press Copybook, 1867–1869, pp. 125–30, 775–79, C. C. Jones, Jr., to Sconyers, April 30, 1867, in Letter Press Copybook, 1864–1867, pp. 695–98, C. C. Jones, Jr., to Enoch Skinner, November 23, 1868, in Letter Press Copybook, 1867–1869, p. 820, all in Jones Papers, University of Georgia Library; Drago, "Black Georgia During Reconstruction," 265. Sconyers was Jones's overseer, and Careless Dawson, his black driver.

55. C. C. Jones, Jr., to F. Edgeworth, May 17, 1867, C. C. Jones, Jr., to Sconyers, June 17, 1867, C. C. Jones, Jr., to Dawson, August 13, 1867, all in Letter Press Copybook, 1864–1867, pp. 777–80, 831–33, 939–46, C. C. Jones, Jr., to Eve, May 27, 1868, C. C. Jones to Pharaoh, August, 1868, both in Letter Press Copybook, 1867–1869, pp. 173, 560–66, 795–97, all in Jones Papers, University of Georgia Library.

tions suffered correspondingly. Most planters, like David Dickson, argued that a successful season depended on the honest treatment of the workers. Those who paid fair wages and treated the blacks fairly confronted fewer labor problems. Moreover, some planters felt legally bound to honor written contracts. One Georgia newspaper advised against such contracts because they gave "the laborer advantage of you, as you may know that he is not doing faithful service, and yet cannot, by contract, turn him off without danger of suit."[56]

The Freedmen's Bureau was instrumental in curbing the fraud and violence practiced against the former slaves. Radical Reconstruction had brought a change in the bureau's administration in Georgia of significant benefit to blacks. The conservative Davis Tillson was replaced in 1867 by Republican Caleb C. Sibley, who reported that many of the native-white agents appointed by Tillson had "shamefully abused their trust, inflicted cruel and unusual punishment on the blacks, and were unfit from their education and belief in slavery to promote the interest of free labor." The following year, Sibley himself was replaced by General John R. Lewis, an avowed friend of the blacks and a partisan Republican. Lewis had also replaced John E. Bryant in 1867 as president of the Georgia Equal Rights and Educational Association and was later appointed by the Republican governor to head the state's first public school system. He remained chief of the bureau until its activities in Georgia ceased in 1870.[57]

With the accession to power of Sibley and Lewis, the bureau attracted more radically inclined agents, like Edwin Belcher, who vigorously protected the rights of the freedmen. Black politicians found Lewis responsive to their pleas for help. When black assemblyman George Clower of Monroe County reported to Lewis that whites were turning off their employees who voted Republican, the general dispatched a young army officer to administer quick punishment to

56. David Dickson, *A Practical Treatise on Agriculture*, 87; Athens *Southern Cultivator*, XXVII (March, 1869), 85; Charles Nordhoff, *The Cotton States in the Spring and Summer of 1875* (New York, 1876), 102; Dalton (Ga.) *North Georgia Citizen*, April 29, 1869.
57. Atlanta *Daily New Era*, January 3, 1868; Howard, *Autobiography*, II, 340; Macon *Georgia Weekly Telegraph*, October 18, 1867; C. Mildred Thompson, *Reconstruction in Georgia*, 335–36; National Archives and Records Service, *Records of the Superintendent of Education*, 2.

the guilty parties in the hope that it would "deter other employers from swindling their employees out of their hard earnings."[58]

A measure of the bureau's tilt toward the blacks was the increasing praise it received from them and the corresponding condemnation from conservative whites. Agents like Belcher won the respect of their black constituents. Houston County blacks praised their local agent, who had "Dispensed justice to all parties without Regard to Color which Some white men Do not like." Concurrently, whites began criticizing the bureau. Frances Leigh charged that "the agent of the Freedmen's Bureau was our master, one always ready to believe the wildest complaints from negroes, and to call the whites to account for the same." According to the Greensboro *Herald*, "the streets have been thronged more or less every day, with negroes leaving their farms and neglecting their business, sauntering around the Bureau office, reporting the best citizens in the county, and forcing them to appear before a *Creole*, or some other specie of the human race in the shape of a man, to answer inquiries relative to transactions as far back as June '65."[59]

But the most important factor in reducing the abuse of the freedmen was peace and prosperity. In December, 1870, the conservatives regained control of the state government. With this victory, the single greatest perpetrator of violence, the Ku Klux Klan, began to disband. Moreover, planters who survived the difficult years of 1865 and 1866 began to prosper. In 1867 John Cobb feared that he would not make the five hundred bales necessary to break even. His fears proved unfounded; he produced over seven hundred bales of cotton. Gradually, the plantations were put into operation again. According to the daughter of a prominent black-belt planter, cotton "was bringing high prices. . . . my father got things started again. He saved every acre of his land." By 1870 Georgia had produced the largest cotton

58. Belcher to J. R. Lewis, September 11, 1867, June 8, 1868, Belcher to Sibley, September 23, 1867, George H. Clower to Lewis, November 19, 1867, Jno. Leonard to Lewis, December 16, 1867, all in Records of the Bureau of Refugees, Freedmen, and Abandoned Lands.

59. Clower to Lewis, November 19, 1867, A. Cobb and Crawford Jones to Sibley, August 22, 1867, both in Records of the Bureau of Refugees, Freedmen, and Abandoned Lands; Leigh, *Ten Years on a Georgia Plantation*, 80; Greensboro *Herald*, June 18, 1868.

crop to date. The planters, said one source, have "astonished even themselves . . . and their success hitherto is the most incontestible assurance of their ultimate triumph over all the obstacles which can be thrown in their way by their tyrannical oppressors." The records of the Bryan plantation near Albany confirm the increasing prosperity. Waverly plantation returned a 30 percent profit in 1871, and a 16 percent profit in 1872. Scotland plantation, operated in 1872, yielded an 8 percent profit.[60]

With the turn towards prosperity, planters began to praise free labor. A Macon paper concluded in 1868 that, with "the improved character and estimate of the freedmen, as farm laborers, most of the talk in the papers about Coolies, Chinamen and other foreign substitutes has ceased. Our farmers see that they can do well with the negro." In May, 1869, a Taylor County planter claimed that the "freedmen are working exceedingly well. They are generally quiet, sober and industrious. They have forgotten politics and are thinking about something more profitable. They deserve a great deal of credit." Similarly, a Decatur County planter wrote in 1871, "I am planting cotton and in good spirits about my crop; negros [sic] work well."[61]

I have made a statistical study of a single Georgia county in the decades after the war to discover how Radical Reconstruction affected the lives of Georgia blacks. Dougherty County was a cotton-producing county in the heart of the black belt of Southwest Georgia. W. E. B. Du Bois, who had examined black landholding in all of Georgia's counties at the turn of the century, pronounced it a "typical black-belt county."[62] There, as elsewhere in Georgia, Radical Reconstruction did not bring blacks the kind of freedom they desired, but it did begin a process that allowed them greater independence from the white man, a chance to strengthen family ties, and an opportunity for some education.

60. John A. Cobb to his wife, October 2, 1867, John A. Cobb to his father, January 31, 1868, both in Cobb Papers; Myrtle Long Candler, "Reminiscences of Life in Georgia," 17; Covington Georgia Enterprise, January 21, 1870; Bryan Papers, IV, 66–67, 86–87, 30–31.
61. Macon Georgia Weekly Telegraph, July 3, 1868; Macon Daily Telegraph, May 15, 1869; T. A. Barrow to his father, April 4, 1871, in Barrow Papers.
62. Du Bois, "The Negro Landholder of Georgia," 683.

The study relied on the federal censuses of 1870, 1880, and 1900, which divided Dougherty County households into three categories: white, black, and mixed (whites and blacks living together). For each of the census years, I selected a random sample of 250 white and 250 black households and identified a number of indicators, including the structure of the household, whether women and children were working, and education and literacy, that told something about black family life in postwar Dougherty County.[63]

Unfortunately, the 1870 census did not list family relationships, but it appears that most of the sample white and black households were nuclear, composed of married couples living with or without unmarried children. The 1880 and 1900 census were more revealing. Although the white population was basically urban and the black rural, most households of both races were nuclear:

	1880	1900
White	42.0%	44.4%
Black	51.6%	42.8%

Moreover, by 1900 there were few black (4.0 percent) or white (3.6 percent) households composed solely of unmarried females with children, divorced persons, or married persons without spouses.

The new economic system evolving in the Georgia black belt after 1870 was conducive to the formation of black nuclear households. Before the war, Dougherty County's six thousand slaves had worked on large plantations in gangs under overseers and had lived in centrally located quarters. The labor system remained substantially the same immediately after the war, except that blacks were paid for their toil.[64] Gradually, however, an important change occurred in the composition of the labor force. Not only were black women and children no longer working in gangs under white overseers, they were disappearing from the fields. In 1870 the majority of black women over age fifteen in the sample households, as well as three-

63. To select an appropriate sample I consulted Hubert M. Blalock, *Social Statistics* (New York, 1972), 213–15. After estimating the probable standard deviations of critical indices, I concluded that the confidence level would not exceed plus or minus 5 percent.
64. Contract dated July 22, 1865, in Yancey Papers.

quarters of their children aged ten to twelve, were not listed as working. Most planters considered the women's withdrawal from the fields pretentious, but it is certain that this change contributed to a labor shortage that ultimately gave the freedmen greater bargaining power and a larger voice in shaping the emerging postbellum labor system.

Between 1870 and 1880, the "one-horse," or family, farm made its appearance. In Dougherty County the number of farms jumped from 221 in 1870 to 975 by 1880. Worked mainly by sharecroppers, most were farms of less than fifty acres, probably too small to support much more than a nuclear family but close in size to the proverbial "forty acres and a mule." By 1900 an even more dramatic change had taken place. The agricultural depression of the 1890s, the scarcity of labor, and the blacks' demand to rent land forced many planters to rent their land to blacks or sell to merchants, who in turn rented to the ex-slaves. Nearly 80 percent of Dougherty County's farms (811 farms) consisted of less than one hundred acres, and most of them were operated by black renters. Since, by Du Bois' estimate, about fifteen hundred black families lived outside of corporate Albany, approximately half of the rural black families in the county lived on one-horse farms. The 1900 census, in describing the "progress" of these farmers, noted: "At first nearly all tenants . . . cultivated small areas of the former plantations under the share system; with the acquisition of property and a better knowledge of farm economics, they adopted the cash system [renting] which carries with it a greater degree of independence."[65]

65. *Agriculture of the United States in 1860; Compiled from the Original Returns of the Eighth Census* (Washington, D.C., 1864), in *House Miscellaneous Documents*, 38th Cong., 1st Sess., unnumbered, p. 196; *The Statistics of the Wealth and Industry of the United States . . .* , Vol. III of *Ninth Census* (Washington, D.C., 1872), in *House Miscellaneous Documents*, 42nd Cong., 1st Sess., unnumbered, p. 348; *Report on the Productions of Agriculture as Returned at the Tenth Census (June 1, 1880) . . .* (Washington, D.C., 1883), in *House Miscellaneous Documents*, 47th Cong., 2nd Sess., No. 42, Pt. III, pp. 40–41; United States Census Office, *Agriculture, Part I: Farms, Livestock, and Animal Products*, Vol. V, 68, and *Agriculture, Part II: Crops and Irrigation*, Vol. VI, 409, in *Census Report: Twelfth Census of the United States, Taken in the Year 1900* (Washington, D.C., 1902); Du Bois, *The Souls of Black Folk*, 106. For the same evolution occurring in another black-belt county, Oglethorpe, see "A Georgia Plantation," 830–36.

A log cabin pictured in W. E. B. Du Bois, "The Negro as He Really Is," *World's Work*, II (May–October, 1901).

With the emergence of these one-horse farms, black women and their children once again returned to work. But now the family had become the basic work unit with the man doing most of the heavy work, aided by his wife and children. In the 1880 sample, half the women over fifteen years of age, and 60 percent of the children aged ten to twelve were working. Twenty years later, three out of every four Dougherty County black women over age fifteen were working, most of them as laborers. There was, however, an important difference in how and where they worked. By 1900, most of them did not work in gangs under overseers, but rather on family farms their husbands or parents rented. Nate Shaw, who operated one of these one-horse farms in a nearby Alabama county around the turn of the century, tried to keep his wife out of the fields. Nevertheless, she often defied his injunction. "I'd be in the field at work and my wife," Shaw recalled, "I'd look around, see her comin out there with a hoe . . . [to] help." Moreover, like his Dougherty County counterparts, Shaw did not want his wife working in white homes. "And I didn't allow her to go about," he remembered, "washin for white folks. I didn't want money comin into my house from that. My wife didn't wait on white folks for their dirty laundry. There was plenty of em would ask her and there'd be a answer ready for em." Indeed, by 1900 few black women or children worked as live-in servants in white households. The mixed household had practically disappeared, falling from 4.3 percent of the households in 1870 to 0.78 percent in 1900.[66]

Life on these one-horse farms was difficult. Most black renters owned little more than a cow, a mule, and a 'possum dog. Many of them barely paid the rent, though they paid it "with great pride," and only one in twenty became a landowner. Their homes were modest and often sparsely furnished and overcrowded, even though the average size of the black household declined from 4.52 persons in 1870 to 4.0 in 1900. Similarly, the average number of children per household, birth to age fifteen, fell from 1.95 in 1870 to 1.68 in 1900. The free blacks' diet remained much the same as it had been when they

66. Theodore Rosengarten, *All God's Dangers: The Life of Nate Shaw* (New York, 1975), 120–21, 191.

were slaves; many continued to subsist on collard greens boiled with a piece of fat meat. Except for an occasional trek into the city of Albany, their social life revolved around the church.[67]

The school, like the church (the local church often served as a school), was important in the life of Dougherty County blacks, who were convinced that education would improve their children's chances for a better life. In 1890 Georgia planter John Dent complained that among the ex-slaves there was a belief that "schooling places them on a higher plane than that of the common field laborer. That is what education is doing for negroes, arousing their ambition to become something they are not qualified for." Like many nineteenth-century Americans, these ex-slaves had an exaggerated notion of what education would do for them; but in a society where labor was based on a written contract, the ability to read was crucial.[68]

Radical Reconstruction brought the establishment of a "separate but equal" public school system for blacks, but when the conservatives regained power, they added the phrase "as far as practicable." Blacks received an inferior education, and most black children attended school only after the "crops were laid by." Nevertheless, the growth of black education in Dougherty County after the Civil War was impressive, particularly in light of the fact that Georgia did not enact a compulsory attendance law until 1916.[69] In 1870 only 19.8 percent of all Dougherty County black children aged ten to twelve were in school; ten years later the figure had reached 36.2 percent. By 1900 more of the county's black children aged ten to twelve (61.1 percent) were in school than white children of the same ages (50.4 percent). In addition, the illiteracy rate among persons over age fifteen in the sample black households declined from 93.6 percent in 1870 to 71.4 percent in 1900. More importantly, while only 15 per-

67. I have recreated this sketch of black family life in the Georgia black belt by using Du Bois, *The Souls of Black Folk*, Chaps. VII–X, and "A Georgia Plantation," 830–36, which describes black family life in Oglethorpe County.

68. Du Bois, *The Souls of Black Folk*, Chaps. VII–X; "A Georgia Plantation," 830–36; Atlanta *Southern Cultivator and Dixie Farmer*, XLVII (July, 1890), 311.

69. Philadelphia *Christian Recorder*, March 2, 1876; C. Mildred Thompson, *Reconstruction in Georgia*, 336–37; Louis R. Harlan, *Separate and Unequal: Public School Campaigns and Racism in the Southern Seaboard States, 1901–1915* (New York: 1968), 230–33.

At just such schools as this one near Albany, Georgia, young blacks received their education.

cent of black children aged ten to fifteen could read in 1870, the percentage reached 55 percent by 1900.

Freedom, then, did not bring Georgia blacks what they fervently desired—ownership of land—though by 1900 many had managed to obtain a degree of independence by renting one-horse farms. The life blacks lived in postwar Georgia, which was so eloquently portrayed by W. E. B. Du Bois in *The Souls of Black Folk*, was never easy. Yet, emancipation and Radical Reconstruction allowed blacks to partially fulfill their desire for a more independent family life, and while Georgia planters retained control over the economic system, they no longer exercised the nearly complete hegemony they had once held as slave-owners. Robert Higgs found that the per capita income of southern blacks rose significantly between 1868 and 1900, for example. Similarly, Edward Meeker argued that, although the life expectancy of blacks in the South declined at the end of the Civil War, by 1880 the trend had reversed itself as economic conditions for the ex-slaves improved. By 1910 black life expectancy was greater than it had been before the war. As hard as life for the blacks was, few would have disputed these words of an aging former Georgia slave: "When I thinks back, it warn't no good feelin' to be bound lak dat. . . . I sho' had rather be free. I guess atter all it's best dat slavery days is over."[70]

70. "Slave Narratives, Georgia," No. 3, p. 213; Robert Higgs, *Competition and Coercion: Blacks in the American Economy, 1865–1914* (Cambridge, 1977); Edward Meeker, "Mortality Trends of Southern Blacks, 1850–1910: Some Preliminary Findings," *Explorations in Economic History*, XIII (January, 1976), 13–42. For a different viewpoint, see Roger L. Ransom and Richard Sutch, *One Kind of Freedom: The Economic Consequences of Emancipation* (Cambridge, 1977).

CHAPTER VI

The Conservative Triumph

The conservative coalition proved the old maxim that politics make strange bedfellows. Although dominated by Democrats, the opposition to Radical or Congressional Reconstruction was an amalgam of all sorts of antebellum political leaders. White supremacy and fear of the federal government had welded a diverse group into one party. Most conservative leaders, members of a planter elite, shared a common ideology. They saw Radical Reconstruction as an immediate threat to their hegemony over Georgia society. The Yankees, they contended, were attempting to foist upon the white South a government dominated by blacks and strangers. Very early in Radical Reconstruction conservative leaders found Georgia whites receptive to their charges that the federal government was attempting to force a black-dominated government on the state. Benjamin H. Hill, Sr., may have been a demagogue, but he accurately expressed the fears of many white Georgians when in October, 1868, he addressed the North: "the Southern whites will never consent to the government of negro. Never! . . . you may burn our cities and murder our people . . . but you will never make them consent to governments formed by negroes and strangers, under the dictation of Congress, by the power of the bayonet."[1]

The conservative ideology was also permeated by the reasoning

1. Isaac Seeley to William E. Chandler, March 26, 1872, in Chandler Papers; Benjamin Harvey Hill, Jr. (comp.), *Senator Benjamin H. Hill of Georgia: His Life, Speeches, and Writings* (Atlanta, 1893), 329.

of the proslavery argument. Conservatives argued that slavery had afforded blacks the external discipline needed to keep their true nature, barbaric and violent, in check. Lacking the restraints once imposed by slavery, the ex-slaves became dangerous. When blacks killed a white man in the suburbs of Savannah in November, 1868, a local newspaper charged: "His murderers were a mob of black savages . . . fully armed and intent upon the commission of any outrage which their brutal instinct might suggest . . . the bloody cruelties of the wild and barbarous negro-chiefs on the banks of the Nile—where the real negro nature is disclosed in its uncontrolled and untamed ferocity." Similarly, a Democratic Macon journal, incensed over an atrocity that it attributed to blacks, concluded in 1869, "The truth is, the restraints and the discipline of slavery were necessary to keep the uneducated African within the pale of civilization. He is a sensualist by constitution. To passions and appetites much stronger than those of the white race, he adds a very small counterbalance of the intellectual and moral faculties."[2]

According to conservatives, the problem of controlling the newly freed slaves was compounded by radical agitators who appealed to the ex-slaves' worst passions. "Society is in a disturbed condition," testified a prominent conservative; "the black man has been our slave, and he has just been emancipated. The white race has uniformly looked upon him as a dangerous element when left absolutely to his own control. Heretofore the white race had controlled and directed him, but they regard him as dangerous when a perfectly free man . . . they have felt that in neighborhoods and localities the very life of society was sometimes endangered by the animosity of the black, stimulated by some white men, against the general body of the white race." Incidents like the Ogeechee uprising on the Savannah rice plantations only confirmed conservatives' fears. Democratic candidate for governor, John B. Gordon, himself a rice planter near Savannah, recalled the hysteria that gripped his community: "We knew that the 'carpet-baggers' . . . were organizing the colored people. . . . We knew of certain instances where great crime had been committed; where overseers had been driven from plantations,

2. Savannah *Morning News*, November 5, 1868; Macon *Telegraph* (n.d.), quoted in Savannah *Morning News*, March 29, 1869.

and the negroes had asserted their right to hold the property for their own benefit. Apprehension took possession of the entire public mind of the State. Men were in many instances afraid to go away from their homes and leave their wives and children, for fear of outrage. Rapes were already being committed in the country."[3]

The conservative ideology had its paternalistic side. Some conservatives were sincerely convinced that the welfare of the freedmen depended on a return to power of the old ruling class. They argued that the planters and ex-slaves were united by a common interest, the cotton economy, and that Radical Reconstruction had only brought a divisiveness that hurt all parties. Aroused by radical agitators, naïve blacks had pursued a course of action contrary to their own best interest. The solution to the chaos spawned by Radical Reconstruction was the removal of the radical agitators and the return of the conservatives to power. Good race relations and peace and harmony would result. According to General Gordon, "if you will remove from our State all but the *bonafide* people of Georgia, there will be the kindliest feeling between the two races." Implied in the argument was the notion that a return to conservative rule would bring with it the wholesome discipline necessary to keep the unbridled nature of the blacks in check. With the return of the external discipline once provided by slavery, the freedmen would again become the "docile" and "obedient" blacks of antebellum days. A white conservative, present when black Union League president Cudjo Fye and other blacks freed a fellow black from jail in 1870, exhibited such logic after Fye and his group were captured: "My sympathies cannot but go out and cling to many of these poor, ignorant, deluded, misled Negroes. I was there in the midst of their excitement, when they were insolent, and vindictive, and full of bravado and threat. I heard their cursings and listened calmly to their bitter anathemas. But now . . . they are the same quiet, docile, humble, dependent people that in olden times were amongst us."[4]

The opponents of Radical Reconstruction were slow to organize, but once they did so, they proceeded to achieve a series of impres-

3. "Ku Klux Klan Report," VI, 122–23, 308.
4. Augusta *Daily Constitutionalist*, April 14, March 16, 1867; "Ku Klux Klan Report," VI, 321; Coulter, "Cudjo Fye's Insurrection," 222.

sive electoral victories. Before the Radical constitutional convention of 1867–1868 the conservative opposition was both disunited and demoralized. The first effective organization occurred in December, 1867, in Macon when delegates from sixty counties gathered and elected Benjamin H. Hill president of the convention. In April, 1868, after other conservative candidates were disqualified by the military or had declined to run, the Democrats nominated John B. Gordon to run as their candidate for governor on a platform that opposed ratification of the Radical constitution. The Democrats were unable to prevent ratification, and Gordon lost the election to Republican Rufus B. Bullock, but Bullock's margin of victory was narrow indeed. In July, 1868, the conservatives endorsed the Democratic presidential electors, and when November arrived, the Seymour-Blair ticket handily defeated the Grant ticket in Georgia. Two years later Republican rule collapsed, and a Democratic legislature was elected. The following year Democrat James M. Smith won the governor's office unopposed.[5]

It is true that divisions within the Republican party hastened its demise as a majority party, but external pressures exerted against it by the conservatives reduced it to almost complete impotence. To crush their opponents, the conservatives employed demagoguery, social ostracism, intimidation, fraud, violence, and the Ku Klux Klan. Demagoguery was hardly confined to the Democratic party. Opportunistic white Republicans told blacks a Democratic victory would mean their reenslavement. Yet there was perhaps more truth in that assertion than the conservatives' campaign rhetoric of a Republican victory resulting in social equality between the races. Republican James Atkins, who turned down the party's nomination for governor in 1871, recalled how the conservatives rallied "all the white men to the support of their interest by crying out 'negro equality,' and by using all the current epithets of the day in order to make the white man feel that there is an intention to make the negroes in every respect equal with them."[6]

5. Avery, *History of the State of Georgia*, 373–75, 383–84, 389–90, 406, 457, 468, 390; "Ku Klux Klan Report," VI, 456.
6. "Ku Klux Klan Report," VI, 522, 529–30.

Given their conservative ideology, it is understandable that the opponents of Radical Reconstruction concentrated their attack on the Republican leaders. Remove these "agitators," their argument implied, and the blacks would again become the humble, obedient servants of the antebellum past. Some of the harassment against white Republican leaders was not planned for political purposes, but resulted from the white community's deep-seated hostility toward anyone willing to enter into an alliance with blacks. In Wilkes County, children would follow the white assistant of black revenue official Edwin Belcher around, chanting "I smell Belcher." In other instances social ostracism was simply a political weapon used to discredit white Republicans. Savannah Republican Dr. James J. Waring, for example, was expelled from the Georgia Medical Society for having "forfeited his position of respectable standing." Waring's chief offenses were posting a bond for local black officeholders and giving legal aid to blacks charged with riot.[7]

The opponents of Reconstruction also threatened and even killed white Republican officeholders. In 1870 a band of men visited Republican congressional candidate George P. Burnett, perhaps the least radical Republican in the state. They fired at the house he was staying in and warned him not to speak. Burnett quickly left the town. Other Republican legislators were harassed, and occasionally they were murdered. George A. Ashburn, after receiving a Ku Klux Klan warning, was assassinated in March, 1868, while visiting Columbus, Georgia. Despite the testimony of eyewitnesses to the killing, a local jury ruled that he had died by shots fired by persons unknown. The military intervened and arrested a number of suspects, including several leading Columbus Democrats, but when Georgia was readmitted into the Union, the defendants were turned over to civilian authorities in Columbus who dropped the matter. "But the truth is," stated black politicians Henry Turner and James Simms, "these men have all been brutally slaughtered because they dared to be Republicans, and possessed such an amount of integrity that they defied both bribes and threats. Had they treacherously deserted their

7. C. Mildred Thompson, *Reconstruction in Georgia*, 371; Georgia Medical Society Minutes (ms in possession of J. Frederick Waring, Savannah), 53, 96–97.

constituents as other men have done in Georgia they would be living to-day."[8]

The black politician was the special object of the conservatives' campaign of violence and intimidation. "There is no especial desire to exterminate a man who has not got any influence," thought Henry Turner, "but any man who is a leader, who is . . . a chairman of a Grant Club or Union League, who is thought to be a center of influence, every such man, in many of the counties, they are determined to kill out. They will kill out all they can kill . . . or they will get up some charge against them, and have them tried, convicted, and sent to the penitentiary." At least one-fourth of Georgia's black legislators were threatened, bribed, beaten, jailed, or killed during the period.[9]

Some black politicians, like Assemblyman Thomas Allen, received threatening notes: "Tom, you are in great danger, you are going heedless with the radicals, against the interest of the conservative white population. . . . stay at home if you value your life, and [do] not vote at all, and advise all of your race to do the same thing. You are marked and watched by the K.K.K." Other black legislators refused bribes and were beaten. Assemblyman Abram Colby of Greene County turned down a five-thousand-dollar bribe and was visited by a vigilante group that gave him over a hundred lashes with a whip. "The worst thing about the whole matter," Colby felt, "was this: My mother, wife, and daughter were in the room when they came and carried me out. My little daughter came out and begged them not to carry me away. They drew up a gun and actually frightened her to death. She never got over it until she died."[10]

Black legislator Abram Turner of Putnam County was murdered, and his colleague from Clarke County, Alf Richardson, barely escaped the same fate. Richardson, according to one conservative account, had "made himself extremely obnoxious to the white people, swelling with insolence and inciting other negroes to devilish deeds." Before he was to testify to a congressional committee investigating

8. C. Mildred Thompson, *Reconstruction in Georgia*, 363, 361, 368, 386; Bloom, "The Georgia Election of April, 1868," 54–56; Simms and Turner to the New York *Tribune*, May 13, 1869, reprinted in Savannah *Morning News*, May 21, 1869.
9. "Ku Klux Klan Report," VII, 1039. See also the Appendix.
10. "Ku Klux Klan Report," VII, 610, 697.

the Ku Klux Klan, he was visited by forty members of the local Klan. Richardson refused to open the door of his house and fled to the attic, whereupon the Klansmen set the house afire. Richardson, escaping the flames, shot one of his attackers before being shot himself. Although left for dead, Richardson survived the attack.[11]

Part of the conservative strategy to neutralize the effectiveness of the black political leaders was to force them to leave their homes. They could then be declared ineligible to sit in the legislature for failing to fulfill residency requirements. Similarly, the conservatives used legal means to harass black leaders. In November, 1872, the son of a prominent conservative family explained the strategy, "We are forestalling the negroes . . . by issuing warrants for some of their ring leaders for riot." Black representative James A. Jackson of Randolph County was arrested for carrying a concealed weapon. (He was later pardoned by Republican Governor Bullock on the grounds that Jackson could not have received a fair trial and that he needed the weapon for his own protection.) State Senator Tunis G. Campbell, Sr., of McIntosh County spent considerable time in court answering legal charges brought against him by the conservatives.[12]

The Democrats also used the carrot and the stick to influence rank-and-file black voters. Black bands were employed at Democratic rallies, and freedmen were hired to stump the state for the Democratic ticket. As employers, Democrats wielded overwhelming economic power over their black employees. Blacks who complied with their wishes were promised jobs; those who refused were threatened with dismissal. Sometimes a promise of reward was accompanied by naked threat. The editor of an Americus newspaper wrote in April, 1868, "let us see that they [black Democrats] never want for employment, and that their families shall never want food and raiment." But he added, "we can make the way of the traitor to his city and State a hard one." Wilkes County Democrats were more explicit during the presidential campaign of 1868. They warned blacks that they "need no longer expect to be employed by those

11. Hull, *Annals of Athens*, 323–24; "Ku Klux Klan Report," VI, 1–19; Macon *American Union*, February 2, 1871.
12. P. B. Bedford to Benjamin F. Butler, January 30, 1871, in Butler Papers; Benjamin W. Barrow to his father, November 6, 1872, in Barrow Papers; Cuthbert *Appeal* (n.d.), quoted in the Atlanta *Constitution*, February 16, 1871.

whom you are working against." And in the presidential election four years later, a Savannah newspaper urged city merchants to make their employees vote the Democratic ticket or not vote at all.[13]

Beginning with the April, 1868, election and continuing until after the presidential election of 1872, the conservatives resorted to intimidation, fraud, and violence to reduce the Republican vote. After the April election in 1868, the Republican Atlanta *Daily New Era* concluded: "From all parts of Georgia there comes up evidence that . . . the disunion party resorted to every means their ingenuity could invent . . . to defeat reconstruction." Privately, conservatives admitted to the *New Era*'s charges and rejoiced over the ease with which they had controlled the black vote. "The result of this election is proof to me that we need never fear negro franchise," thought John Cobb, Sumter County planter and Democratic assemblyman. "We can control it with little trouble—the only trouble before was that we did not know how to go about it. . . . Every man who voted the Radical ticket in this county was watched & his ticket marked & all are now known & they will never cease to regret it, as long as they live."[14]

Ironically, the Republicans had furnished their foes with the perfect means of disfranchising the blacks, the poll tax. The constitution of 1868 required a poll tax to help finance public education. Most Republicans probably never realized the detrimental impact of the tax upon the black vote. The legislature of 1866 had already required that all adult male Georgians, including ex-slaves, pay a poll tax. When a freedman could not pay the tax, his employer was required to deduct it from his wages. But after the April, 1868, election many planters refused to pay it, and even when they did, their employees could not convince Democratic election officials that it had been paid. Moreover, a considerable number of freedmen simply could not afford to pay it. In desperation Republican Governor Rufus

13. Americus *Weekly Sumter Republican*, October 4, 1872; *Daily Columbus Enquirer*, July 15, 1868; Matthews, "The Negro in Georgia Politics," 56–57; Americus *Sumter Tri-Weekly Republican*, April 30, 1868, quoted *Ibid.*, 57; Washington (Ga.) *Gazette*, October 9, 1868, quoted in Matthews, "The Negro in Georgia Politics," 57; Savannah *Morning News*, October 2, 1872.

14. Atlanta *Daily New Era*, May 17, 1868, quoted in Bloom, "The Georgia Election of April, 1868," 62; John A. Cobb to his wife, April 26, 1868, in Cobb Papers.

B. Bullock suspended the poll tax before the November, 1868, presidential election, but most county officials were Democrats, and they refused to honor his proclamation. The tax, coupled with violence and intimidation, disfranchised many black voters.[15] The returns from ten counties that elected black representatives to the constitutional convention or assembly of 1868 illustrate the dramatic drop in the black vote.

| | Registered Voters | | April Election | | November Election | |
County	White	Black	Bullock	Gordon	Grant	Seymour
Jasper	696	988	789	665	5	873
Hancock	746	1545	1394	525	85	958
Wilkes	598	1362	979	672	86	1332
Oglethorpe	830	1158	1144	557	116	849
Stewart	925	1533	752	940	63	482
Talbot	822	1256	1057	758	49	963
Warren	751	1219	1224	544	188	881
Schley	380	501	389	374	69	454
Randolph	954	1193	687	1113	1	969
Columbia	669	1854	1222	457	1	1120

Source: "Ku Klux Klan Report," VI, 456–57.

In 1870 the Georgia legislature, with the blacks reseated, nullified the poll tax, but with the triumph of the conservatives in December of that year, it was reinstated. During the presidential election of 1872 the poll tax and intimidation again sharply reduced the black vote. According to a state Union League official writing to the secretary of the National Republican Committee in 1872, "the KK intimidations, and the poll tax" were "very *serious* if not *insurmountable* obstacles."[16]

15. "Ku Klux Klan Report," VII, 927–28; *House Miscellaneous Documents*, 40th Cong., 3rd Sess., No. 52, pp. 8, 61; D. T. Wilson to Office of the Collector, Columbia County, September 19, 1867, in Joseph Belknap Smith Papers, Manuscript Department, William R. Perkins Library, Duke University, Durham, N. C.; Matthews, "The Negro in Georgia Politics," 65; "Ku Klux Klan Report," VI, 456–57.
16. "Ku Klux Klan Report," VII, 927–28; C. Mildred Thompson, *Reconstruction in Georgia*, 275; Savannah *Morning News*, November 2, 1872; Seeley to Chandler, March 26, 1872, in Chandler Papers.

The black urban vote was further reduced by a series of election riots that resulted from the conservatives' nearly hysterical fear of urban elections as a prelude to black insurrection. A planter's wife living near Augusta confided to her diary in 1868: "Tuesday will be the day for the Presidential election and the South feels instinctively that she is standing upon the mouth of a volcano, expecting any moment an eruption. . . . Tonight it is reported that all of the houses in the neighborhood are to be burnt up." Similarly, a Savannah doctor wrote in his diary during the same election that "the fear of the torch, so often invoked by Radical orators White and Black, was upon us, & we kept watch all night, & a fire would have been the funeral Pyre of any radical Scoundrel who might have kindled it." A Savannah newspaper in November, 1868, reported, "A Body of Armed Negroes from the Ogeechee March on the City." After an election disturbance in Starkville in 1870, the Atlanta *Constitution* published a charge that it was the "fruits of a concocted scheme to whet the appetites of the negroes for blood, intimidate the whites and carry the election."[17]

Events in Savannah, Elberton, and Augusta in 1868 and in Macon in 1872 were similar enough to suggest a typical election riot scenario. Early on election morning November, 1868, Savannah blacks gathered at the city court house to exercise their franchise. When fifty white railroad employees approached the court house to vote, the sheriff ordered the blacks to stand aside. Police were called to the scene and began using their clubs. A fight broke out, shots were fired, and a riot ensued. Two blacks and one white were killed; many on both sides were wounded. Afterwards, the freedmen "kept away from the polls." Similar riots occurred in Augusta and Elberton on the same day, and in Macon during the next presidential election.[18]

There is evidence to suggest that these incidents were part of the conservatives' plan to control the black vote. In 1875 a visiting re-

17. Ella Gertrude (Clanton) Thomas Diary (ms in Ella Gertrude (Clanton) Thomas Papers, Manuscript Department, William R. Perkins Library, Duke University, Durham, N.C.), 1868–1870, p. 4; Arnold, *Letters of Richard D. Arnold*, 143; Savannah *Morning News*, November 4, 1868; Atlanta *Constitution*, December 15, 1870.

18. *House Miscellaneous Documents*, 40th Cong., 3rd Sess., No. 52, pp. 8, 14–16; Savannah *Morning News*, November 4, 1868; Matthews, "The Negro in Georgia Politics," 65–66.

porter wrote that "in Georgia other means have been used to over-come the colored vote—means not at all justifiable. In some cities, for instance, as in Atlanta and Savannah, insufficient voting-boxes were provided, and the negro voters are crowded out and prevented from casting their full vote." Planned or not, such riots aided the Democratic cause. "I guess you have heard . . . of our little fight on election day," an Eatonton conservative wrote in 1871, "which re-sulted in a glorious victory to the democratic party; it looked like we were going to have a real war for a while the negroes made very bold demonstrations but . . . a few shots made them run like frightened sheep & [they] could not be induced to return. We elected our entire ticket by a large majority."[19]

However, the Ku Klux Klan was without doubt the single most effective organization implementing the conservatives' program of violence and intimidation against the Republican opposition. The Klan entered Georgia before the April, 1868, election. Wealthy con-servatives welcomed it, supported its work, and composed its leader-ship. In March, 1868, a Democratic Augusta newspaper reported, "Klan has been organized in this place. . . . Success say we to the Ku Klux Klan!" According to an influential planter in Clarke County, the Klan was "aided and abetted by older men of character and means, members of the various churches and esteemed for their worth." Democratic candidate for governor John B. Gordon thought it was composed of "some of the very best citizens of the State—some of the most peaceable, law-abiding men, men of large property, who had large interest in the State." Similarly, the editor of the Atlanta *Constitution* acknowledged that he "knew all about it, and shared in its legitimate work. It combined the best men of the State, old, virtuous, settled, cautious citizens."[20]

Little distinction can be drawn between the Ku Klux Klan and the Democratic party; Democratic newspaper editors and political lead-ers alike were involved in Klan activities. The editor of the Atlanta

19. Nordhoff, *The Cotton States*, 103; Frank of Leverett and Co., to Guilmartin and Co., August 14, 1871, in Lawrence J. Guilmartin and John Flannery Papers, Manu-script Department, William R. Perkins Library, Duke University, Durham, N.C.

20. Augusta *Chronicle*, March 25, 1868, quoted in C. Mildred Thompson, *Recon-struction in Georgia*, 369; Hull, *Annals of Athens*, 323; "Ku Klux Klan Report," VI, 308; Avery, *History of the State of Georgia*, 382, 402.

Constitution, prominent in the Democratic party's hierarchy, was a klansman. John B. Gordon, the Democratic candidate for governor in 1868, was reputed to be the head of the Georgia Klan. The chief of the Klan in Oglethorpe County had been a Democratic candidate for the assembly in the same election. His immediate superior was Democratic congressional candidate and ex–Confederate general Dudley M. DuBose, the son-in-law of Robert Toombs.[21]

The primary purpose of the Klan was the political objective of restoring the Democrats to power. It was most active in black-belt counties where freedmen were capable of electing Republican candidates. Black politician Romulus Moore, after a visit by the local Columbia County Klan, was convinced that the purpose of the Klan was to control the black vote. "You think that you negroes and radicals are going to control this country," the vigilante visitors told him, "but white men at the North, the aristocracy of the North, have always controlled the poorer classes of people, and we intend to do it here." Privately, influential Democrats admitted their dependence upon the Klan. L. N. Trammell, later elected president of the Georgia State Senate, advised a friend in March, 1868, that "the negroes should as far as possible be *kept from the polls*. I think that the organization of the KKK might effect this more than anything else." The head of the Klan in Oglethorpe County publicly admitted years later that "the Reconstruction acts and fifteenth amendment put the Southern negroes in politics. The Klan organized to put them out, and it succeeded."[22]

Contemporaries thought that it was an equally important function of the Klan to control labor. The Republican sheriff of Warren County, a victim of the Klan's wrath, argued that the purpose of the Klan was "to control the State government and control the negro labor, the same as they did under slavery." Planters plagued by labor problems welcomed the emergence of the Klan. Charles Stearns reported that in Columbia County labor problems "induced all the planters at first to hail with delight the formation of the Ku-Klux or-

21. Avery, *History of the State of Georgia*, 382, 402, 374; Allen P. Tankersley, *John B. Gordon: A Study in Gallantry* (Atlanta, 1955), 248–49; *Uncle Remus Magazine*, I (January, 1908), 24.
22. "Ku Klux Klan Report," VII, 611, 739; L. N. Trammell to Alex [Irwin?] March 30, 1868, in Cobb Papers; *Uncle Remus Magazine*, I, (January, 1908), 24.

der, promising as it did, to rectify all these abuses, as well as to promote the political welfare of the country." Black laborers who too "saucily" addressed their mistress, or disputed their wages, were liable to be severely beaten by the Klan. Moreover, the Klan's method of disciplining the recalcitrant freedmen resembled the tactics of the old slave patrol. According to Romulus Moore, "there has always been a patrol law in this country; and this is the same, only in worse form." The Klan, like the slave patrol, used "nigger hounds" to catch their victims and the whip to punish them.[23]

The death of George Ashburn and the attack on Richardson suggest that the Klan played a central role in the statewide terroristic campaign of the Democrats to regain political power. Most of the Klan's other activities are difficult for the historian to document because they were shrouded in secrecy, but in one county the Klan's actions were eventually well publicized. In 1908 John C. Reed, captain of the Klan in Oglethorpe County, described in a series of articles how the Klan operated. Reed's exploits were not as spectacular as those of the Klan in nearby Warren County, but they were more representative. Unlike the Warren County Klan, those in Oglethorpe County and probably elsewhere did not resort to murder to achieve their ends.[24]

Prior to the presidential election of 1868, Oglethorpe County had been solidly Republican. The county sent Republicans, including one black, to the constitutional convention of 1867–1868 and elected a Republican to the assembly in April, 1868. One of the defeated Democratic candidates for the assembly, John C. Reed, turned to fellow ex-Confederate Dudley M. DuBose for solace and advice. DuBose persuaded the former Confederate army captain to take command of the Klan in Oglethorpe County.[25]

For Reed the cause was a holy one, saving the South from Africanization. "What we must do would look to outsiders like criminal law-

23. "Ku Klux Klan Report," VI, 213, 12, 242, VII, 739, 645–50, 669; Stearns, *The Black Man of the South*, 364.

24. Allen W. Trelease, *White Terror: The Ku Klux Klan Conspiracy and Southern Reconstruction* (New York, 1971), has given considerable attention to the Klan in Warren County. This county, however, was hardly typical. See Reed's exploits in John Calvin Reed, "What I Know of the Ku Klux Klan," *Uncle Remus Magazine*, I (January–November, 1908).

25. *Uncle Remus Magazine*, I, (January, 1908), 24.

lessness and wicked conspiracy," remembered Reed. "But the cause
—the protection of our dear women and sweet children, the preservation of civilization, the true welfare of both Southern whites and
blacks—demanded that we endure all pains, penalties and ignominy
that might befall us in our conscience-commanded cause." According to Reed, the klansmen were "as conscientious as their fore-
fathers who fought at . . . Lexington, and Bunker Hill." But beneath
the high-minded rhetoric was a partisan objective. "I emphasize
again," he wrote. "We resolved that the whites should win every
election possible." Reed's first objective was to eliminate the leadership of the white Republicans, all native-born Georgians. Reed and
his men threatened most of them into silence, and prevented any
meetings of white farmers seeking debtor relief. Next, the Klan
turned to the blacks, breaking up their meetings and terrorizing
those freedmen who dared show any independence. They tied one
victim to a tree, whipped him, and then paraded him through the
black community in a show of force.[26]

Reed's ultimate triumph came during the presidential election of
1868. According to his plan, the Klan was responsible for controlling
the precinct at Lexington, where many freedmen voted. Reed succeeded in getting the Democrats to nominate him and a fellow klansman superintendents of the election. On election day, he and other
Democratic election officials persuaded the lone Republican superintendent to ignore Bullock's proclamation suspending the poll tax.
When another white Republican demanded that the governor's proclamation be publicly read, Reed threatened to have him arrested.
Moreover, the Klan was ready for any contingency. They had their
own force at the polls, and were ready to cooperate with the local
sheriff to put down any black resistance. The drastic drop in the Republican vote from April to November, 1868, is a tribute to Reed's
efficiency. In April, Bullock defeated Gordon 1,444 to 557, but in
November Seymour defeated Grant 849 to 116.[27]

After the Democratic triumph in the 1870 elections, the Klan in
Oglethorpe, and probably elsewhere in the black belt, began to dis-

26. *Ibid.* (February, 1908), 20, (January, 1908), 26, (February, 1908), 20, (March, 1908),
23, (April, 1908), 17–18.
27. *Ibid.* (February, 1908), 20–21; "Ku Klux Klan Report," VI, 457.

band. Reed claimed that the Klan lasted "until we virtually restored
the supremacy of our race by carrying the three days' election in December, 1870." With the police power of the state safely in the hands
of the conservatives, there was no longer any need for the Klan to
control labor. By 1872 the conservatives had reassembled most of
their prewar military companies. "In the Spring of 1872," wrote a
Democratic legislator, "quite a sudden military ardor took possession of our people, and one after another our old Volunteer Companies began to re-organize." So, too, was the planters' disdain of
Klan activity growing as violence was becoming counterproductive.
Their freedmen were terrorized to the point that they could not
work at all. Gradually, conservatives began denouncing the Klan's
violence against the freedmen. In 1871 an Augusta paper that had
once welcomed the Klan to Georgia concluded that "there is now no
longer any need whatever of a *secret* armed organization, at least
in our locality." But violence against blacks continued, especially
in northern Georgia, where blacks were relatively few. The Klan,
once the preserve of conservatives, provided illicit distillers of liquor
in northern Georgia an effective means of protecting their operations from federal revenue officials and any curious blacks who hap-
pened to discover them. While Reed disassociated himself from
"bogus Ku-Klux" who came after him, he and other conservatives involved in the Klan were nonetheless responsible for spawning the
vigilante organization supported by violence that survived Radical
Reconstruction.[28]

With Klan support the conservatives were victorious and, once in
power, consolidated their victory. They restored the poll tax of 1868,
virtually disfranchising many freedmen. Likewise, they altered the
registration law by allowing the registry book to be opened only during the three months of the year that coincided with planting time,
when most blacks could not afford to leave their crops to register. In
1876 only six hundred out of six thousand adult black males were
registered to vote in Chatham County. Democrats also began to vig-

28. John Calvin Reed, *The Brothers' War* (Boston, 1905), 422, xiii; George A. Mercer Diary (typed copy in Col. George A. Mercer Papers, Georgia Historical Society,
Savannah), December 22, 1872; "Ku Klux Klan Report," VI, 9, 417, 232, 403, 464, 470,
491, 509–510, VII, 601, 643–44, 865, 1134; C. Mildred Thompson, *Reconstruction in
Georgia*, 369; Fitz-Simmons, "The Ku Klux Klan in Georgia," 90.

orously investigate the activities of the Republican administration. Gross corruption was found in the leasing of convict laborers, in the purchasing and leasing of the state capital, and in state subsidies to railroads, particularly those connected with Bullock's close friend Hannibal I. Kimball. Bullock himself was later tried and acquitted of any personal wrongdoing.[29]

The Democrats eliminated the Republican programs that commanded the least popular support. For instance, they repudiated a large part of the state debt, accrued in subsidizing railroads. However, they hesitated to dismantle the more popular measures of the Republican administration, such as debtor relief and public education. The Democrats did modify provisions for public schooling to the detriment of blacks, however. The Reconstruction legislature of 1870 had passed a public school act that required separate but equal facilities for both races. The Democrats added the phrase "as far as practicable" in 1872, and thereafter black educator William S. Scarborough labeled the state's educational system a "mere farce." According to Scarborough, white children received first-rate educations, but black children were taught in dilapidated schools by incompetent white southerners, "rebels of the bitterest stamp," who were "pledged to . . . keep them in the rear of the whites."[30]

The Constitutional Convention of 1877 had the potential of becoming Georgia's Thermidor. The delegates unanimously elected former governor Charles J. Jenkins president. Robert Toombs, archreactionary, dominated the assembly as chief of the all-important Committee on Revision. The convention slightly stiffened the residency requirements for voting but did not explicitly disfranchise the blacks. The provisions of the constitution of 1868, given a proper interpretation and used in conjunction with the reinstated poll tax, had been sufficient to render black participation in politics improbable.[31]

The failure to legally disfranchise the blacks proved embarrassing

29. Savannah *Colored Tribune*, July 8, 1876; C. Mildred Thompson, *Reconstruction in Georgia*, 275, 272–74.

30. C. Mildred Thompson, *Reconstruction in Georgia*, 275, 336–37; Philadelphia *Christian Recorder*, March 2, 1876.

31. Albert Berry Saye, *A Constitutional History of Georgia, 1732–1945* (Athens, 1948), 280–84.

to the Democrats and allowed the blacks to play a minimal role in state politics until 1906. In 1880 the Democrats split over their choice of governor, and both candidates actively wooed the black vote. The election reawakened all the old antagonisms between black and white Republicans. John E. Bryant's plan to field a Republican candidate was denounced by ex-Congressman Jefferson F. Long. Long apparently felt that the party should endorse the Democratic candidate with the most to offer them. Challenging Bryant, Long declared: "Black men have long lost confidence in most white Republicans. You white Republicans destroyed the party in the South." The Republicans refused to endorse either candidate or to nominate their own. But with the Democrats split and actively courting the black vote, five blacks were elected to the assembly. At least one black sat in the state legislature from then until 1906, two years before Georgia blacks were legally disfranchised.[32]

A half dozen black politicians remained active in Republican politics in Georgia until the turn of the century. Although the party was no longer a significant force in state politics, Georgia Republicans fought bitterly over national patronage and the control of the state delegation to the Republican national conventions. In 1877 a number of white Republicans, joined by black former assemblymen James M. Simms and W. H. Harrison, contested John E. Bryant's claim to the chairmanship of the State Central Committee. In a letter to the president of the United States, they accused Bryant of both selling out to the Democrats in 1870 and taking money from railroads to influence his vote. Several black reconstructionists, including Madison Davis, received federal appointments. In 1890 President Benjamin Harrison named Davis postmaster for Athens, Georgia.[33]

In 1876 Georgia's three most prominent black reconstructionists, A. A. Bradley, Tunis G. Campbell, Sr., and Henry M. Turner, had left the political scene. Bradley had opposed the Republican administration, thereby splitting the party in Chatham County, and found him-

32. Bacote, "The Negro in Georgia Politics," 38–39, 43–44, 87, 524–25, 521.
33. For an account of the black reconstructionists after Reconstruction, see Bacote, "The Negro in Georgia Politics"; *Letter to the President of the United States Relative to the Character and Antecedents of John E. Bryant, with a Letter form Gen. Davis Tillson, Late U.S.A.* (Savannah, n.d.); Bacote, "The Negro in Georgia Politics," 134, 130–31.

This photograph of Henry M. Turner in later life appeared in Charles Alexander, *One Hundred Distinguished Leaders* (Atlanta: Franklin, 1899).

self without political allies. He was anathema to both parties and turned his attention to other matters. After various abortive efforts to use the legal system to silence Tunis G. Campbell, Sr., the conservatives finally succeeded in 1876 in having him jailed for malfeasance in office. In 1875 Henry M. Turner publicly expressed his disillusionment with the Republican party. "The party has repeatedly planked its platforms with the high sounding gush of '*security of life and person*,'" he noted, "and the whole balderdash would end with the campaigns." Turner left politics for the pulpit in 1876, becoming manager of the AME Publication Department in Philadelphia. In 1880 he returned to Georgia as a bishop and later became chancellor of Morris Brown College in Atlanta. Three years later Turner interrupted his church affairs long enough to write a blistering attack on the United States Supreme Court for nullifying the Civil Rights Act of 1875.[34]

Though Henry M. Turner eventually became a proponent of a back-to-Africa scheme, he never abandoned his theological version of history. He merely adapted it to fit new circumstances. In 1888 Turner thought he saw God's hand in the Prohibition party. "It is a divine party," he declared. "There is nothing between the democratic or republican parties but a little scramble for office. No issue divides them, but both parties have dropped the Negro. . . . The republican party seems to have become too aristocratic for the Negro. This party will grow and be a blessing to our children's children." At the end of the nineteenth century Turner was still predicting God's retribution on an erring United States people. He told a gathering of AME ministers in 1899 that "God would pour his wrath out upon his people."[35]

34. Coulter, *Negro Legislators in Georgia*, 94–108, 170, 31–36; Philadelphia *Christian Recorder*, November 11, 1875.
35. Macon *Daily Telegraph*, April 25, 1868; Atlanta *Constitution*, November 1, 1899, quoted in Bacote, "The Negro in Georgia Politics," 127, 34, 282.

Conclusion

From its inception, Radical Reconstruction in Georgia was tenuous. The federal government never imposed black rule on Georgia. Under the Congressional Reconstruction Acts of 1867, the blacks were simply allowed to participate in the calling of a constitutional convention and in the April, 1868, election of state officials. The only real intrusion of federal power occurred under the Congressional Reorganization Act of 1869, when General Alfred H. Terry restored the black legislators expelled in 1868 and removed those white members ineligible under the terms of the Fourteenth Amendment. Except for Terry's actions, military interference in Georgia was relatively mild; there were too few northern troops in the state to protect the freedmen, let alone enforce bayonet rule.

Since Georgia was predominantly white, there was little chance that the electoral process would lead to black domination. Most voters were southern whites who voted for Democrats as a matter of course. In the April, 1868, election, the state nearly elected Ku Klux Klan chief John B. Gordon governor. Although 90 percent of Republican voters were black, the party was controlled by southern whites, who excluded blacks from most political offices during the period. On the county and city level, black officeholding was minimal, and almost all of the state's elected officials were white. Blacks never numbered more than 20 percent of the legislature, and Georgia had only one black congressman, Jefferson F. Long, who filled a short term.

160

Although dependent on black votes, Georgia's white Republicans did little for their black constituents, except adopt a segregated public schools system. Nearly all native-born Georgians, they were heavily influenced by Joseph Brown and shared their white opponents' antipathy towards blacks. Most became reconstructionists to assure white domination of Georgia politics, and many were more interested in building railroads than in furthering black rights. In September, 1868, the Georgia legislature, despite a Republican majority in both houses, expelled its black members.

White racism alone, however, cannot fully explain why Radical Reconstruction in Georgia was so short-lived. After all, in Alabama, where whites also outnumbered blacks, Radical Reconstruction lasted longer. Alabama's black political elite, not dominated by ministers, was more aggressive than Georgia's. Working with a healthy sprinkling of Yankees and Freedmen's Bureau officials, Alabama's eighteen black delegates to the Constitutional Convention of 1868 were able to produce a more progressive constitution.[1]

The ephemeral quality of Radical Reconstruction in Georgia can be attributed to the unique nature of the state's black political leadership. Lacking the sizable, affluent, and experienced antebellum free-black class that existed in South Carolina and Louisiana, Georgia freedmen turned almost exclusively to their ministers for political leadership. These ministers, by expounding a providential version of history that nourished the rapid growth of republicanism among the ex-slaves and helped them overcome feelings of inferiority ingrained in them by the peculiar institution, were able to rally the freedmen to the Republican cause. Yet, their domination of black politics proved costly. As antebellum preachers, slave and free, they had mastered the art of compromise in order to bring the Gospel message to the slaves. Implicit in the message, even in freedom, was an otherworldliness, fatalism, and tendency to view all men, even the former slave-owners, as created in God's image and deserving of his mercy. Translated into politics, this produced a certain conservatism.

Ironically, although as preachers and artisans Georgia's black pol-

1. Berlin, *Slaves Without Masters*, 396–97, 136–37. For the breakdown of the Alabama convention, see Du Bois, *Black Reconstruction in America*, 490–92. On the role of Alabama's ministers in politics, see Kolchin, *First Freedom*, 120–21, 165–66.

iticians probably had stronger roots in their local communities than did their more secular and affluent counterparts in South Carolina and Louisiana, they were no more radical. They were inexperienced in institutions like the army and Freedmen's Bureau, and they were acutely aware of the intellectual and material gulf between themselves and the native-born white delegates, who greatly outnumbered them. Nor were there many northern-born delegates to provide allies at the convention. Predominantly ministers attuned to the ideals of Christian mercy, the blacks voted at the constitutional convention to remove the disabilities of their political opponents, and they refused to support a provision that would have explicitly guaranteed their right to hold office. Without the latter provision, they were expelled from the legislature in September, 1868, and in their absence, Radical Reconstruction was practically aborted. Emboldened by the blacks' expulsion, the Democrats organized one of the largest, best-disciplined, and most effective Ku Klux Klans in the South. In December, 1870, less than a year after the blacks were reseated, the conservatives, relying heavily on the terrorism of the Klan, won an overwhelming electoral victory, virtually nullifying the black vote.

It is tempting to brand Radical Reconstruction in Georgia a complete failure, but to do so would be to ignore the historical context. It is certain that Georgia blacks exercised an influence over the electoral process that seemed radical to contemporaries. In 1870 a Republican newspaper proclaimed the election of a black alderman in Macon "a most complete revolution in our city government. Heretofore, the negro has not even been allowed to vote for any city officer, much less be voted for." Moreover, as the study of Dougherty County has suggested, emancipation and Radical Reconstruction provided Georgia freedmen considerable leverage in shaping the postbellum labor system. In addition, the black political movement matured rather than collapsed after the blacks' expulsion. Georgia's minister-politicians realized that to effectively challenge white hegemony they had to be more militant, self-reliant, and black oriented. Their subsequent efforts in the face of stiff opposition from both their opponents and their white Republican allies resulted in the Second Reconstruction of Georgia. "These unlettered men went to work to do their business of retribution and recovery of their privileges in an extraordinarily practical way," recalled Isaac W. Avery, klansman and editor of the Atlanta *Constitution*. "The colored leaders, deserted in this valued matter by their white allies, for the first and only time in the protracted play of Reconstruction, self-reliantly took the bit in their own mouths and organized a race victory."[2] Had Georgia blacks been given the political and civil rights sought by their leaders, the emergence of a really "New" South, which we are now witnessing, might have begun decades earlier. W. E. B. Du Bois was not mistaken in describing Radical Reconstruction as a "splendid failure."

2. Macon *American Union*, December 15, 1870; Avery, *History of the State of Georgia*, 405–406.

Appendix: Black Legislators and Convention Delegates, 1867–1872

Black Legislators and Convention Delegates, 1867–1872

Name	Office*	Birth-place	County	Prewar Status	Color†	Occupation Prewar/War	Occupation Postwar	Literacy‡	Value of Property, 1870 Real	Personal	Intimidation	Sources
Alexander, Robert	C	NC	Clay	—	—	—	AME minister	—	—	—	—	1,5
Allen, Thomas	H	SC	Jasper	slave	—	Baptist minister/shoemaker	same	literate	—	—	received KKK note	2,4
Anderson, Isaac	C,S	GA	22nd District/Houston	—	—	—	CME minister	—	—	—	—	1,5
Atkinson, A. F.	H	—	Thomas	—	—	—	—	illiterate	—	—	—	17
Barnes, Eli	H	GA	Hancock	slave	—	—	mechanic	literate	—	—	visited by a band of men	2
Battle, Jasper	H	—	Thomas	—	—	—	—	—	—	—	—	
Beard, Simeon	C	SC	Richmond	—	—	—	Methodist minister/teacher	literate	—	—	—	1,4,5,9
Beard, Thomas	H	—	Richmond	—	—	—	grocer	—	—	—	—	14
Belcher, Edwin	H	SC	Wilkes	—	—	U.S. army	Freedmen's Bureau agent	literate	—	—	—	28
Bell, Jack R.	C	VA	Oglethorpe	—	—	—	—	—	—	—	—	1
Bentley, Moses H.	C	GA	Chatham	—	—	—	—	—	—	—	arrested for riotous behavior	1,25
Blue, James	H	—	Glynn	—	B	—	railroad worker	illiterate	$1000	$200	—	31

Name	Color[*]	State	County/District	Status[§]	Census[†]	Occupation	Occupation	Literacy[‡]			Notes	Refs
Bradley, Aaron A.	C,S	SC	1st District/Chatham	S/F^s	—	shoemaker	lawyer	literate	—	—	—	1,4,25
Brown, J.	H	—	Monroe	—	—	—	AME minister	—	—	—	—	2,33
Bruton, Adam N.	H	—	Decatur	—	—	—	—	—	—	—	—	
Campbell, Tunis G., Sr.	C,S	NJ	2nd District/McIntosh	free	B	AME Zion minister	same/Freedmen's Bureau agent	literate	$500	$300	jailed, offered bribe	2,18,31
Campbell, Tunis G., Jr.	H	NY	McIntosh	free	B	waiter/storekeeper	—	literate	$500	$300	—	2,4,31
Casey, James C.	C	GA	Marion	—	—	—	—	illiterate	—	—	—	1,15
Chatters, George W.	C	SC	Stewart	—	—	body servant	—	—	—	—	—	1,9
Claiborne, Malcolm	C,H	SC	Burke	slave	—	—	minister/teacher	literate	—	—	received warning from Klan	1,2,4,16
Cobb, Samuel A.	C	GA	Houston	—	—	—	—	—	—	—	—	1
Clower, George A.	H	—	Monroe	—	—	—	—	—	—	—	threatened	22
Colby, Abram	H	GA	Greene	S/F^s	M	barber	day laborer/minister	illiterate	0	0	whipped	2,31
Costin, John T.	C,H	VA	Talbot	—	—	—	AME Zion minister	—	—	—	life threatened	1,5,21

* C signifies a delegate to the Constitutional Convention of 1868; H is used for a member of the Georgia House of Representatives; S indicates a Georgia state senator.

† Color was determined from information in the 1870 MS Census. M indicates mulatto, and B signifies black.

‡ For purposes of this table, a man was considered literate if he could read and write.

§ A slave who was freed before the war.

Black Legislators and Convention Delegates, 1867–1872—continued

Name	Office*	Birth-place	County	Prewar Status	Color†	Occupation Prewar/War	Occupation Postwar	Literacy‡	Value of Property, 1870 Real	Value of Property, 1870 Personal	Intimidation	Sources
Crayton, Thomas	C,S	GA	20th District/Stewart	—	—	—	AME minister	—	—	—	—	1,5
Crumley, Robert	C	GA	Warren	—	—	—	AME minister	—	—	—	—	1,5
Davis, Madison	H	GA	Clarke	slave	M	wheelwright	fireman	literate	$700	$100	—	31,33
Deveaux, James B.	S	—	21st District	—	—	—	minister/teacher	literate	—	—	—	4,6,19
Dinkins, Jesse	C	GA	Schley	—	B	—	farmer/AME minister	illiterate	0	$300	—	1,30,31
Dukes, Abram	H	SC	Morgan	—	B	—	farm laborer	illiterate	0	0	received warning from Klan	2,17,31
Floyd, Monday	H	GA	Morgan	slave	—	—	minister/carpenter	literate	—	—	received warning from Klan	2,4
Fyall, F. H.	H	SC	Macon	slave	—	—	railroad worker	—	—	—	jailed	13,16
Gardner, Samuel	H	—	Warren	—	—	—	—	—	—	—	—	
Golden, William A.	C,H	GA	Liberty	—	B	—	—	illiterate	0	$150	—	1,31
Guilford, William A.	C,H	GA	Upson	—	B	—	—	literate	0	$200	—	1,31
Harrison, William H.	C,H	GA	Hancock	slave	—	body servant	farmer/railroad	literate	—	—	received warning	1,2,20

Name		State	County	Status	B			Literacy			Event	Ref.
Houston, Ulysses L.	H	SC	Bryan	slave	—	Baptist minister/servant	Baptist minister	literate	$500	$125	—	7,31
Hutchings, Jacob	H	—	Jones	slave	—	stonemason	teacher	literate	—	—	—	4,6,7
Jackson, James	C,H	VA	Randolph	—	—	—	—	—	—	—	jailed	1,26
Joiner, Philip	C,H	VA	Dougherty	—	—	—	—	—	—	—	shot at during Camilla riot	1,32
Jones, Van	C	GA	Muscogee	—	—	—	AME minister	—	—	—	—	1,5
Lewis, J.	H	—	Stewart	—	—	—	—	—	—	—	—	
Linder, George	C,H	GA	Laurens	—	B	—	farm laborer	literate	0	$700	—	1,31
Long, Jefferson	Cong.	GA	Bibb	slave	—	—	tailor	literate	—	—	threatened	2,12,27
Lumpkin, Robert	C,H	VA	Macon	slave	—	—	—	illiterate	—	—	—	1,4,13
Moore, Romulus	C,H	GA	Columbia	S/F§	—	blacksmith	Baptist minister/boarding-house keeper	literate	—	—	visited by a band of men	1,2,4
Noble, W. H.	C	ALA	Randolph	—	—	—	AME minister	—	—	—	—	1,5
O'Neal, Peter	H	GA	Baldwin	—	B	—	—	—	$300	$200	—	31
Ormond, George	H	—	Houston	—	—	—	—	—	—	—	threatened with a pistol	23
Palmer, Daniel	C	GA	Washington	—	B	—	Baptist minister	—	$500	$200	—	1,3,31
Pope, Lewis	C	GA	Wilkes	—	—	—	—	—	—	—	—	1
Porter, James	H	SC	Chatham	free	B	tailor	tailor/minister/teacher	literate	$3000	$4000	—	3,8,10,31

Black Legislators and Convention Delegates, 1867–1872—continued

Name	Office*	Birth-place	County	Prewar Status	Color†	Occupation Prewar/War	Occupation Postwar	Literacy‡	Value of Property, 1870 Real	Value of Property, 1870 Personal	Personal Intimidation	Sources
Reynolds, W. H. D.	C	GA	Chatham	—	—	—	—	—	—	—	—	1
Richardson, Alfred	H	GA	Clarke	slave	—	—	carpenter/grocer	literate	—	—	shot, house burned	2,4,19
Sikes, Benjamin	C	VA	Dougherty	—	—	—	—	—	—	—	—	1
Simms, James	H	GA	Chatham	S/F§	M	carpenter	Baptist minister/editor	literate	0	0	—	7,11,31
Simmons, A.	H	VA	Houston	—	B	—	carpenter	—	0	$200	—	31
Smith, Abraham	H	GA	Muscogee	—	B	—	minister	literate	0	$500	—	4,31
Smith, Samuel	H	—	Coweta	—	—	—	—	—	—	—	—	
Stewart, James	C	NC	Chatham	—	—	—	—	—	—	—	—	1
Stone, Alexander	C,H	GA	Jefferson	—	B	—	—	literate	0	$900	—	1,31
Strickland, Henry	C	GA	Greene	—	—	—	AME minister	—	—	—	—	1,5
Turner, Abraham	H	GA	Putnam	—	—	—	—	—	—	—	killed	2,31
Turner, Henry M.	C,H	SC	Bibb	free	—	AME minister/U.S. army chaplain	AME minister/Freedmen's Bureau official	literate	—	—	life threatened	1,2,4
Wallace, George	C,S	GA	12th District/	—	B	—	—	literate	0	$100	warrant issued for	1,24,31

Whitehead, Robert	C	GA	Burke	—	—	—	—	—	—	1
Whitaker, J.	C	GA	Terrell	—	—	—	—	AME minister	—	1,5
Williams, Samuel	C,H	NC	Harris	—	—	—	—	—	—	1

Sources:

1. Allen D. Candler (comp.), *Confederate Records of Georgia*, VI, 1020–27.
2. "Ku Klux Klan Report," VI, 1–19, VII, 272, 607–18, 695–707, 735–43, 854–64, 922–32, 979, 954–59, 1034–42, 1057–62, 1194.
3. *Proceedings of the Freedmen's Convention*, 1–7, 21; *Proceedings of the Council of the Georgia Equal Rights Association*, 5, 8; *Proceedings of the Convention of the Equal Rights and Educational Association*, 1–3; Macon *Georgia Weekly Telegraph*, October 18, 1867.
4. Lawe, "The Black Reconstructionist in Georgia," 52–53.
5. Philadelphia *Christian Recorder*, February 1, 1868, January 27, 1866; Macon *American Union*, April 16, 1869.
6. Hutchings, *Hutchings Bonner Wyatt*, 195, 198.
7. Simms, *The First Colored Baptist Church*, 172, 262–63.
8. "Colloquy with Colored Ministers," 89–90; Lawe, "The Black Reconstructionist," 36.
9. Augusta *Daily Constitutionalist*, April 14, 1867, March 31, 1868.
10. Savannah *Freemen's Standard*, February 15, 1858.
11. Emanuel King Love, *History of the First African Baptist Church, from Its Organization, January 20th, 1788, to July 1st, 1888* (Savannah, 1888), 165.
12. Steward, *Fifty Years in the Gospel Ministry*, 129.
13. Willard E. Wight (ed.), "Negroes in the Georgia Legislature: The Case of F. H. Fyall of Macon County," *Georgia Historical Quarterly*, XLIV (March, 1960), 88–90, 92, 95, 96.
14. Augusta *Colored American*, December 30, 1865.
15. J. Casey Papers, Georgia Department of Archives and History, Atlanta.
16. *House Executive Documents*, 41st Cong., 2nd Sess., No. 288, pp. 56, 85.
17. *Georgia House Journal*, 1871, p. 129.
18. Drago, "Black Georgia During Reconstruction," Chap. V.
19. Hull, *Annals of Athens*, 323–24; *Georgia House Journal*, 1872, p. 8; Macon *American Union*, February 2, 1871.
20. Macon *American Union*, April 2, 1869.
21. Wight [ed.], "Reconstruction in Georgia," 85.
22. George H. Clower to Rufus B. Bullock, December 14, 1870, in Reconstruction File, Georgia Department of Archives and History, Atlanta.
23. George Ormond to Captain Hill, July 21, 1868, in Executive Department, Correspondence of Bullock.
24. Benjamin W. Barrow to his father, November 6, 1872, in Barrow Papers.
25. Savannah *Daily News and Herald*, February 6, 1868.
26. Cuthbert, *Appeal*, n.d., as quoted in Savannah *Morning News*, February 27, 1871.
27. Savannah *Daily Times*, February 19, 1890.
28. Edwin Belcher to Caleb C. Sibley, May 14, 1867, Belcher to Alexander H. Stephens, March 5, 1869, both in Records of the Bureau of Refugees, Freedmen, and Abandoned Lands.
29. Coulter, *Negro Legislators in Georgia*, 37, 164.
30. Gaines, *African Methodism in the South*, 22.
31. 1870 MSS Census, Population schedule.
32. Fitz-Simons, "The Camilla Riot," 121.
33. Redkey, *Respect Black*, 32, Gamble, "Athens," 71.

Bibliography

PRIMARY SOURCES

MANUSCRIPTS

Atlanta Historical Society
  Benjamin F. Conley Papers
  Minutes of the City Council of Atlanta
  S. P. Richard Papers
Emory University, Atlanta
  Dr. Robert Battey Papers
  John S. Dobbins Papers
  Alexander H. Stephens Papers
  William Syndor Thomson Papers
Georgia Department of Archives and History, Atlanta
  Amos T. Akerman Papers
  Moses H. Bentley Papers
  Marion Billups Papers
  Foster Blodgett Papers
  Tunis G. Campbell, Sr., Papers
  Tunis G. Campbell, Jr., Papers
  J. C. Casey Papers
  Howell Cobb Papers
  Benjamin F. Conley Papers
  Convict Roster, 1817–1871
  Thomas Crayton Papers
  Executive Department, Correspondence of Rufus B. Bullock, July 4, 1868, to October 29, 1871
  William Guilford Papers
  William H. Harrison Papers

Joshua Hill Papers
Herschel V. Johnson Papers
Negroes File
E. A. Nisbet Papers
Pater O'Neal Papers
James Porter Papers
Reconstruction File
A. T. Reeve Papers
Alexander Stone Papers
Davis Tillson Papers
Richard W. White Papers
Georgia Historical Society, Savannah
    E. C. Anderson's Beverly and Berwick Plantation Book, 1872–1876
    Col. George A. Mercer Papers
    W. W. Paine Papers
    Register of Free Persons of Color, Chatham County, 1860–1863
    Harvey Moore Watterson Papers
Library of Congress
    Benjamin F. Butler Papers
    Simon Cameron Papers
    William E. Chandler Papers
    Salmon P. Chase Papers
    Federal Writers' Project, Georgia Narratives, Nos. 1–4 of "Slave Narra-
        tives: A Folk History of Slavery in the United States from Interviews
        with Former Slaves." Typewritten records assembled by the Library of
        Congress Project, Work Projects Administration for the District of Co-
        lumbia, 1936–1938.
    William T. Sherman Papers
    Alexander H. Stephens Papers
National Archives
    "Population," Schedule I of "Returns of the United States Census," Ninth
        Census, 1870, Tenth Census, 1880, Twelfth Census, 1900 (Georgia)
    Record Group 105
        Records of the Bureau of Refugees, Freedmen, and Abandoned Lands
        Service Record of Edwin Belcher, Company E, 73rd Pennsylvania
        Infantry
Private Papers
    Georgia Medical Society Minutes, copy in possession of J. Frederick War-
        ing, Savannah
Southern Historical Collection, Library of the University of North Carolina
    at Chapel Hill
    Edward Clifford Anderson Papers
    Garnett Andrews Papers, #1839

Arnold-Screven Papers
George W. Bryan Papers
W. W. Gordon Papers
Duff Green Papers
Thomas Butler King Papers, #1252
William King Papers
MacKay-Stiles Papers
Manigault Papers
Benjamin C. Yancey Papers, #2594
University of Georgia Library, Athens
  Baber-Blackshear Papers
  Col. David C. Barrow Papers
  William Starr Bassinger Reminiscences
  Joseph E. Brown Papers, Felix Hargrett Collection
  Howell Cobb Papers
  Cobb-Irwin-Lamar Papers
  Charles Colcock Jones, Jr., Papers
  M. Dennis MS Ledger
  Henry P. Farrow Papers
  Latimer Plantation Record Book, 1855–1868
  Telamon-Cuyler Papers
Manuscript Department, William R. Perkins Library, Duke University, Durham, N.C.
  Charles E. Bridges Papers
  Samuel Houston Brodnax Papers
  John E. Bryant Papers
  Chatham County, Georgia, Court Records (Sentence Book), 1869–1881
  L. S. Ellington Papers
  Georgia Broadsides
  Georgia Papers
  Lawrence J. Guilmartin and John Flannery Papers
  Edward R. Harden Papers
  Herschel Vespian Johnson Papers
  Charles Colcock Jones, Jr., Papers
  N. B. Moore Farm Journal and Day Book, 1841–1870
  E. A. Nisbet Papers
  Joseph Belknap Smith Papers
  Alexander H. Stephens Papers
  Missouri H. Stokes Papers
  William Henry Talbot Papers
  Ella Gertrude (Clanton) Thomas Papers
  William Norwood Tillinghast Papers
  E. W. Webster Papers

OFFICIAL RECORDS AND DOCUMENTS

PUBLICATIONS OF THE UNITED STATES GOVERNMENT

Agriculture of the United States in 1860: Compiled from the Original Returns of the Eighth Census. Washington, D.C.: United States Census Office, 1864. In *House Miscellaneous Documents*, 38th Cong., 1st Sess., unnumbered, p. 196.

Congressional Globe, 39th–42nd Congs.

U.S. Census Office. *Agriculture, Part I: Farms, Livestock, and Animal Products.* Vol. V of *Census Reports: Twelfth Census of the United States, Taken in the Year 1900.* Washington, D.C.: United States Census Office, 1902.

————. *Agriculture, Part II: Crops and Irrigation.* Vol. VI of *Census Reports: Twelfth Census of the United States, Taken in the Year 1900.* Washington, D.C.: United States Census Office, 1902.

U.S. Bureau of the Census. *Negro Population, 1790–1915.* Washington, D.C.: Government Printing Office, 1918.

————. *Ninth Census of the United States: Statistics of Population.* Washington, D.C.: Government Printing Office, 1872.

House Executive Documents, 39th Cong., 1st Sess., Nos. 34, 99, 42nd Cong., 2nd Sess., Nos. 82, 288.

House Miscellaneous Documents, 40th Cong., 3rd Sess., No. 52, 41st Cong., 1st Sess., No. 34.

"House of Representatives, Report No. 30, Report of the Joint Committee on Reconstruction, Part III. Georgia, Alabama, Mississippi, Arkansas." *Reports of the Committees of the House of Representatives*, 39th Cong., 1st Sess., Vol. II.

"Ku Klux Klan Report, Georgia Testimony: Report of the Joint Select Committee to Inquire into the Affairs of the Late Insurrectionary States." *Senate Reports of Committees*, 42nd Cong., 2nd Sess., Vol. II, Pts. VI and VII.

National Archives and Records Service, General Services Administration. *Records of the Superintendent of Education for the State of Georgia Bureau of Refugees, Freedmen, and Abandoned Lands, 1865–1870. National Archives Microfilm Publications Pamphlet Accompanying Microcopy No. 799.* Washington, D.C.: Government Printing Office, 1969.

Report on the Productions of Agriculture as Returned at the Tenth Census (June 1, 1880) . . . Washington, D.C. Government Printing Office, 1883. In *House Miscellaneous Documents*, 47th Cong., 2nd Sess., No. 42, Pt. III, 40–41.

Senate Executive Documents, 39th Cong., 1st Sess., Nos. 2, 27, 2nd Sess., No. 6.

The Statistics of the Wealth and Industry of the United States . . . Vol. III of *Ninth Census.* Washington, D.C.: Government Printing Office, 1872. In

House Miscellaneous Documents, 42nd Cong., 1st Sess., unnumbered, p. 348.

The War of the Rebellion: A Compilation of the Official Records of the Union and Confederate Armies. Washington, D.C.: Government Printing Office, 1880–1901, additions and corrections inserted in each volume, 1902.

PUBLICATIONS OF THE GEORGIA STATE GOVERNMENT

Acts of the General Assembly of the State of Georgia, 1866–1872.

Annual Reports of the Comptroller General of the State of Georgia, 1860–1873.

Candler, Allen D., comp. *The Confederate Records of the State of Georgia*. Vols. I–IV, VI. Atlanta: C. P. Byrd, 1909–1911.

Clark, R. H., T. R. R. Cobb, and D. Irwin, preps. *The Code of the State of Georgia*. Rev. and corr. David Irwin. Atlanta: Franklin Steam Printing House, 1867.

———, preps. *The Code of the State of Georgia*. Rev., corr., annot. David Irwin, George Lester, and W. B. Hill. 2nd ed., rev. Macon: J. W. Burke, 1873.

Georgia House Journal, 1866–1872.

Georgia Reports.

Georgia Senate Journal, 1866–1872.

Reports of Committees and Replies

   Evidence Taken by the Joint Committee of the Legislature Appointed to Investigate the Management of the State Road Under the Administration of R. B. Bullock and Foster Blodgett. Atlanta: n.p., 1872.

   Majority and Minority Reports of the Committee to Investigate the Fairness of the State Road Lease, Testimony, 1872.

   Proceedings of Committee Appointed to Investigate Charges Made by Angier Against Bullock. Report of the Committee.

   Proceedings of the Joint Committee Appointed to Investigate the Condition of the Georgia Penitentiary N.p.: [1870].

   Reply of Henry Clews and Company to the Annual Report of N. L. Angier, 1872.

   Report of the Committee of the Legislature to Investigate the Bonds of the State of Georgia, 1872.

   Report of the Finance Committee on the Report of N. L. Angier, Treasurer, on the Condition of the Treasury. Macon: 1869.

   Report of the Joint Committee to Investigate the Condition of the Western and Atlantic R.R. Atlanta: Samuel Bard, 1869.

   Testimony Taken by the Committee to Investigate the Official Conduct of Rufus B. Bullock, 1872.

PUBLICATIONS OF GEORGIA CITY GOVERNMENTS

Directory of the City of Savannah for 1870. Savannah: Alex Abrams, 1870.

Duncan, William. *Tabulated Mortuary Record of the City of Savannah, from January, 1854, to December 31, 1869. Compiled from the Mortuary Reports on File in the Mayor's Office.* Savannah: Morning News Steam-Power Press, 1870.

Hanleiter's Atlanta City Directory for 1872. Atlanta: Plantation, 1872.

Report of Edward C. Anderson, Mayor of Savannah, for the Year Ending September 30, 1866. Savannah: n.p., 1866.

Report of John Screven, Mayor of the City of Savannah, for the Year Ending September 30, 1871. Savannah: Morning News Steam-Power Press, 1871.

PUBLISHED ACCOUNTS BY BLACKS

Campbell, Tunis Gulic. *Sufferings of the Rev. T. G. Campbell and His Family, in Georgia.* Washington, D.C.: Enterprise, 1877.

Carter, Edward R. *The Black Side: A Partial History of the Business, Religious and Educational Side of the Negro in Atlanta, Ga.* Atlanta: n.p., 1894.

"Colloquy with Colored Ministers: A Civil War Document." *Journal of Negro History,* XVI (January, 1931), 88–94.

Gaines, John Wesley. *African Methodism in the South; or, Twenty-five Years of Freedom.* Atlanta: Franklin, 1890.

Hood, James Walker. *One Hundred Years of the African Methodist Episcopal Zion Church; or The Centennial of African Methodism.* New York: A.M.E. Zion Book Concern, 1895.

Love, Emanuel King. *History of the First African Baptist Church, from Its Organization, January 20th, 1788, to July 1st, 1888.* Savannah: Morning News Print, 1888.

Lynch, James. *The Mission of the United States Republic: An Oration Delivered by Rev. James Lynch, at the Parade Ground, Augusta, Ga., July 4, 1865.* Augusta: Steam Power Press, 1865.

Phillips, Charles Henry. *The History of the Colored Methodist Episcopal Church in America: Comprising Its Organization, Subsequent Development, and Present Status.* Jackson, Tenn.: C.M.E. Church, 1898.

Ponton, Mungo Melanchthon. *Life and Times of Henry M. Turner: The Antecedent and Preliminary History of the Life and Times of Bishop H. M. Turner, His Boyhood, Education and Public Career, and His Relation to His Associates, Colleagues and Contemporaries.* Atlanta: A. B. Caldwell, 1917.

Proceedings of the Convention of the Equal Rights and Educational Association of Georgia, Assembled at Macon, October 29th, 1866, Containing the Annual Address of the President, Captain J. E. Bryant. Augusta: The Convention, 1866.

*Proceedings of the Council of the Georgia Equal Rights Association, As-
sembled at Augusta, Ga., April 4th, 1866. Containing the Address of the
President, Captain J. E. Bryant, and Resolutions Adopted by the Council.* Augusta: The Council, 1866.

*Proceedings of the Freedmen's Convention of Georgia, Assembled at Au-
gusta, January 10th, 1866. Containing the Speeches of Gen'l Tillson,
Capt. J. E. Bryant, and Others.* Augusta: The Freedmen's Convention,
1866.

Simms, James Meriles. *The First Colored Baptist Church in North America. Constituted at Savannah, Georgia, January 20, A.D. 1788.* Philadelphia: J. B. Lippincott, 1888.

Steward, Theophilus G. *Fifty Years in the Gospel Ministry.* N.p., n.d.

Tanner, Benjamin Tucker. *An Apology for African Methodism.* Baltimore:
n.p., 1867.

Taylor, Susie King. *Reminiscences of My Life in Camp with the 33d United
States Colored Troops, Late 1st S.C. Volunteers.* Boston: The author, 1904.

Thomas, Edgar Garfield. *The First African Baptist Church of North America.* Savannah: n.p., 1925.

Turner, Henry M. "Speech on the Eligibility of Colored Members to Seats in
the Georgia Legislature. . . . Delivered Before That Body September 3d,
1868," in George A. Singleton, *The Romance of African Methodism: A
Study of the African Methodist Episcopal Church.* New York: Exposition
Press, 1952, Appendix B, 1–16.

Wayman, Alexander Walker. *My Recollections of African M. E. Ministers;
or, Forty Years' Experience in the African Methodist Episcopal Church.*
Philadelphia: A.M.E. Book Rooms, 1881.

Williams, George Washington. *History of the Negro Race in America from
1619 to 1880. Negroes as Slaves, as Soldiers, and as Citizens; Together
with a Preliminary Consideration of the United of the Human Family, an
Historical Sketch of Africa, and an Account of the Negro Governments of
Sierra Leone and Liberia.* 2 vols. New York: G. P. Putnam's Sons, 1883.

PUBLISHED TRAVEL ACCOUNTS

Andrews, Sidney. *The South Since the War, as Shown by Fourteen Weeks of
Travel and Observation in Georgia and the Carolinas.* Boston: Ticknor
and Fields, 1866.

Botume, Elizabeth Hyde. *First Days Amongst the Contrabands.* New York:
Arno Press and the New York Times, 1968.

Dennett, John Richard. *The South As It Is, 1865–1866.* Ed. Henry M. Christian. New York: Viking Press, 1965.

Muir, John. *A Thousand-Mile Walk to the Gulf.* Ed. William Frederick Bade.
Boston: Houghton Mifflin, 1916.

Nordhoff, Charles. *The Cotton States in the Spring and Summer of 1875.*
New York: Burt Franklin, 1876.

Powers, Stephen. *Afoot and Alone: A Walk from Sea to Sea by the Southern Route, Adventures and Observations in Southern California, New Mexico, Arizona, Texas, Etc.* Hartford, Conn.: Columbian, 1872.

Reid, Whitelaw. *After the War: A Tour of the Southern States, 1865–1866.* Ed. C. Vann Woodward. New York: Harper and Row, 1965.

Somers, Robert. *The Southern States Since the War, 1870–1.* University: University of Alabama Press, 1965.

Trowbridge, John Townsend. *The South: A Tour of Its Battle-fields and Ruined Cities, a Journey Through the Desolated States, and Talks with the People; Being a Description of the Present State of the Country—Its Agriculture—Railroads—Business and Finances—Giving an Account of Confederate Misrule, and of the Sufferings, Necessities and Mistakes, Political Views, Social Condition and Prospects of the Aristocracy, Middle Class, Poor Whites and Negroes.* Hartford, Conn.: L. Stebbins, 1867.

PUBLISHED ACCOUNTS BY WHITE CONSERVATIVES

Andrews, Eliza Frances. *The War-Time Journal of a Georgia Girl, 1864–1865.* New York: D. Appleton, 1908.

Arnold, Richard Dennis. *Letters of Richard D. Arnold, M.D., 1808–1876.* Papers of the Trinity College Historical Society, Double Series XVIII–XIX. Durham, N.C.: Seeman Press, 1929.

Avary, Myrta (Lockett). *Dixie After the War: An Exposition of Social Conditions Existing in the South During the Twelve Years Succeeding the Fall of Richmond.* New York: Doubleday, Page, 1906.

Avery, Isaac Wheeler. *The History of the State of Georgia from 1850 to 1881, Embracing the Three Important Epochs; the Decade Before the War of 1861–5; the War; the Period of Reconstruction, with Portraits of the Leading Public Men of This Era.* 1881. Reprint New York: AMS Press, 1972.

Candler, Myrtle Long. "Reminiscences of Life in Georgia During the 1850s and 1860s, Part V," *Georgia Historical Quarterly,* XXXIV (March, 1950), 10–18.

Dickson, David. *A Practical Treatise on Agriculture; to Which Is Added the Author's Published Letters.* Ed. J. Dickson Smith. Macon, Ga.: J. W. Burke, 1870.

Gay, Mary Ann Harris. *Life in Dixie During the War, 1861, 1862, 1863, 1864, 1865.* Atlanta: Charles P. Byrd, 1897.

"A Georgia Plantation." *Scribner's Monthly,* XXI (April, 1881), 830–36.

Haygood, Atticus Green. *Our Brother in Black: His Freedom and His Future.* New York: Phillips and Hunt, 1881.

Hill, Benjamin Harvey, Sr. *Notes on the Situation, as Published in the Chronicle and Sentinel.* Augusta: Chronicle and Sentinel Presses, 1867.

Hill, Benjamin Harvey, Jr. *Senator Benjamin H. Hill of Georgia: His Life, Speeches, and Writings.* Atlanta: T. H. P. Bloodworth, 1893.

Hood, John Bell. *Advance and Retreat: Personal Experiences in the United States and Confederate States Armies.* Bloomington: Indiana University Press, 1959.

Howard, Frances Thomas. *In and Out of the Lines: An Accurate Account of Incidents During the Occupation of Georgia by Federal Troops in 1864–1865.* New York: Neale, 1905.

Hull, Augustus Longstreet, ed. *Annals of Athens, Georgia, 1810–1901.* [Athens]: Banner Job Office, 1906.

Jones, Mary Sharpe, and Mary Jones Mallard. *Yankees A'Coming: One Month's Experience During the Invasion of Liberty County, Georgia, 1864–1865.* Ed. Haskell Monroe. Tuscaloosa, Ala.: Confederate, 1959.

Le Conte, Joseph. *'Ware Sherman: A Journal of Three Months' Personal Experience in the Last Days of the Confederacy.* Berkeley: University of California Press, 1937.

Leigh, Frances Butler. *Ten Years on a Georgia Plantation Since the War.* New York: Negro Universities Press, 1969.

Morgan, Mrs. Irby [Julia]. *How It Was: Four Years Among the Rebels.* Nashville: Methodist Episcopal Church, South, 1892.

Myers, Robert Manson, ed. *The Children of Pride: A True Story of Georgia and the Civil War.* New Haven: Yale University Press, 1972.

Phillips, Ulrich B., ed. *The Correspondence of Robert Toombs, Alexander H. Stephens, and Howell Cobb.* Annual Report of the American Historical Association for the Year 1911. Vol. II. Washington, D.C.: Government Printing Office, 1913.

Reed, John Calvin. *The Brothers' War.* Boston: Little, Brown, 1905.

———. "What I Know of the Ku Klux Klan." *Uncle Remus Magazine*, I (January–November, 1908).

Robertson, James I., Jr., ed. *The Diary of Dolly Lunt Burge.* Athens: University of Georgia Press, 1962.

PUBLISHED ACCOUNTS BY WHITE REPUBLICANS OR FREEDMEN'S BUREAU OFFICIALS

Alvord, John Watson. *Eighth Semi-annual Report on Schools for Freedmen, July 1, 1869.* Washington, D.C.: Government Printing Office, 1869.

———. *Letters from the South, Relating to the Condition of the Freedmen, Addressed to Major General O. O. Howard, Commissioner Bureau R., F., and A. L. by J. W. Alvord, Gen. Sup't Education.* Washington, D.C.: Howard University Press, 1870.

———. *Ninth Semi-annual Report on Schools for Freedmen, January 1, 1870.* Washington, D.C.: Government Printing Office, 1870.

———. *Seventh Semi-annual Report on Schools for Freedmen, January 1, 1869.* Washington, D.C.: Government Printing Office, 1869.

———. *Tenth Semi-annual Report on Schools for Freedmen, July 1, 1870.* Washington, D.C.: Government Printing Office, 1870.

————. *Third Semi-annual Report on Schools for Freedmen, January 1, 1867.* Washington, D.C.: Government Printing Office, 1867.

Brown, Joseph Emerson. *Ex-Governor Brown Replies to B. H. Hill's Notes on the "Situation."* Augusta: Georgia Printing, 1867.

Bullock, Rufus Brown. *Address of Rufus B. Bullock to the People of Georgia. A Review of the Revolutionary Proceedings of the Late Repudiating Legislature. The Slanders and Misrepresentations of the Committees Exposed. A Republican Administration Contrasted with the Corrupt and Reckless Action of the Present Usurping Minority, Under the Lead of General Toombs.* N.p., 1872.

————. *Have the Reconstruction Acts Been Fully Executed in Georgia? Speech at Albion, New York, October 17, 1868.* Washington, D.C.: Chronicle Print [1868].

————. "Reconstruction in Georgia, 1865–70." *Independent,* LV (March 19, 1903), 670–74.

————. *Remarks of Gov. Bullock to the Judiciary Committee of the Senate, in Reconstruction of Georgia, March 2, 1870.* Washington, D.C.: Chronicle Print, 1870.

Caldwell, John H. *Reminiscences of the Reconstruction of Church and State in Georgia.* Wilmington, Del.: J. M. Thomas, 1895.

Howard, Oliver Otis. *Autobiography of Oliver Otis Howard, Major General, United States Army.* 2 vols. Freeport, N.Y.: Books for Libraries Press, 1971.

Letter to the President of the United States Relative to the Character and Antecedents of John E. Bryant, with a Letter from Gen. Davis Tillson, Late U.S.A. Savannah: Savannah Times Steam Print, n.d.

Stearns, Charles. *The Black Man of the South, and the Rebels; or, The Characteristics of the Former, and the Recent Outrages of the Latter.* 1872. Reprint New York: Negro University Press, 1969.

Wight, Willard E., ed. "Reconstruction in Georgia: Three Letters by Edwin G. Higbee." *Georgia Historical Quarterly,* XLI (March, 1957), 81–90.

Yulee, Elias. *An Address to the Colored People of Georgia.* Savannah: Republican Job Office, 1868.

PUBLISHED ACCOUNTS BY MILITARY MEN

Angle, Paul M., ed. *Three Years in the Army of the Cumberland: The Letters and Diary of Major James A. Connolly.* Bloomington: Indiana University Press, 1959.

Athearn, Robert G., ed. "An Indiana Doctor Marches with Sherman: The Diary of James Comfort Patten." *Indiana Magazine of History,* XLIX (December, 1953), 405–22.

Boyle, John Richards. *Soldiers True: The Story of the One Hundred and Eleventh Regiment Pennsylvania Veteran Volunteers and of Its Cam-*

paigns in the War for the Union, 1861–1865. New York: Eaton and Mains, 1903.

Bradley, George S. *The Star Corps; or, Notes of an Army Chaplain During Sherman's Famous "March to the Sea."* Milwaukee: Jermain and Brightman, 1865.

Conyngham, David Power. *Sherman's March Through the South.* New York: Sheldon, 1865.

DeWolfe, M. A., ed. *Marching with Sherman: Passages from the Letters and Campaign Diaries of Henry Hitchcock, Major and Assistant Adjutant General of the Volunteers, November, 1864–May, 1865.* New Haven: Yale University Press, 1927.

Foote, Corydon Edward. *With Sherman to the Sea: A Drummer's Story of the Civil War, as Related by Corydon Edward Foote to Olive Deane Hormel.* New York: John Day, 1960.

Higginson, Thomas Wentworth. "Fair Play the Best Policy." *Atlantic Monthly*, XV (May, 1865).

———. *Army Life in a Black Regiment.* East Lansing: Michigan State University Press, 1960.

[Kellogg, Mary E.], comp. *Army Life of an Illinois Soldier, Including a Day by Day Record of Sherman's March to the Sea: Letters and Diary of the Late Charles W. Wills. . . .* Washington, D.C.: Globe Printing, 1906.

Nichols, George Ward. *The Story of the Great March: From the Diary of a Staff Officer.* New York: Harper and Brothers, 1865.

Sherman, William Tecumseh. *Memoirs of General William T. Sherman by Himself.* Bloomington: Indiana University Press, 1957.

Stormont, Gilbert R., comp. *History of the Fifty-eighth Regiment of Indiana Volunteer Infantry, Its Organization, Campaigns, and Battles from 1861–1865. From the Manuscript Prepared by the Late Chaplain John J. Hight, During His Service with the Regiment in the Field.* Princeton, Ind.: Press of the Clarion, 1895.

Winther, Oscar Osburn, ed. *With Sherman to the Sea: The Civil War Letters, Diaries, and Reminiscences of Theodore F. Upson.* Baton Rouge: Louisiana State University Press, 1943.

NEWSPAPERS AND JOURNALS

Albany
  Patriot
Americus
  Tri-Weekly Republican
  Weekly Sumter Republican
Athens
  Southern Banner
  Southern Cultivator
  Southern Watchman

Atlanta
  Constitution
  Daily Atlanta Intelligencer
  Daily New Era
  Daily Opinion
  Daily Sun
  Gate City Guardian
  Methodist Advocate
  Southern Cultivator and Dixie Farmer
Augusta
  Colored American
  Daily Chronicle and Sentinel
  Daily Constitutionalist
  Loyal Georgian
Columbus
  Daily Columbus Enquirer
  Daily Sun
Covington
  Georgia Enterprise
Dalton
  North Georgia Citizen
Dawson
  Weekly Journal
Greensboro
  Herald
Griffin
  American Union (Moves to Macon)
  Semi-Weekly Star
  Tri-Weekly Star
Hawkinsville
  Dispatch
Macon
  American Union
  Daily Telegraph
  Journal and Messenger
  Georgia Journal and Messenger
  Georgia Weekly Telegraph
  Southern Confederacy
Milledgeville
  Federal Union
  Southern Recorder
New York
  Herald

Nation
Times
Philadelphia
  Christian Recorder
Rome
  Tri-Weekly Courier
  Weekly Courier
Sandersville
  Central Georgian
Savannah
  Colored Tribune
  Daily Advertiser
  Daily Herald
  Daily News and Herald
  Daily Republican
  Freemen's Standard
  Morning News
Thomaston
  Georgia Herald
Valdosta
  South Georgia Times
Washington, Ga.
  Gazette

SECONDARY SOURCES

ARTICLES

Abzug, Robert. "The Black Family During Reconstruction." In Daniel Fox, Nathan Huggins, and Martin Kilson, eds. *Key Issues in the Afro-American Experience.* 2 vols. New York: Harcourt Brace Jovanovich, 1971, pp. 26–41.

Bacote, Clarence Albert. "William Finch, Negro Councilman, and Political Activities in Atlanta During Early Reconstruction." *Journal of Negro History*, XL (October, 1955), 341–64.

Blassingame, John W. "Before the Ghetto: The Making of the Black Community in Savannah, Georgia, 1865–1880." *Journal of Social History*, VI (1973), 463–88.

Bond, Horace Mann. "Social and Economic Forces in Alabama Reconstruction." *Journal of Negro History*, XXIII (July, 1938), 290–348.

Cason, Roberta F. "The Loyal League in Georgia." *Georgia Historical Quarterly*, XX (June, 1936), 125–53.

Coulter, E. Merton. "Cudjo Fye's Insurrection." *Georgia Historical Quarterly*, XXXVIII (September, 1954), 213–25.

————. "The New South: Benjamin H. Hill's Speech Before the Alumni Society of the University of Georgia, 1871." *Georgia Historical Quarterly,* LVII (Sumer, 1973), 179–99.

Drago, Edmund L. "How Sherman's March Through Georgia Affected the Slaves." *Georgia Historical Quarterly,* LVII (Fall, 1973), 361–75.

————. "Militancy and Black Women in Reconstruction Georgia." *Journal of American Culture,* I (Winter, 1978), 838–44.

Du Bois, W. E. B. "Georgia Negroes and Their Fifty Millions of Savings." *World's Work,* XVIII (May, 1909), 1150–54.

————. "The Negro as He Really Is." *World's Work,* II (May–October, 1901), 848–65.

Escott, Paul D. "The Context of Freedom: Georgia's Slaves During the Civil War." *Georgia Historical Quarterly,* LVIII (Spring, 1974), 79–104.

Fitz-Simons, Theodore Barker, Jr. "The Camilla Riot." *Georgia Historical Quarterly,* XXXV (June, 1951), 116–25.

Flanders, Ralph B. "The Free Negro in Ante-Bellum Georgia." *North Carolina Historical Review,* IX (July, 1932), 250–72.

Gottlieb, Manuel. "The Land Question and Georgia During Reconstruction." *Science and Society,* III (1939), 356–88.

House, Albert V., Jr. "Deterioration of a Georgia Rice Plantation During Four Years of Civil War." *Journal of Southern History,* IX (February, 1943), 98–113.

————. "A Reconstruction Share-Cropper Contract on a Georgia Rice Plantation." *Georgia Historical Quarterly,* XXVI (June, 1942), 156–65.

McKelvey, Blake. "Penal Slavery and Southern Reconstruction." *Journal of Negro History,* XX (April, 1935), 153–79.

Matthews, John M. "Negro Republicans in the Reconstruction of Georgia," *Georgia Historical Quarterly,* LX (Summer, 1976), 145–64.

Meeker, Edward. "Mortality Trends of Southern Blacks, 1850–1910: Some Preliminary Findings." *Explorations in Economic History,* XIII (January, 1976), 13–42.

Meier, August. "Negroes in the First and Second Reconstructions of the South." *Civil War History,* XIII (1967), 114–30.

Mohr, Clarence. "Before Sherman: Georgia Blacks and the Union War Effort." *Journal of Southern History,* XLV (August, 1979), 331–52.

Pleck, Elizabeth H. "The Two-Parent Household: Black Family Structure in Late Nineteenth-Century Boston." *Journal of Social Studies,* VI (Fall, 1972), 1–31.

Redkey, Edwin S. "Bishop Turner's African Dream." *Journal of American History,* LIV (September, 1967), 271–90.

Ripley, C. Peter. "The Black Family in Transition, 1860–1865." *Journal of Southern History,* XLI (August, 1975), 369–80.

Russ, William A., Jr. "Radical Disfranchisement in Georgia, 1867–1871." *Georgia Historical Quarterly,* XIX (September, 1935), 175–209.

Shifflet, Crandal A. "The Household Composition of Rural Black Families: Louisa County, Virginia, 1880." *Journal of Interdisciplinary History*, VI (Autumn, 1975), 235–60.

Taylor, A. Elizabeth. "The Origin and Development of the Convict Lease System in Georgia." *Georgia Historical Quarterly*, XXVI (June, 1942), 113–28.

Taylor, Alrutheus A. "Negro Congressmen a Generation After." *Journal of Negro History*, VII (April, 1922), 127–71.

Wight, Willard E., ed. "Negroes in the Georgia Legislature: The Case of F. H. Fyall of Macon County." *Georgia Historical Quarterly*, XLIV (March, 1960), 85–97.

Woodman, Harold D. "Post–Civil War Southern Agriculture and the Law." *Agricultural History*, LIII (1979), 319–37.

———. "Sequel to Slavery: The New History Views the Postbellum South." *Journal of Southern History*, XLIII (November, 1977), 523–54.

BOOKS

Bacote, Clarence Albert. *The Story of Atlanta University: A Century of Service, 1865–1965.* Atlanta: Atlanta University, 1969.

Banks, Enoch Marvin. *The Economics of Land Tenure in Georgia.* New York: Columbia University Press, 1905.

Bentley, George R. *A History of the Freedmen's Bureau.* Philadelphia: University of Pennsylvania Press, 1955.

Berlin, Ira. *Slaves Without Masters: The Free Negro in the Antebellum South.* New York: Vintage, 1976.

Blalock, Hubert M. *Social Statistics.* Ed. David M. Edwards. 2nd ed. New York: McGraw-Hill, 1972.

Blassingame, John W. *The Slave Community: Plantation Life in the Antebellum South.* New York: Oxford University Press, 1972.

Bond, Horace Mann. *The Education of the Negro in the American Social Order.* New York: Prentice-Hall, 1934.

Brooks, Robert Preston. "The Agrarian Revolution in Georgia, 1865–1912." *Bulletin of the University of Wisconsin*, No. 639. History Series, Vol. III, No. 3. Madison: University of Wisconsin, 1914.

Bryan, Thomas Conn. *Confederate Georgia.* Athens: University of Georgia Press, 1953.

Bullock, Henry Allen. *A History of Negro Education in the South from 1619 to the Present.* Cambridge, Mass.: Harvard University Press, 1967.

Conway, Alan. *The Reconstruction of Georgia.* Minneapolis: University of Minnesota Press, 1966.

Coulter, E. Merton. *Negro Legislators in Georgia During the Reconstruction Period.* Athens: Georgia Historical Quarterly, 1968.

———. *The South During Reconstruction, 1865–1877.* Baton Rouge: Louisiana State University Press, 1947.

Du Bois, W. E. B. *Black Reconstruction in America: An Essay Toward a History of the Part Which Black Folk Played in the Attempt to Reconstruct Democracy in America, 1860–1880.* New York: Atheneum, 1975.
———. *The Negro American Family.* 1908. Reprint edition. New York: Negro Universities Press, 1969.
———. "The Negro Landholder of Georgia." *Bulletin of the Department of Labor,* No. 35 (July, 1901). Washington, D.C.: Government Printing Office, 1901.
———. *The Souls of Black Folk: Essays and Sketches.* Greenwich, Conn.: Fawcett, 1964.
Elon, Amos. *Herzl.* New York: Holt, Rinehart, and Winston, 1975.
Fielder, Herbert. *A Sketch of the Life and Times and Speeches of Joseph E. Brown.* Springfield, Mass.: Press of Springfield Printing, 1883.
Flanders, Ralph Betts. *Plantation Slavery in Georgia.* Chapel Hill: University of North Carolina Press, 1933.
Flippin, Percy S. *Herschel V. Johnson of Georgia, State Rights Unionist.* Richmond: Press of Dietz Printing, 1931.
Foner, Eric. *Free Soil, Free Labor, Free Man: The Ideology of the Republican Party Before the Civil War.* New York: Oxford University Press, 1970.
Garrett, Franklin Miller. *Atlanta and Environs: A Chronicle of Its People and Events.* 3 vols. New York: Lewis Historical Publishing, 1954.
Genovese, Eugene D. *Roll, Jordan, Roll: The World the Slaves Made.* New York: Vintage, 1976.
Granger, Mary, ed. Savannah Writers' Project. *Savannah River Plantations.* Savannah: Georgia Historical Society, 1947.
Gutman, Herbert. *The Black Family in Slavery and Freedom, 1720–1925.* New York: Pantheon Books, 1976.
Hammond, Edmund Jordan. *The Methodist Episcopal Church in Georgia, Being a Brief History of the Two Georgia Conferences of the Methodist Episcopal Church, Together with a Summary of the Causes of Major Methodist Divisions in the United States and of the Problems Confronting Methodist Union.* [Atlanta]: The author, 1935.
Harlan, Louis R. *Separate and Unequal: Public School Campaigns and Racism in the Southern Seaboard States, 1901–1915.* New York: Atheneum, 1968.
Higgs, Robert. *Competition and Coercion: Blacks in the American Economy, 1865–1914.* Cambridge: Cambridge University Press, 1977.
Holt, Thomas. *Black over White: Negro Political Leadership in South Carolina During Reconstruction.* Urbana: University of Illinois Press, 1977.
Hutchings, Richard Henry. *Hutchings Bonner Wyatt: An Intimate Family History.* Utica, N.Y.: Hutchings family, 1937.
Jones, Jacqueline. *Soldiers of Light and Love: Northern Teachers and Georgia Blacks, 1865–1873.* Chapel Hill: University of North Carolina Press, 1980.

Kolchin, Peter. *First Freedom: The Responses of Alabama's Blacks to Emancipation and Reconstruction*. Westport, Conn.: Greenwood, 1972.

Levine, Lawrence W. *Black Culture and Black Consciousness: Afro-American Folk Thought from Slavery to Freedom*. New York: Oxford University Press, 1978.

Litwack, Leon F. *Been in the Storm So Long: The Aftermath of Slavery*. New York: Alfred A. Knopf, 1979.

————. *North of Slavery: The Negro in the Free States, 1790–1860*. Chicago: University of Chicago Press, 1965.

McFarland, Andrew Stuart. *Power and Leadership in Pluralist Systems*. Stanford: Stanford University Press, 1969.

Morrow, Ralph Ernest. *Northern Methodism and Reconstruction*. East Lansing: Michigan State University Press, 1956.

Nathans, Elizabeth Studley. *Losing the Peace: Georgia Republicans and Reconstruction, 1865–1871*. Baton Rouge: Louisiana State University Press, 1968.

Parks, Joseph H. *Joseph E. Brown of Georgia*. Baton Rouge: Louisiana State University Press, 1977.

Perdue, Robert E. *The Negro in Savannah, 1865–1900*. New York: Exposition Press, 1973.

Quarles, Benjamin. *The Negro in the Civil War*. Boston: Little, Brown, 1953.

Raboteau, Albert J. *Slave Religion: The "Invisible Institution" in the Antebellum South*. New York: Oxford University Press, 1980.

Range, Willard. *A Century of Georgia Agriculture, 1850–1950*. Athens: University of Georgia Press, 1954.

————. *The Rise and Progress of Negro Colleges in Georgia, 1865–1949*. Athens: University of Georgia Press, 1951.

Ransom, Roger L., and Richard Sutch. *One Kind of Freedom: The Economic Consequences of Emancipation*. Cambridge: Cambridge University Press, 1977.

Redkey, Edwin S. *Respect Black: The Writings and Speeches of Henry McNeal Turner*. New York: Arno Press and New York Times, 1971.

Reed, Wallace Putnam, ed. *History of Atlanta, Georgia, with Illustrations and Biographical Sketches of Some of Its Prominent Men and Pioneers*. Syracuse: N.Y.: D. Mason, 1889.

Rosengarten, Theodore. *All God's Dangers: The Life of Nate Shaw*. New York: Alfred A. Knopf, 1975.

Saye, Albert Berry. *A Constitutional History of Georgia, 1732–1945*. Athens: University of Georgia Press, 1948.

Shadgett, Olive Hall. *The Republican Party in Georgia from Reconstruction Through 1900*. Athens: University of Georgia Press, 1964.

Simmons, William J. *Men of Mark: Eminent, Progressive, and Rising*. Cleveland: G. M. Rewell, 1887.

Smith, Samuel Denny. *The Negro in Congress, 1870–1901*. Chapel Hill: University of North Carolina Press, 1940.

Swint, Henry Lee. *The Northern Teacher in the South, 1862–1870*. New York: Octagon Books, 1967.

Tankersley, Allen P. *John B. Gordon: A Study in Gallantry*. Atlanta: Whitehall Press, 1955.

Thompson, C. Mildred. *Reconstruction in Georgia: Economic, Social, Political, 1865–1872*. New York: Columbia University Press, 1915.

Thompson, Edward P. *The Making of the English Working Class*. London: Victor Gollancz, 1965.

Trelease, Allen W. *White Terror: The Ku Klux Klan Conspiracy and Southern Reconstruction*. New York: Harper and Row, 1971.

Vincent, Charles. *Black Legislators in Louisiana During Reconstruction*. Baton Rouge: Louisiana State University Press, 1976.

Wade, Richard C. *Slavery in the Cities: The South, 1820–1860*. New York: Oxford University Press, 1964.

Walker, Clarence E. *A Rock in a Weary Land: The African Methodist Episcopal Church During the Civil War and Reconstruction*. Baton Rouge: Louisiana State University Press, 1981.

Wiener, Jonathan M. *Social Origins of the New South, 1860–1885*. Baton Rouge: Louisiana State University Press, 1978.

Wiley, Bell Irvin. *Southern Negroes, 1861–1865*. New Haven: Yale University Press, 1938.

Woodson, Carter Godwin. *The Education of the Negro Prior to 1861: A History of the Education of the Colored People of the United States from the Beginning of Slavery to the Civil War*. New York: G. P. Putnam's Sons, 1915.

Woolley, Edwin C. *The Reconstruction of Georgia*. Columbia University Studies in History, Economics, and Public Law, Vol. XIII, No. 3. New York: Columbia University Press, 1901.

Young, Ida, Julius Cholson, and Clara Nell Hargrove. *History of Macon, Georgia*. Macon: Lyon Marshall and Brooks, 1950.

THESES, DISSERTATIONS, AND UNPUBLISHED PAPERS

Bacote, Clarence Albert. "The Negro in Georgia Politics, 1880–1908." Ph.D. dissertation, University of Chicago, 1955.

Benson, Alexa Wynelle. "Race Relations in Atlanta as Seen in a Critical Analysis of the City Council Proceedings and Other Related Works, 1865–1877." M.A. thesis, Atlanta University, 1966.

Bloom, Charles G. "The Georgia Election of April, 1868: A Re-examination of the Politics of Georgia Reconstruction." M.A. thesis, University of Chicago, 1963.

Christler, Ethel Maude. "Participation of Negroes in the Government of Georgia 1867–1880." M.A. thesis, Atlanta University, 1932.

Drago, Edmund L. "Black Georgia During Reconstruction." Ph.D. dissertation, University of California, Berkeley, 1975.

Fitz-Simons, Theodore Barker, Jr. "The Ku Klux Klan in Georgia, 1868–1871." M.A. thesis, University of Georgia, 1957.

Frankel, Noralee. "Rural Black Women in Mississippi: Their Withdrawal from the Work Force, 1865–1868." A paper read at the Organization of American Historians Convention, April, 1980.

Freeman, Henri H. "Some Aspects of Debtor Relief in Georgia During Reconstruction." M.A. thesis, Emory University, 1951.

Hassler, Nancy G. "A Dream Deferred: The Nature of Black Leadership During Reconstruction." Unpublished research paper, University of California, Berkeley, 1969.

Gamble, Robert S. "Athens: The Study of a Georgia Town During Reconstruction, 1865–1872." M.A. thesis, University of Georgia, 1967.

Lawe, Theodore Maxwell. "The Black Reconstructionist in Georgia, 1865–1877." M.A. thesis, Atlanta University, 1966.

McDaniel, Ruth Douglas Currie. "Georgia Carpetbagger: John Emory Bryant." Ph.D. dissertation, Duke University, 1973.

Matthews, John M. "The Negro in Georgia Politics, 1865–1880." M.A. thesis, Duke University, 1967.

Mohr, Clarence Lee "Georgia Blacks During Secession and Civil War, 1859–1865." Ph.D. dissertation, University of Georgia, 1975.

Owens, James L. "The Negro in Georgia During Reconstruction, 1864–1872: A Social History." Ph.D. dissertation, University of Georgia, 1975.

Quattelbaum, Edwin. "The Absence of Sambo in Georgia Reconstruction." Unpublished research paper, University of California, Berkeley, 1967–68.

Reidy, Joseph P. "The Unfinished Revolution: White Planters and Black Laborers in the Georgia Black Belt, 1865–1910." A paper read at the Organization of American Historians Convention, April, 1980.

Sanford, Paul Laurence. "The Negro in the Political Reconstruction of Georgia, 1865–1872." M.A. thesis, Atlanta University, 1947.

Sweat, Edward Forrest. "The Free Negro in Antebellum Georgia." Ph.D. dissertation, Indiana University, 1957.

Young, Edward Barham. "The Negro in Georgia Politics, 1867–1877." M.S. thesis, Emory University, 1955.

Index

194   Index

Bentley, Moses H., 67
Black code: postwar modification of, 103
Black Reconstruction. *See* Reconstruction, Radical
Blacksmiths, black, 39
Blodgett, Foster, 36
Bounty hunters, northern, 12
Bradley, Aaron A.: as delegate to Constitutional Convention, 40, 41, 44; background of, 41–43; political career of, 45, 59, 60, 62–63, 64, 67, 71–72, 85, 87, 95, 157–58
Brooks County, 60
Brown, Andrew, 22
Brown, Joseph E., 30, 40, 41, 42, 44, 46, 47, 48, 49–50, 54, 55, 56, 64, 65, 68, 72, 161
Bryan, George W., 120
Bryan County, 73
Bryant, John E., 28, 29–30, 36, 40, 44, 45, 53, 54, 55, 56, 60, 131, 157
Bryant, Lem, 126
Bullock, Rufus B.: and Constitutional Convention, 30, 36, 42–43, 44, 45; and "New Era" ideology, 50–51; as governor of Georgia, 28, 47, 48, 53–56, 62, 63, 71, 94, 144, 147, 148–49, 154; background of, 50; defeat and resignation of, 57, 58, 65; mentioned, 59, 60, 64, 67, 72, 88, 156
Burke County, 120, 129
Burnett, George P., 41, 145
Businessmen, black, xii, 108
Butler, Benjamin F., 54, 59, 69–70

Cameron, Simon B., 64, 65
Camilla riot, 51, 52, 53, 93
Campbell, Tunis G., Jr., 82
Campbell, Tunis G., Sr., 40, 44, 45, 67, 80, 82–84, 85, 86, 87, 147, 157, 158
Candler, Milton A., 48
Capital, state, 50, 68, 97, 156. *See also* Atlanta; Milledgeville
Carnegie, Andrew, 64
Carpenters, black, 38
Carpetbaggers, 35, 36, 49, 52, 63, 142
Carter, Edward R., 4
Carter, Lewis, 33
Caste system, 68, 103
Census, federal, xii, 37, 39, 134, 135
Central Railroad, 64. *See also* Railroads
Chaplains, black, 12, 24
Charismatic leaders, black. *See* Ministers, black

Charleston, 27, 38
Chatham County, 13, 60, 62, 71, 85, 91, 98, 155
Chinese workers, 133
Christler, Ethel Maude, 45
Churches, black: and black society, 16, 18, 20, 21, 72, 138; property of, 18, 22, 26. *See also* Ministers, black; Religion, black
City councilmen, black, 80, 81
Civil and Political Rights Association, 53, 54
Civil War, 24–26, 30
Claiborne, Malcolm, 67
Clarke County, 4, 52, 70, 79, 89, 119, 146, 151
Class antagonism, 30, 36
Clews, Henry, 72
Clift, Joseph W., 63
Clower, George, 131
Cobb, Howell, 36
Cobb, Howell, Jr., 78–79
Cobb, John, 94, 124, 132, 148
Colby, Abram, 37, 67, 94, 146
Colby, William, 37
Colfax, Schuyler, 48
Colored Methodist Episcopal church, 19
Columbia County, 39, 52, 106, 112, 115, 152
Columbus, 26, 31, 145
Committee on the Franchise, 40. *See also* Constitutional Convention
Confederate States of America, 1, 3
Confederates, former: civil disabilities of, 36, 45, 56. *See also* Conservatives, white; Democratic party
Congregational church, 13, 33
Congress, U.S., 54, 60, 65
Congressional Reconstruction Acts, 31, 33, 160. *See also* Reconstruction, Radical
Congressional Reorganization Act of 1869, pp. 55, 57
Conley, Benjamin, 36
Conscription: of slaves, by Confederate government, 1
Conservatives, white, xiii, 44, 46, 51, 56, 141, 142, 143, 144, 146, 147–48, 161, 162. *See also* Democratic party; Ku Klux Klan
Constitution of 1868: black leaders on, 44; provisions of, 43, 95, 98, 99, 148, 156; ratification of, 47; weaknesses of, 44–45